GANDHI, WOMEN, AND THE NATIONAL MOVEMENT, 1920-47

GANDHI, WOMEN, AND THE NATIONAL MOVEMENT, 1920-47

Anup Taneja

Under the auspices of
AIWC

HAR-ANAND PUBLICATIONS PVT LTD
E-49/3, Okhla Industrial Area, Phase-II, New Delhi-110020
Tel.: 41603490
E-mail: info@haranandbooks.com/haranand@rediffmail.com
Shop online at: www.haranandbooks.com

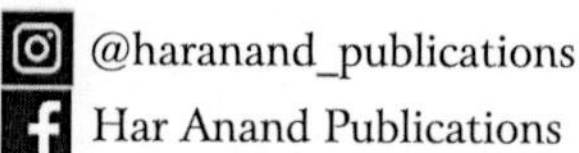

Reprint, 2024

Published by Ashok Gosain and Ashish Gosain for
Har-Anand Publications Pvt Ltd

Printed in India

Dedication

This book is dedicated to my mother,
the late Shrimati Kamla Taneja

Acknowledgements

To start with, I would like to place on record my sincere thanks to Professor Aparna Basu, President, AIWC, who very kindly gave her consent to the publication of this book under the sponsorship of AIWC. She was also kind enough to spare some of her valuable time in going through the typed-script and in offering her invaluable suggestions during various stages of its preparation.

I may also express my deep sense of gratitude to Dr. Sanghmittra, Deputy Director (Research), ICHR, who had motivated me to undertake research in this area of Gender Studies. Thanks are also due to the late Shri M.A. Farooqui, Assistant Director (L), ICHR, for extending his wholehearted cooperation by way of making readily available various books and records as and when required.

Above all, my deep feelings of indebtedness are also due to my parents, wife and daughter who had patiently borne with me, particularly during periods when I was so deeply involved in my research work that I could not devote much time to my family and home.

Last, but not the least, the professional competence shown by M/s. Har-Anand Publications in bringing out this high quality production in a very short period of time, deserves the highest accolade.

(Women need to be educated not for the purpose of seeking a job, but for becoming instrumental in educating their children.)

In yet another article, Padmavati Kumariji expressed her opinion as follows:

> *Ladkiyon ko padhane ka arth yeh kadapi nahin ki unhe B.A., M.A., ki digrian dilayee jain, balki avashyakta hai unhe greh sambandhi karyon ki shiksha di jaye.*[6]

(It is not essential to give women such education which could enable them to collect degrees. Need is to give them such education which could enable them to carry out their household functions competently.)

Several articles published in *Madhuri* and *Chand*[7] impressed upon the women the need to inculcate virtues like patience, mercy, tolerance, surrender, etc. The basic idea behind inculcation of such virtues was to suppress women's ability to question male domination in the family. Interestingly, women often justified their demand for political rights by saying that in doing so the traditional notion of womanhood would not be put into jeopardy. Thus, in an article titled "Striyon ke Samanta ke Adhikar" (Equal Rights for Women), Indra argued:

> *Ek dharmik pativrata patni rajnitik matadhikar prapt karne par bhi waisi hi sati sadhavi aur patibhakt reh sakti hai, jaise un vishesh adhikar ke bina.*[8]

(A religious and virtuous wife would continue to remain equally virtuous, devoted and faithful even after obtaining the right to vote.)

[6] Smt. Padmavati Kumariji, "Kanyaon ki Shiksha", *Chand* (December 1923), p. 255.

[7] Laxmi Devi Johari, "Striyon ki Susthir Pratishtha", *Madhuri* (January-July 1923); Chand Bai Jain, "Hamari Shaktiyan", *Madhuri* (January-July 1923); Smt. Krishna Devi Srivastava, "Mahila", *Chand* (December 1923).

[8] Indra, "Striyon ke Samanta ke Adhikar", *Madhuri* (August 1926), p. 403.

(Women are required to perform the task of bearing and rearing children and this the man cannot perform .... It is the duty of the father to earn and make available all things required for the upbringing of children. He also ought to protect his wife and children from enemies.)

Femininity was identified with efficient performance of duties by a woman as a mother and as a wife. In her article titled "Stri Kartavya" (Duties of a Woman), Indumati Sharma expressed the following opinion :

> *Striyon ka pradhan kartavya hai apne balakon ka palan poshan tatha grihasti ka kaam.*[3]

(The prime duty of a woman is to look after her house and her family.)

In regard to the type of education to be imparted to women, the following opinion was expressed:

> *Vidya stri aur purush dono ke liye avashyak hai kintu wahi shiksha usi roop main ladkiyon ke liye upayogi nahin ho sakti, dono ke marg aur kartavya bhina bhina hain.*[4]

(Education is essential for both man and woman, but education of a similar kind as that meant for a man cannot be useful for a woman in the same way. The paths and duties of both are entirely different.)

Thus, women should be educated not to enable them to seek a job, but to perform their domestic and social duties to the best of their abilities. To quote Indumati Sharma in this connection:

> *Woh agar padhengi, to naukari nahin, apna tatha apne balakon ka udhar karengi.*[5]

[3]Smt. Indumati Sharma, "Stri Kartavya", *Madhuri* (January-July 1923), p. 683.

[4]Smt. Janak Dulari Pandey, "Striyon ki Shiksha", *Madhuri* (July-December 1922), p. 404.

[5]Smt. Indumati Sharma, "Striyan Padhkar Kya Karengi", *Madhuri* (July-December 1923), p. 95.

Contents

CHAPTER I

INTRODUCTION: THE PRE-GANDHIAN PHASE

I

Position of Women in Indian Society: The White Man's Burden

The position and status of women in society truly reflect a country's civilization and cultural attainments. India has a rich cultural heritage, and many women have left an indelible impression in the annals of Indian history in different periods. Even from the numerous finds of Mohenjodaro (like the depiction of the cult of mother-worship, female figures richly adorned, a bronze of a dancing-girl) it becomes evident that women were given due importance in the social structure of those times. But with the advent of asceticism in Buddhism and Jainism, the position of women in society began to deteriorate. Under the patriarchal Indian society, a woman's place became so miserable that she began to be treated like a chattel to be gifted away by the husband.

In the early part of the nineteenth century, a number of social ills like child-marriage, female infanticide, *purdah*, sati, dowry, prohibition of widow remarriage, indignities suffered by widows, etc. had started manifesting in all their ugliness. Lack of proper education among women made matters worse; the basic idea behind giving education to women was to establish on a firm footing the traditional notions of femininity. It would be interesting to note in this connection Rousseau's observations in 'Emile': "Thus women's entire education should be placed in relation to men, to please men, to be useful to them, to win over their love and respect, to raise them as children, care for them as adults...".

The nineteenth century social reformers echoed similar ideas on women's education. Even the minds of women in the concerned period were conditioned in such a manner that they had accepted their subordinate status within the patriarchal system without much resistance. And in keeping with the patriarchal norms there was complete division in the duties, rights and responsibilities of a man and a woman within the family. The existence of this differentiation was considered of paramount importance so as to ensure peace and harmony within the family and society:

> *Shrishti ne stri purush ka jo bhed paida kiya hai, usme kuch arth hai, aur is bhed ke karan striyon aur purushon ke sansarik kartavyon me bahut antar pad jata hai.*[1]

(To some extent the difference created by nature between man and woman is meaningful and due to this the worldly duties of both the sexes differ widely.)

Thus the work of bearing and rearing children devolved on the woman, and providing her the means to accomplish this was the responsibility of the man.

> *Striyon ko santati janan aur palan poshan ka kaam karna hai aur yeh kaam kisi prakar se purshon se nahin ho sakta...*
>
> *Pita ka kartavya hota hai is palan poshan ke liye jo samagri zaroori hai use kama kar lain aur stri tatha bachchon ki sab shatruon se raksha karein.*[2]

[1]Gopal Damodar Tamaskar, "Samaj main Striyon ka Sthan", *Madhuri* (January-July 1925), p. 62.

[2]Ibid.

independence) was in itself a highly commendable one. The very experience of working outside home, and of participating shoulder to shoulder with men for a noble cause, went a long way in infusing a spirit of self-confidence and self-respect among the women of India, and in enhancing their status in society. Indeed, Gandhi was right in his assertion that the contribution made by women to the cause of India's independence "should be written in letters of gold".

ANUP TANEJA

Indian Council of Historical Research
New Delhi

1995); Geraldine Forbes, *Women in Modern India* (Cambridge University Press, 1996); and Aparna Basu and Anup Taneja, ed, *Breaking out of Invisibility* (ICHR Monograph Series-7, New Delhi, 2002).

The present book (*Gandhi, Women, and the National Movement, 1920-47*) attempts a critical assessment of the success achieved by Gandhi in mobilizing women on a mass scale and motivating them to participate in the national movement. It examines in detail the role played by women (from different walks of life) in the freedom struggle in different regions of the country through their association with various Gandhian movements like the Non-cooperation, the Civil Disobedience and the Quit India. Indeed, at Gandhi's call women began to come out of the narrow confines of their homes to participate in constructive programmes like spinning of *charkha*, wearing *khadi* clothes, picketing, boycott of foreign goods, etc.

However, notwithstanding the phenomenal success achieved by Gandhi, it would not be incorrect to say that he never directed his attention to raising the consciousness of women to a level where they could start seeing the world from an altogether different perspective. In Gandhi's scheme of things, radical change in the traditional framework based on male-dominated patriarchal norms was never envisaged. According to him, a woman's place is in the home, while man is responsible for providing woman with the necessary means to enable her to run her home efficiently. Besides, the idea of economic independence of women was not acceptable to Gandhi. Little wonder then that the majority of women who came under the influence of Gandhi reverted to their age-old traditional roles at home after the attainment of the country's independence. But given the constraints of the conservative social environment of the times when Gandhi lived and also the fact that India had remained a colony of Britain for a long time, Gandhi's achievement (of mobilizing women on a mass scale for the cause of the country's

Preface

During the last few decades, the scope of history has vastly expanded: it is no longer a chronicle of kings and statesmen, but a study of the masses, of men and women representing different strata of society. The focus has shifted from the study of rulers or kings to the study of peoples. There can be no two opinions about the fact that women constitute a significant section of society and are an integral part of it. Wars could not have been fought, nor for that matter industrialization could have taken place, had the complementary support of women not been there. The basic purpose of women's studies—a relatively new field of research in India—therefore, is to highlight the role of women in every sphere of life, be it politics, national movement, religion or their role as reformers and revolutionaries, searching for their own identity, particularly those women working at the grassroots level, whose contributions have till now remained obscure in the annals of history.

In the post-independence period very little work was done on women, but with the publication of B.R. Nanda's pioneering work titled *Indian Women: From Purdah to Modernity* (Vikas, New Delhi, 1976), gender came to be recognized as a fundamental category of social, cultural and historical reality, perception and study. Women are no longer invisible in history. In the recent past there has been a growing interest on the question of gender within historical research. The most outstanding examples in this respect are: Kumkum Sangari and Sudesh Vaid, ed, *Recasting Women* (Kali for Women, New Delhi, 1989); J. Krishnamurthi, ed, *Women in Colonial India* (OUP, New Delhi, 1989); Leela Kasturi and Vina Mazumdar, ed, *Women and Indian Nationalism* (Vikas, New Delhi, 1994); Bharati Ray, ed, *From the Seams of History* (OUP, New Delhi,

This lucidly written and meticulously researched book will, therefore, be of great interest to the AIWC members as well as students and scholars of modern India.

11 August, 2004

APARNA BASU
President, AIWC

Foreword

The women's question seems to have acquired a centrality today, so that issues concerning women are discussed and debated at various fora. This ubiquity of women's issues should, however, not obscure the fact that it is but recently that the majority has sought to find out its recent past. Contrary to the apparent situation today, it has in fact been a difficult task to visualize women at all in history.

Women's history in India began as an act of reclamation. Women's role in the freedom struggle is an area in which considerable work has been done. There are descriptive accounts of women's participation in various phases of the freedom struggle since 1857. Many women who took part in the freedom movement, both Gandhian and revolutionary, have written about their own experiences.

While women were visible on the Indian political scene from the foundation of the Indian National Congress in 1885, and especially during the Swadeshi movement from 1905-1911, it was Mahatma Gandhi who gave women a definite role and involved them in a big way in the freedom movement. Dr. Anup Taneja here attempts a critical assessment of the success achieved by Gandhi in mobilizing women on a mass scale to participate in the Civil Disobedience and Quit India movements and the impact these had on their lives, perceptions and activities.

The All India Women's Conference is proud to be associated with this project; many of the past presidents of AIWC such as Sarojini Naidu, Rajkumari Amrit Kaur, Vijaylakshmi Pandit, Hansa Mehta, Kamaladevi Chattopadhyay and scores of other members of AIWC took an active part in the freedom struggle.

Lokmanya Tilak, a political leader of great stature, had a very narrow outlook on the question of women's education. He protested against the idea of imparting higher education to women and strongly criticized the curriculum of the female high school—the reason being that it was on par with the curriculum of boys and therefore socially unacceptable. To quote him:

> Every middle class man wants his wife to be literate and well-trained in household duties, to spend her leisure hours in reading religious texts in order to improve her mind, and to help him in domestic duties. Just as a trade is of primary importance to a craftsman and training is secondary, so are household duties generally primary for women and education incidental.... By the age of 15-16 a woman should be well-trained in housework, and this training will never be available in a school as much as at home. The marital home is the workshop of female education.[9]

Thus, in a male-dominated patriarchal Indian society, the type of education which was sought to be imparted to women re-emphasized their familial roles—as a daughter she was supposed to be obedient to her father; as a wife she was supposed to be dutiful to her husband (even though the latter might be cruel and disloyal to her); and in her old age she was to be an appendage of her son. There was virtually no opportunity for women to assert their individuality and to express their opinion in important matters having a bearing upon their lives. It would be no exaggeration to say that woman in Indian society was a mere shadow of man having no entity of her own.

The first references to the position of women in modern India were made by the historians belonging to the Old Imperialist School. The main works of this school are:

[9]Bal Gangadhar Tilak, *Samagra Lokamanya Tilak*, Vol. 5 (Kesari Prakashan, Pune, 1976), pp. 219-20.

James Mill's *History of British India* (1818), Henry Beveridge's *Comprehensive History of India* (published around 1862), and the works of J.C. Marshman, a missionary who wrote around the 1830s. The accounts of foreign travellers, missionaries and officials deal at length with the laws promulgated by the British to put an end to social ills like sati, prohibition of widow remarriage, polygamy, etc.

The British, in order to assert their cultural superiority and to legitimize their rule, tried to capitalize on the pathetic condition of women in India. The works of this school of thought—while dealing with the condition of women and other ills affecting the society—focussed on the concept of the **white man's burden** to redeem the uncivilized Indian society from various social evils. Thus, the "woman question" became not only an essential item in the cultural background between the rulers and the ruled, but was also sought to be utilized by the colonialists to establish a peculiar sort of moral *raison d'etre* for the perpetuation of the British Raj in India.[10]

Evangelical missionaries were mainly responsible for projecting a negative picture about the people, society and culture of India. It was their firm conviction that India was in a state of darkness and urgently needed the 'light' of the gospel. The basis of their arguments was the prevalence of customs such as sati, female infanticide, *purdah*, polygamy and, above all, lack of education among women. Charles Grant, who was an important personality in missionary circles, produced an influential tract in 1792 —*Observations on the State of Society among the Asiatic Subjects of Great Britain*[11]—which explained the relationship between Britain and India. He believed that his

[10]Rajan Mahan, *Women in Indian National Congress, 1921-1931* (Rawat Publications, Jaipur and New Delhi, 1999), p. 25.

[11]Charles Grant, "Observations on the State of Society among the Asiatic Subjects of Great Britain, Particularly with respect to Morals, and on the means of improving it. Written Chiefly in the year 1792", in *Parliamentary Papers*, 1812-13, X, Paper 282 and *Parliamentary Papers*, 1831-32, VIII, Paper 734.

Observations would go a long way in framing a future policy vis-à-vis India, and that the British Empire could be established on a firm footing through the spread of Christianity. His *Observations* greatly influenced the missionary opinion. In the opinion of Grant: "While men were bound by no moral restraints and lived with 'the insensibility of brutes', Indian women were doomed to a life of servitude and self-imprisonment and a violent and premature death".[12] Introduction of Christianity, according to Grant, would make the Indians "rise in the scale of civilization".[13] His main idea was that the Raj should establish itself firmly in India. He thus argued: "By planting our language, our knowledge, our opinions, and our religion in our Asiatic territories...we shall probably have wedded the inhabitants of these territories to this country...".[14]

It may thus be seen that the portrayal of a negative picture of Indian culture by Evangelical missionaries was highly motivated—it was a serious attempt to establish a sanction for permanent British rule in India.[15] Little wonder then that this view became widely accepted later for it provided a justification for British rule in India.[16] With this object in mind, British missionary women began to arrive in India in the later part of the nineteenth century.

Another group which thoroughly condemned the Indian civilization was the Radicals and Utilitarians. This group too left no stone unturned in portraying an extremely negative picture of the Indian culture which ultimately exercised considerable influence on the eventual policy followed by the British vis-à-vis India.[17] The chief

[12]A.T. Embree, *Charles Grant and British Rule in India* (London, 1962), p.145.

[13]Charles Grant, "Observations", op. cit., p. 83.

[14]Ibid., pp. 59-60.

[15]A.T. Embree, op. cit., p. 142.

[16]Ibid., p.156.

[17]Erik Stokes, *English Utilitarians and India* (Oxford, London, 1962). Also see G.D. Bearce, *British Attitudes Towards India, 1734-1858* (Oxford, London, 1961) and Thomas Metcalf, *The Aftermath of Revolt* (Princeton University Press, New Jersey, 1965).

spokesman of this school was James Mill whose *History of British India* (1818) aptly reflected the basic Utilitarian approach towards India. This monumental work of six volumes served as a big boost to Mill's career (he was rewarded with one of the Company's most coveted posts – Asstt. Examiner of India Correspondence) by virtue of which he was able to influence greatly the British policy formation and implementation.

Some of the important observations made by Mill are: "In truth, the Hindu like the Eunuch, excels in the qualities of a slave";[18] "In the still more important qualities, which constitute what we call the moral character, the Hindu ranks very low".[19] Through the downright condemnation of the Indian politico-legal system and socio-religious institutions, Mill advocated complete overhauling and transformation of the Indian society. In regard to the position of women, Mill states: "The condition of women is one of the most remarkable circumstances in the manners of nations. Among rude people, the women are generally disregarded; among civilised people they are exalted".[20] Thus, for Mill the British were a civilized people, while the Indians were rude. He asserted that "nothing can exceed the habitual contempt which the Hindus entertain for their women".[21] Mill's Rationalist-Utilitarian approach became "the most important single influence moulding English opinion about India for the fifty years from its publication".[22] This goes to show the extent to which Mill's approach had become popular among the British. Thus, the "woman question" provided the British with one of their favourite justifications for the presence and perpetuation of the Raj.[23]

[18]James Mill, *The History of British India*, 6 volumes (London, 1820), Vol. II, p. 365.

[19]Ibid., p. 306.

[20]James Mill, op. cit., Vol. I, p. 445.

[21]Ibid., p. 386.

[22]T.G.P. Spear, "British Historical Writing in the Era of the National Movements", in C.H. Philips, ed, *Historian*, p. 405.

[23]Rajan Mahan, op. cit., p. 30.

It is interesting to note that although the official policy of the British was non-interference in Indian culture and religion,[24] yet they promulgated a number of legislations on issues affecting women like sati, female infanticide and child-marriage, raising the age of consent and allowing widow remarriage. Between 1795 and 1930, the British enacted laws on as many as six issues relating to women: sati in 1829; widow remarriage in 1856; age of consent was raised to 12 in 1891; female infanticide was prohibited by the Acts of 1795, 1804 and 1870; child-remarriage was forbidden in 1929.

Another point which needs to be emphasized in this connection is that in enacting these legislations the British had the tacit support of the Indian social reformers of the time, especially Rammohun Roy (on the prohibition of sati) and Ishwar Chandra Vidyasagar (in support of widow remarriage).

II

Social Reformers, the Nationalist Ideology and the Women's Question

The growing popularity of English language coupled with the encouragement to Christian missionaries to popularize Christianity greatly influenced some Indian social reformers in the early 19th century, particularly Raja Rammohun Roy and Ishwar Chandra Vidyasagar. Rightly described as the father of India's modern enlightenment, Rammohun Roy's efforts in improving the position of women in India mark the starting point in the 19th century social reform movement in Bengal. He was very much critical of the manner in which the early British missionaries condemned the religious beliefs of the Indians at street corner meetings. He was of the firm opinion that India would be able to make great strides in the political

[24]In addition to repeated assurances of British administrators, this policy of non-interference had also been embodied in the famous Queen's Proclamation of 1858.

field by acquiring modern knowledge through English language. He said that it was because of education that Europe had been able to register immense progress in the field of industrialization, and that the contemporary ideas of national freedom, democracy and equality of sexes in Europe could be attributed to English language. "It was through the English language that successive generations of Indians including Gandhiji and Jawaharlal Nehru became acquainted with the best Western minds: Thomas Jefferson and Abraham Lincoln; Voltaire and Rousseau; Marx, Engels and Lenin; women suffragette leaders on both sides of the Atlantic; the nationalist revolutionaries of Ireland; Tolstoy, Ruskin and Thoreau; and such stimulating thinkers as George Bernard Shaw and Bertrand Russell. This intellectual interaction with the West helped to enrich the content of Indian nationalism".[25]

In the year 1818—ten years before he established the Brahmo Samaj—Rammohun started his anti-sati campaign with utmost zeal and fervour. One of the main motivating factors behind this was Rammohun's personal experience of the death of his sister-in-law. He condemned the practice of sati both on humanitarian grounds and on the basis of Hindu scriptures, with emphasis on the latter. In a pamphlet published in 1818, he bitterly criticized the society's apathy towards the ill-treatment of women in India: "What I lament is, that, seeing the women thus dependent and exposed to every misery, you feel for them no compassion that might exempt them from being tied down and burnt to death".[26]

Rammohun, however, had a tough time in communicating his point of view to a society where religion reigned supreme. And to make matters worse he had to contend

[25]Aruna Asaf Ali, *The Resurgence of Indian Women* (Radiant Publishers, New Delhi, 1991), p. 30.

[26]"First & Second Conferences between an Advocate for and an Opponent of the Practice of Burning of Widows Alive" (ISIS, Calcutta, 1820), cited in Sumit Sarkar, "Rammohun Roy and the Break with the Past", in V.C. Joshi, ed, *Rammohun Roy and the Process of Modernization in India* (New Delhi, 1975), p. 52.

with the orthodox elements who were not amenable to social reforms. Both the social reformers and the orthodox elements took shelter in the scriptural authority to substantiate their respective points of view. Rammohun quotes from Manu as follows: "Manu in plain terms enjoins a widow to continue till death for giving all injuries, performing austere duties, avoiding every sexual pleasure, and cheerfully practising the incomparable rules of virtue which have been followed by such women as were devoted to only one husband".[27] While comparing the relative advantages of sati and ascetic life, Rammohun gave preference to the latter; and in substantiation of this he cited from the Vedas: "From a desire during life, of future fruition, life ought not to be destroyed".[28]

The orthodox elements on their part tried to prove that the condemnation of sati by the East India Company was based on misinterpretation of the scriptures, as is evident from the following statement: "But we humbly submit that in a question so delicate as the interpretation of our sacred books, and the authority of our religious usages, none but Pandits and Brahmans, and teachers of holy lives, and known learning, ought to be consulted—not men who have neither any faith nor care for the memory of their ancestors or of their religion".[29] Thus, the orthodox elements firmly believed that sati was a far better option than asceticism simply because it "involves temporary suffering and heavenly blessings; ascetic widowhood is of lesser spiritual value though it involves a life-time of suffering".[30] It may be pointed out that in recent times this debate has focussed more on the ideational form of discourse. There can be no denying that this is of

[27]Ibid. Also see J.C. Ghose, ed, *The English Works of Raja Ram Mohan Roy* (New Delhi, 1982), Vol. II.

[28]Maitrayee Chaudhuri, *Indian Women's Movement—Reform and Revival* (New Delhi, 1993), p. 19.

[29]"Petition of the Orthodox Community etc.", in J.N. Majumdar, ed, *Raja Rammohun Roy and Progressive Movements in India* (Calcutta, 1941), p. 157.

[30]Maitrayee Chaudhuri, op. cit.

considerable importance, but at the same time: "Consideration of power and conflict, allegiance and control were of no less consequence. While writings in the past have probably confined themselves entirely to questions of interests and powers, recent writings have tended to gloss over them. The petition of the orthodoxy would however suggest that the awesome power of the state and machinations of vested interests cannot be underplayed".[31] The petition reads: "None of our countrymen feel a pleasure in hearing anything to the disadvantage of the honourable company; they always pray for the welfare of the government .... We have been subject to no distress under the government of the company; it is only the abolition of suttee, sic, which has given disquietude".[32] It may thus be seen that the evolution of the women's question right up to the present day has two divergent aspects : one is the politics of power and state control, and the other is the idiom of discourse.

The scriptural context of the sati debate exercises a great deal of influence on the women's question. It leads to an analysis of sati purely at the level of religion. Also, it leads to the rewriting of history. According to Lata Mani, women became the focal point around which tradition was debated and reformulated.[33] Besides, tradition takes the shape of brahmanic scriptures, meaning thereby that all the popular forms of customs and beliefs pave the way for a new tradition. Above all, an equation of tradition with scriptures means a necessary break with Islamic influence. All the social evils are thus attributed to the Islamic rulers.[34] In this context, Rammohun's approach was genuinely original to start with. His idea was to strike a

[31]Ibid.

[32]*Samachar Chandrika*—quoted by John Bull on 9 March 1830 in J.N. Majumdar, op. cit., p. 330.

[33]Lata Mani, "Contentious Traditions : The Debate on Sati in Colonial India", in Kumkum Sangari and Sudesh Vaid, ed, *Recasting Women: Essays in Colonial History* (Kali for Women, New Delhi, 1989).

[34]Maitrayee Chaudhuri, op. cit., p. 20.

harmony among the Hindu, Islamic and Western culture and tradition.[35] But, subsequently, Rammohun towed the line of other Hindu intellectuals of the 19th century in their belief that the British rule was a welcome relief from the Muslim tyranny.[36] Thus, while on the one hand Rammohun—in the process of condemning the sati practice —asked the Hindu women to deviate from the *pativrata* ideal, on the other, "his attempt to cleanse Hinduism of its popular form and identify it with solely the Vedanta tradition led to a hegemonization of the upper caste world-view".[37]

Uma Chakravarty[38] deals with Rammohun's rewritings on religion and its implication for both sati in particular and the status of women in general. She points out that the goal for women according to the ancient Hindu legislatures was *pativrata dharma* (devotion to husband). But Rammohun believed that the ultimate goal of all Hindus was total surrender to the Divine essence—a merger which could not be effected through the practice of sati. It is in this context that Rammohun presented his arguments against the miserable plight of women. And he further substantiated his arguments by using the Maitreyi Yajnavalkya episode. He emphasized that women had great spiritual potential, and that they were no less than men in this respect. This, in effect, meant that the position of women in ancient Indian society was quite high in comparison to that of contemporary women. "This was part of the process to reconstitute and ideologize the glorious Hindu past, a process which built an entire gamut of ideas about India and about what legitimately constitutes India, which stretched beyond Rammohun and onto the

[35]Susobhan Sarkar, *Bengal Renaissance and other Essays* (New Delhi, 1981), pp. 5-9.

[36]Maitrayee Chaudhuri, op. cit., p. 20.

[37]Ibid.

[38]Uma Chakravarti, "Whatever Happened to the Vedic Dasi? Orientalism, Nationalism and the Script for the Past", in Kumkum Sangari and Sudesh Vaid, op. cit.

entire colonial period as later debates in women's organizations and political parties would show".[39]

Credit, however, goes to Rammohun Roy—and not Governor-General Bentinck who signed the decree—for the abolition of sati in December 1829. He has been rightly hailed as the father of Indian Renaissance.

If Rammohun is remembered for his anti-sati campaign, Vidyasagar's role in his campaign to legalize remarriage is no less significant. His efforts resulted in the enactment of the Hindu Women's Remarriage Act in 1856. In the light of the following words of Pandita Ramabai relating to the plight of the widow in Hindu society, Vidyasagar's achievement becomes even more significant: "Among the Brahmans of the Deccan the heads of all widows must be shaved regularly every fortnight. The widow must wear a single coarse garment. She must eat only one meal during the twenty-four hours of a day. She must never take part in family feasts. A man or woman thinks it unlucky to behold a widow's face before seeing any other object in the morning".[40] However, despite a number of widow remarriages which took place as a result of Vidyasagar's efforts, it did not become an acceptable norm of society. Vidyasagar became an object of severe criticism, and the Act remained a "dead letter". Above all, "Even those lower castes which allows them tend to give them up, believing that if they assimilate their social observances to those of the higher caste, they will enhance the prestige and facilitate their rise to the same level as the latter".[41]

This oppressiveness which is an integral part of the structure of the Hindu caste system needs to be emphasized. Though the process of Sanskritization allows positional upward mobility within the ladder, yet this

[39]Maitrayee Chaudhuri, op. cit., p. 21. Meredith Borthwick, *The Changing Role of Women in Bengal, 1849-1905* (Princeton University Press, New Jersey, 1984), p. 28.

[40]Aruna Asaf Ali, op. cit., p. 33.

[41]Charles Heimsath, *Indian Nationalism and Hindu Social Reform* (Princeton University Press, New Jersey, 1964), p. 80.

process has proved to be negative as far as women are concerned. This is a problem which the social reformers found difficult to tackle, more so when we consider that "the operational Hinduism which comes not in its 'spirit', its 'anarchic federation of sub-cultures and textual authorities' but as a caste-based organisation most often vested with both power and violence welding abilities".[42]

A study conducted by the Census of 1931 revealed that less than 10 per cent of the population of the Indian subcontinent was affected by ban on divorce and widow re-marriage.[43] These were essentially high caste Hindu customs and the bans did not extend to the rest of the society. For the majority, the marriage laws were fairly flexible and permissive. *Purdah* was a custom which was common among the high caste women and the women from the lower castes and classes were not touched by it as is evident from their participation in the labour force in agriculture, industry and other services. Their problems were not *purdah*, widow remarriage, divorce and education. Their problems were rooted in poverty; in discrimination in the payment of wages which were very low; in their helplessness against exploitation of many kinds; etc. The social reformers of the 19th century had remained silent on these issues. Thus one of the greatest failures of the reform movement was the inability of the social reformers to expose the nature of oppression that affected women in different layers of our society. Their stress was more on emancipation from above rather than addressing the problem from below. Sumit Sarkar is right in his assertion that: "Fundamental elements of social conservatism such as maintenance of caste distinctions and patriarchal forms of authority in the family, acceptance of the sanctity of shastras, preference for symbolic rather than substantive changes in social practices, all of them were conspicuous in the reform movements of early and mid

[42]Maitrayee Chaudhuri, op. cit., p. 23.
[43]Vina Mazumdar, *Symbols of Power* (Mumbai, 1979), p. xi.

19th century".[44] What reformers were trying was merely to raise the position of women in society and that too within the framework of the patriarchal norms. They never questioned the power imbalance that was structured in the man-woman relationship.

In regard to the reform movements of the 19th century it may be noted that most of the leaders of those times were mainly from the middle classes and upper castes and so were their followers. Hence the reforms which they sought to bring about were mainly governed by the considerations of social and economic advancement of their respective groups. Moreover, these reform movements were greatly influenced by the presence of the British missionaries who were trying to take advantage of the pathetic state of women in Indian society by asserting their cultural superiority.

Even reform movements like the Arya Samaj left crucial areas untouched. Swami Dayanand in his writings does not show much concern about women as individuals. He only recognizes women in familial roles as wives and mothers. Neither in theory nor in practice did this movement question the power imbalance which was structured in the husband-wife relationship in the existing family system. The Arya Samaj did make substantial contributions by way of bringing about social reforms such as the removal of untouchability, prohibition of widow remarriage, etc., but, by and large, the Samaj essentially functioned within the paradigm of the patriarchal system.

The Arya Samajists also took up the cause of female education, but their focus was on the upper caste women. It is evident from the list of subscribers and donors published in the Samaj journals, that the financial support came from the commercial and trading classes. The curricula of Samaj's schools was based on the perception of men in regard to the education to be given to women. Too

[44]Sumit Sarkar, "The Women Question in 19th Century Bengal", in Kumkum Sangari and Sudesh Vaid, ed, *Women and Culture* (Mumbai, 1985), pp. 157-72.

much emphasis was laid on religion and domestic economy in the curricula. Basically, this sort of education was not geared towards making women financially independent but towards inculcating in them such qualities that would make them modern, educated housewives. The unwillingness to question the legitimacy of certain institutional forms of women's oppression defined the narrow limits within which the Arya Samaj movement operated. In this context Madhu Kishwar has very rightly stated : "They wanted women 'enlightened' but 'dependent'; they wanted to give them 'dignity' but not 'freedom' ".[45] According to her, the Arya Samaj had sought to reform women rather than the social condition which made their position miserable.

Prem Chowdhary has successfully brought out the peculiar condition in the prevailing dominant customs and attitudes in rural Haryana in relation to women in the colonial period.[46] She says that while on the one hand prevalence of customs like bride price, widow remarriage, equal economic work partnership indicate a high status, on the other, the importance given to a male child; extremely unequal female sex ratio as compared to the male; *purdah* and *ghunghat* (veil) custom; neglect of female education and denial of the right of inheritance to property and the custom of *karewa*[47] (on the death of her husband, the woman was required to marry the younger brother of her husband or his cousin or in some cases even his elder brother), reflect the low status of women who were not only exploited at the socio-economic level, but also at the sexual level.

Thus, the 19th century social reformers wished to bring about some improvement in the condition of women, but at the

[45]Madhu Kishwar, "The Daughter of Aryavarta", in J.Krishnamurthy, ed, *Women in Colonial India* (OUP, New Delhi, 1989), p. 103.

[46]Prem Chowdhary, "Customs in Colonial Haryana", in Kumkum Sangari and Sudesh Vaid, ed, *Recasting Women*, op. cit.

[47]Ibid., p. 314. Also known as *Karao* or *Chadder Andezi.*

same time they never raised their voice against the position or power enjoyed by men within the patriarchal society. The male dominated familial culture reduced women to the level of objects of sexual gratification. Sex symbols and sex roles stereotyping were the means through which women were subjected within the framework of patriarchy.

Veena Das and Dagmar Engels have argued that the British were not really concerned with the pathetic condition of Hindu women but in employing what they took to be their acute deprivation as evidence for moral unfitness of the Hindu society itself.[48] Therefore, while discussing the position of women in India in the late 19th century, due cognizance has to be given to the presence of the British in India. Both, the early 19th century and the late 19th century reform movements, were greatly influenced by the Western ideas of liberty and rationality. The constant interaction of these reformers with Western culture greatly affected their thinking; this motivated them to take up those issues which had been condemned by the British. The late 19th century reformers have to be seen within the framework of growing nationalist activity. The need of the hour had demanded glorification of India's rich cultural heritage, and the reformers started talking about equality for women in accordance with the stipulations of the Vedic texts. Literature of the 19th century depicted apprehensions in regard to Westernization of Bengali women. The literature of parody and satire in the first half of the 19th century clearly contained much that was prompted by straightforward defence of tradition and outright rejection of Western influence. The idea of a Bengali woman trying to imitate the style of European *memsahibs* was just not acceptable, particularly in terms of new items of clothing such as blouse, petticoat, shoes, use of Western cosmetics, reading novels, etc.

[48]Veena Das, "Gender Studies, Cross Cultural Comparison and Colonial Organization of Knowledge", *Berkshire Review* (1986) and Dagmar Engels, "The Age of Consent Act, 1891: Colonial Ideology in Bengal", *South Asia Research*, Vol. III, No. II (1983).

III

The Nationalist Resolution to the Women's Question

Thus towards the end of the nineteenth century with the upsurge of the national movement, two contrary pulls could be seen in nationalist ideology: while on the one hand there was a tendency to glorify India's past and its rich cultural heritage, on the other there was a desire to change and to bring about a radical transformation of the traditional institutions and opinions in favour of new identities. The nationalists thus were faced with the uphill tasks of simultaneously defending the Indian culture and bettering the lot of women in Indian society. This was because the position of women was extremely crucial to India's preparedness for self-rule. The "woman question" was, however, so ticklish and complicated that the nationalists found it difficult to find an appropriate solution to it. Sivanath Sastri's frank admission that "women are fishbones in our throats; we cannot cough them up, and we dare not swallow them",[49] aptly reflects the dilemma in which the Indian nationalists were placed. It also points to the significance attached to the "woman question" in the nationalist endeavour.

A resolution to this anomaly was sought to be explained by representing women as the dynamic aspect of the Divine, an authentic body of national tradition, embodying the principle of continuity, and men as the progressive agents of national modernity embodying the static aspect of the Divine, the principle of discontinuity. No need was now felt to plead before the British to bring about social reforms. According to Partha Chatterjee, the reason why the issue of female emancipation had disappeared from the public agenda of nationalist agitation in the late 19th century was not because it was overtaken by more emotive

[49]Quoted in *The Foreign Missionary*, Vol. XII, No. 2, February 1891, p. 14.

issues concerning political power, but because of the refusal of nationalism to make the women's question an issue of political negotiation with the colonial state. The problems relating to women were now to be looked upon as internal matter which had to be resolved without any kind of British intervention. In the words of Chatterjee: "In the entire phase of national struggle, the crucial need was to protect, preserve and strengthen the inner core of the national culture, its spiritual essence. No encroachments by the colonizer must be allowed in that inner sanctum. In the world, imitation of and adaptation to Western norms was necessity, at home they were tantamount to annihilation of one's very identity".[50]

Chatterjee argued that the contradictory pulls in the Indian nationalist ideology in its struggle against colonial domination were amicably resolved through demarcation of culture into two distinct spheres—the material and the spiritual. The material domain lies outside us, the spiritual within, which is our true self and has to be preserved to retain our cultural identity. This inner/outer distinction was applied to day-to-day living and you get a separation of the social space into the home and the world. The world is the external, the material, the home, the family, the inner spiritual realm. To quote Partha Chatterjee: "The world is the external, the domain of the material; the home represents our inner spiritual self, our true identity. The world is a treacherous terrain of the pursuit of material interests where practical considerations reign supreme. It is also typically the domain of the male. The home in its essence must remain unaffected by the profane activities of the material world—and woman is its representation".[51]

[50]Partha Chatterjee, " The Nationalist Resolution to the Women's Question", in Kumkum Sangari and Sudesh Vaid, ed, *Recasting Women*, op. cit., pp. 240-41.

[51]Ibid., pp. 238-39.

IV

Awakening of Women's Consciousness

The Emergence of Women's Organizations

In view of the fact that the social reform movement of the nineteenth century could not transcend the constraints imposed by the patriarchal norms of the society and women were continued to be treated as mere objects on whom judgement was to be passed, an urgent need was felt for writing a new script for the past which would impart strength to the process of making India a great nation and reflect its new social-cultural and political aspirations. Women's question had therefore to be properly dealt with in the reconstruction of historical consciousness and search for the golden age.

The growing awareness among women in regard to their low position in the male-dominated patriarchal society at different levels motivated them to fight for their rights. By the end of the nineteenth century many women representing the elite classes began to form their own organizations. This marked the emergence of a rudimentary women's movement in India. And the role played by the Tagore family went a long way in the direction of formation of women's organizations. Credit goes to Swarnakumari Devi, sister of Rabindranath Tagore, for organizing the Sakhi Samiti in 1882. Subsequently, it became a craft centre for widows. The year 1882 also saw the founding of another organization for women—Arya Mahila Samaj—credit for which goes to Pandita Ramabai. She also established the Sharada Sadan with the purpose of providing employment and education to women, widows in particular. Ramabai Ranade, wife of Justice Ranade, established the Seva Sadan. Gujarati Stree Mandal was started in 1908. Branches of Mahila Seva Samaj were established in Mysore and Pune in the years 1913 and 1916 respectively. But the first major attempt to organize women on an all-India basis took place with the

establishment of Women's Indian Association (WIA) in 1917. By 1921 the WIA had established 48 branches with membership in excess of 2700. Annie Besant, Margaret Cousins and Dorothy Jinarajadasa were the founding members of this organization.

Another major women's organization to have been established in the post-World War I period was the All-India Women's Conference (AIWC). It was established in 1927 and its principal objective has been to elevate the status of women and bring about an increase in their legal and constitutional rights. The AIWC has also been making systematic efforts to create social awareness among women. It is indeed a premier women's organization that has attracted the most talented and capable Indian women such as Sarojini Naidu, Vijaylakshmi Pandit, Rajkumari Amrit Kaur, Rameshwari Nehru, Dhanvanthi Rama Rau, Kamaladevi Chattopadhyay, Muthulakshmi Reddy, Charulata Mukherjee, Vidyagauri Neelkanth, Hansa Mehta, and many others. Professor Aparna Basu, who is presently the President of the AIWC, has been rendering yeoman service to the cause of women's emancipation in India through her association with the AIWC.

Women's organizations, particularly the AIWC, served as a powerful medium through which "women's opinion" on various issues could be freely expressed. They went a long way in the development of women's personalities in such a manner that they could gain the necessary confidence to take up leading roles in politics and social institutions.

Role of Popular Hindi Journals and Magazines

The Indian women's movement did not derive its inspiration from the West, but from its realization that the women's dependence upon male 'charity', 'benevolence', and spiritual concern could not ensure for them autonomy, rights and power. This movement gained its strength from its prolonged and active association with the anti-colonial struggle in India. The main purpose behind the Indian

women's movement was to mobilize under a common platform those women who had been silently suffering in the male-dominated patriarchal society. And in order to highlight the manner in which women were being victimized in the male-dominated patriarchal society, the enlightened women started taking recourse to the media with the basic purpose of carving new spaces and roles for women who, like men, had an equally important role to play in society.

There was a remarkable mushrooming of women's journals in Hindi in the early years of the 20th century which went a long way in giving visibility and voice to their target group who were being victimized merely by virtue of their being females. These journals focussed on issues like female education, child marriage, mismatched marriage, polygamy, *purdah*, female backwardness, etc. *Stree Darpan* was the pioneer in women-oriented journalism, credit for which goes to Rameshwari Nehru,[52] who had started this journal in 1909. Another important magazine to have been introduced in 1909 was *Grihalakshmi* which mainly focussed on the traditional role of women and education and it generally echoed the views of *Stree Darpan.*[53] *Saraswati* and *Madhuri*[54] were two women-oriented journals which were edited by men. *Mahila Sarvasu* was another women-oriented journal which was published by a man, namely Pandit Devdutt Sharma, and was mediocre in content.[55] One of the better women-oriented journals of those times was *Chand* which was first published in 1922 from Allahabad. Its editors

[52]Rameshwari Nehru (1886-1966) was the wife of Brijlal, a government official. She had edited the *Stree Darpan* during the period 1909-25. She had also served the AIWC as President during the years 1940-41. After partition she had worked as Director of Women's Section, Ministry of Relief and Rehabilitation.

[53]*Pratap,* 15 March 1920 (Kanpur). It reported "the most unparalleled narrative on women's education".

[54]Available at MSL, Old Delhi: *Madhuri*'s editor was Shri Dularelal Bhargava.

[55]*Stree Darpan*, January 1919. It commented: "The Journal needs improvement".

were Ramrikh Sehgal and Ramkrishna Mukund Laghate, while Vidyavati Sehgal was its manager.[56]

Since the editors of most of the women's journals of those times were men who had coopted their wives as editors, *Stree Darpan*'s place was unique as it was launched independently by a woman—Rameshwari Nehru. The special feature of this journal was that it helped women in gaining proficiency in writing and expressing their feelings. With the purpose of making its readers familiar with the methodology of writing, this journal also published the Hindi translated versions of novels written in Bengali and other languages. The contents of this journal included commentaries, short-stories, poems, articles and book reviews.[57] Through the medium of *Stree Darpan*, Rameshwari Nehru wanted the orthodox and self-centred men to realize that women were in no way inferior to men, and that it was high time that a proper and healthy environment was created for women so that they could extend their wholehearted cooperation to men as equals and not as their subordinates. Above all, through the medium of this journal, she also wanted to provide communication space to women in order that they could locate them in the mainstream perspective of the national movement for India's independence.[58]

During the period 1911 to 1920, *Stree Darpan* mainly focussed on the theme of education and the need for opening schools and colleges for women. It was argued that a wide gap had developed between men and women within middle-class urban families mainly because the men had access to Western education. And because of the constant interaction of these men with their English

[56]MSL, Old Delhi, *Chand*, 1922.

[57]Kumkum Sangari and Sudesh Vaid, ed, *Recasting Women: Essays in Colonial History* (Kali for Women, New Delhi, 1989), p. 211.

[58]Rameshwari Nehru's editorials published in the issues of *Stree Darpan* (October 1915; July and December 1916; and December 1919) discuss the aims and objectives of the publication of this Journal.

colleagues and bosses, their perceptions had undergone a radical change as a result of which they began looking down upon their tradition-bound and illiterate wives. The gender specific roles within the family when seen in the light of the new socio-cultural and politico-economic situation tended to widen the gap even more. This in consequence led to the social agony of women and they became victims of constant humiliation at the hands of their Westernized husbands. This is aptly illustrated from the following:

> *Sabhyata ki poshak ke ander abhi*
> *bahut se sankiran bhaav ke hriday*
> *chupe rathe hain jo ki ante karan*
> *se stri jaati ko paon tale rakhna*
> *pasand karte hain.*[59]

(Even today, a number of men hide their narrow and reactionary views about women behind their civilized appearance. It is their heartiest desire to keep women under their foot.)

The enlightened women of those times were quick to realize that it was because of lack of education that women's position in society had become so embarrassing. They thus began to vehemently oppose the prevalent customs like child marriage and *purdah* which they thought were great obstacles to women's education. Rameshwari Nehru played a big role in creating awareness among both men and women through the columns of *Stree Darpan.* A number of poems and stories which were published in *Stree Darpan* reflected the Editor's ceaseless endeavours in demonstrating the deep-rooted social prejudice against women's education. In her editorial "Deshi aur Vilayti Nari Shiksha", the Editor pointed out that among the various advantages of education, the most important one was that it enabled women to inculcate in them a sense of pride in being Indians.[60] The result of

[59]Kailash Rani Baatal, "Striyon Ka Mahatav Tatha Purushoan Ka Kartavya", *Stree Darpan*, December 1915.

[60]*Stree Darpan*, August 1918.

these efforts was that a number of social and religious institutions and women's organizations established girls' schools in the northern part of India, especially Lahore, Jullunder, Benaras, Aligarh, Allahabad, etc. Through the columns of *Stree Darpan* Rameshwari Nehru kept the readers informed about the opening of new educational institutions, particularly those that had boarding facilities for girls. She also made fervent appeals to people to extend their wholehearted cooperation by way of generous donations to these institutions.

Apart from women's education another important theme which found wide coverage in *Stree Darpan* was *purdah.* Satyawati had pointed out that mere abolition of the custom of *purdah* would not serve any useful purpose unless it was accompanied by imparting education to women and removal of other social evils affecting women.[61] Satyawati was of the opinion that the custom of *purdah* was a big stumbling block in the way of women's education. Bhagyavati too had strongly condemned the custom of *purdah*, as can be seen from the following extract: "If India is to recapture its past glory and to progress, women's potentialities ought to be given full scope for development. In order to achieve this objective, the custom of *purdah*, the inveterate enemy of woman's health, has to be discarded for ever".[62]

In an article titled "Purdeh ki Visham Vedana", Rajdulari emphasized that it was high time that an end was put to gender discrimination, and to work out ways and means whereby the code of conduct for men and women framed by the society is reformulated keeping in mind the progressive trend of the world. While impressing upon the society the urgent need to uproot and demolish pernicious social customs like *purdah*, child marriage, mis-matched marriage, dowry exchange, etc., she pointed out that

[61]Smt. Satyawati, "Striyan aur Purdah", and Smt. Bhagyavati, "Adhunik Purdah Pranali Tatha Us Se Haniyan", *Stree Darpan*, December 1918.

[62]*Stree Darpan*, August 1918.

women were in no way less than men at the intellectual level and were therefore competent enough to take part in the national welfare activities. She also stressed upon the need to impart vocational training to women, particularly widows, so that they could earn their livelihood and become financially independent.

The themes of child marriage, mis-matched marriage and widow remarriage also found adequate coverage in the columns of *Stree Darpan*. A woman who wrote under anonymity drew attention to Gandhi's advice that child marriage should be completely stopped, and there should be no restriction to the remarriage of those widows whose marriage had not consummated. A series of articles was published in Hindi journals in favour of widow remarriage. Yet another woman wrote that young men should not hesitate in marrying *pati vihina abala* (weak women without husband).[63]

A number of cases were reported where old men married girls who were young enough to be their daughters or even grand-daughters. This often led to widowhood among young girls which made them feel extremely insecure. This is aptly reflected in the following statement made by a child widow: "As yet my milk teeth have not fallen, how shall I be able to pass my life".[64] In one case a greedy man sold his daughter to an elderly man for seven thousand rupees.[65] A cartoon under the caption "Marriage in old Age" was published with these satirical comments : "Everybody ran helter-skelter to see the bridegroom, as soon as the news travelled people began to say between themselves, whether to call him bridegroom or bride's grandfather".[66] Gulab Devi Chaturvedi from Kota reported the marriage of a man of 60 years with a girl of 14 and sarcastically commented: "bless them, bless them".[67]

[63]*Stree Darpan*, January to June 1920.
[64]*Stree Darpan*, November 1920.
[65]*Stree Darpan*, March 1919.
[66]"Bal-Vivah aur Vartaman Durdasha", *Chand*, May 1936.
[67]*Stree Darpan*, February 1918.

In yet another case, a widow who had suffered a lot was forced to lead an immoral life by her in-laws. She was bold enough to write that those who were laughing at her misfortune must be aware of the fact that 75 per cent of the widows were forced to undergo abortions. In her opinion widows should lead chaste lives provided they could restrain their biological urges. And in case they could not do so, they should not hesitate to remarry. She did not find anything wrong in this because by adopting this course they could save themselves from the life of vice.[68]

Glorification of widowhood and suppression of sexuality of widows had been a dominant feature of the middle class psyche underlying the process of construction of new woman by Swami Dayanand and Mahatma Gandhi. The former had advocated widow remarriage with the purpose of effecting an improvement in the Hindu race.[69] Gandhi, on the other hand, had recommended remarriage for child widows on compassionate grounds; and for adult widows he advocated remarriage in order to save them from moral corruption. But he was firm in his opinion that if widows lived a pure life, they could contribute a great deal to the field of social welfare and national reconstruction.

As far as the viewpoint of the growing band of thinking women on the issue as reflected in the columns of *Stree Darpan* is concerned, it may be noted that the majority of the contributors—young housewives, middle-aged mothers and teenaged daughters, etc.—tried to locate the problem of widows and social resistance to their remarriage in the context of the position of women in Indian society. In this connection it would be important to refer to Hukma Devi's article titled, "Stree Unnati Kaise Ho" in which she had drawn attention to the low status of women in society which was reflected in the eagerness of widowers to

[68]"Hindu Samaj Ka Kacha Chittha", *Chand*, November 1929.

[69]See Swami Dayanand, *Satyarth Prakash*, tr. by Chiranjiv Bharadwaj (Agra, 1915), pp. 22-32.

remarry immediately after the death of their wives.[70] This, in her opinion, was the biggest reason for the devaluation of women. According to her, "... men were far more grieved if their pet animals and birds died or flew away than if their wives fell ill and died, because a woman's status is of as little consequence as a man's shoe – if it wears out you can always replace it".[71]

In her article titled, "Ardhangani Ya Paon Ki Jooti", Hukma Devi sarcastically used the expression "Paon Ki Jooti" to show the manner in which women were humiliated in society. She further wrote: "In the present time India is plagued by the atrocities within the institution of marriage. Not a single household is exempt from this. You lose one wife, you marry another, the second dies and a third is ready...".[72] She therefore implored upon women to wake up from their slumber and fight against the atrocities perpetrated against them.[73]

Through the publication of poems, articles and stories in its various issues, *Stree Darpan* was able to successfully spread the message of gender-discrimination in society. In an article titled "Ek Vidhwa Ki Jiwani", an anonymous writer drew a comparison between the privileged position of a widower and the ignominy suffered by a widow in society. She held the male-dominated patriarchal system responsible for this sorry state of affairs. She also vehemently criticized the women for silently suffering at the hands of men, as can be seen in the following assertion: "In the mistaken perception of Indian society, men seem to be more useful than women. It may be conceded that men have been unjust to women". But the question is: why women did not protest against this injustice. Why did they not assert their individuality and

[70]*Stree Darpan*, August 1917.

[71]Vir Bharat Talwar, "Feminist Consciousness in Women's Journals in Hindi, 1910-20", in Kumkum Sangari and Sudesh Vaid, op. cit., p. 213.

[72]Ibid., p. 215.

[73]Ibid.

rights? Women share more responsibility for their own degradation.[74]

The select band of enlightened women made efforts to channelize the growing discontent among women into an organized social resistance. Uma Nehru, elder daughter-in-law of Nandlal Nehru, was the most progressive of the feminists of the period. Her article titled "Hamare Samaj Sudharak" serves as a prominent example in this respect. She vehemently criticized the policy of double standards followed by the social reformers. While on the one hand they eulogized the Sita-Savitri ideal and exhorted the Indian women to emulate this, on the other they themselves preferred to acquire English knowledge and to follow the Western lifestyle. Regarding the social reformers as hypocrites, she wrote:

> *Sita aur Savitri banane ke liye Ramchandra, Krishna, Bharat aur Yudhishtir ki aavashkta hoti hai. Coat, patloon, aur necktie collar sharier par aur pashchimi aarthik adarshoan ki tarang dil mein lekar aisi stri jati ke utpann karne ki abhilaasha akaashpushp dhundne ke samaan hai.*[75]

(The task of producing model women like Sita and Savitri seems incongruent with a social situation which does not oblige men to become a Ramchandra, a Krishna, a Bharat or a Yudhishter. Dressed in coat, pant and necktie, and inebriated with the ambition to emulate Western economic ideals, Indian men's craving for such ideal women is akin to search for the proverbial mythical flower.)

In yet another article titled "Hamare Hriday", Uma Nehru pointed out that while on the one hand Indian men were greatly concerned about India's freedom, on the other they had shown complete apathy to the enslavement of women both at the physical and spiritual levels. She

[74] *Stree Darpan*, December 1915.

[75] *Stree Darpan*, March 1918. Also see Vir Bharat Talwar, op. cit., p. 228.

criticized the hallowed ideal of self-sacrifice as a woman's *dharma* (duty). "Such self sacrifice which clearly destroys one's own body and soul and makes others greedy, selfish, unjust and tyrannical is not self sacrifice, it is suicide".[76] She ridiculed the discriminatory attitude followed in gender-relations in India. She never liked the traditional model wherein the relationship between man and woman was akin to the master-slave relationship.[77] She believed that man-woman relationship should be based on mutual love and respect. She was particularly critical of the manner in which Indian men tried to suppress woman's sexuality and fertility and exploited her labour by calling her *Grihalakshmi*.

Thus as a result of the contributions made by the popular Hindi journals, *Stree Darpan* in particular, through the publication of a number of thought-provoking articles, poems and stories, there began to emerge a change in attitudes in traditional families. Definitely, their perceptions on gender-relations had undergone a perceptive change. The traditional perception of women as *ardhangini* which had reduced her to the level of a mere shadow of her husband devoid of any independent thinking, began to show a perceptible change. The new woman represented both the traditional image of womanhood capable of performing her household duties efficiently and the modern, enlightened image capable of assuming responsibilities outside the four walls of her home.

This new role-model for women was accepted by the progressive women thinkers of those times because under the new model due recognition was given to women's independent thinking, their intellectual capabilities and their existence as individuals in their own right.[78] The *patidharma* concept which required women to completely surrender their individuality to their husbands at every

[76]Vir Bharat Talwar, op. cit., pp. 228-29.

[77]*Stree Darpan*, April 1918.

[78]Rameshwari Nehru, "Stri Jati Aur Desh Ki Swadhinta", *Stree Darpan,* August 1921.

level—mind, body, soul—was put under scrutiny.[79] Women felt that on a reciprocal basis their husbands also should follow the ideal of *patnivrata dharma*[80] and remain totally loyal to their wives. Thus, in the new equation of gender-relations, both the husband and wife were to be treated on an equal footing. They could retain their individual identities and personal freedom. The earlier master-slave relationship between husband and wife paved the way for a more dignified relationship based on the spirit of mutual love and respect.

Stage was now set for women to make their presence felt in the ongoing national movement. And in this respect, the contribution made by Annie Besant, both to the cause of the freedom struggle and women's emancipation, deserves a special mention. The formation of the Home Rule League in 1916 under the able leadership of Annie Besant was indeed a very significant event to have taken place in the history of India's national movement and women's resurgence. This is mainly because it was for the first time that a woman led the movement.

It was largely due to the efforts of Annie Besant that an organized movement was formed for placing before the British authorities the demand for the political rights of women. Her leadership qualities served as a source of

[79]Surya Devi, "Nari Vilap", *Stree Darpan,* December 1918; Dharampatni Kalindi Narayanan Verma, "Pativrata Dharm aur Swatantarta", *Stree Darpan,* August 1921. The fact that the author articulated her radical ideas under the name of her husband showed the deep-rooted impact of the social norm of the merger of wife's identity with that of her husband's.

[80]Smt. Hira Devi, "Stri Vrat", *Stree Darpan,* July 1910. In her articles, Kailash Rani Baatal, a regular contributor to *Stree Darpan*, often drew attention to the contradiction between the public postures and private behaviour of Indian men who flaunted the liberal ideal of "duties towards women" as a rhetoric. Her article "Strion Ka Mahatava Tatha Purushon Ka Kartavya", *Stree Darpan,* December 1915, was an eloquent articulation of these ideas. Also see, Uma Nehru, "Hamara Samajik Dhancha", *Stree Darpan,* April 1918.

inspiration for women of India who felt motivated to contribute their humble mite to the cause of the country's freedom. And with the advent of Gandhi on the political scene of India, women's involvement in the political affairs of the country assumed a new dimension. C.M. Reddi had rightly stated that "Dr. A. Besant prepared the ground for the Gandhian freedom movement in which women have played a prominent part".[81]

However, before we embark on a detailed discussion of the role played by women in different Gandhian movements like the Non-cooperation, the Civil Disobedience and the Quit India, it would be appropriate to first dwell on Gandhi's ideology and perception in regard to the role he had envisaged for women both in society and freedom struggle and to understand the various influences that had shaped Gandhi's vision of women.

[81]C.M. Reddi, "The Religion and Social Reforms", in J.H. Cousins, ed, *The Annie Besant Centenary Book*. Also see Manmohan Kaur, *Women in India's Freedom Struggle* (Sterling, New Delhi, 1985), p. 112.

CHAPTER II

GANDHI'S PERCEPTION OF WOMEN

I

Creation of Counter-Hegemonic Influence of Nationalist Ideology

It would not be incorrect to say that in the history of revolutions and national liberation struggles of the twentieth century, the Gandhi-led mass movement occupies a unique position. Thus far the revolutions of twentieth century took place only in those countries which were non-bourgeois in character such as Tsarist Russia, Colonial China, Vietnam and Cuba. In such states, it was by virtue of armed revolts that the movements succeeded in overthrowing the oppressive rules and in bringing back the power. In contrast, in the highly centralized, bureaucratic colonial state in India, the Britishers were able to curtail the civil liberties of the Indians by using repressive measures through the rule of law and powerful military strength at its command which became evident only when it faced challenge from a formidable mass movement. Since the Britishers were able to exercise considerable authority, influence and prestige over the minds of the Indians, it could be called a semi-hegemonic state.

Gandhi was the first to realize that it was virtually impossible to overthrow such a powerful state through armed/insurrectionary movement. He believed that the Indians should find ways and means to reduce the impact of the prestige and authority of the colonial state and to create the counter-hegemonic influence of nationalist ideology and leadership. He was of the firm conviction that only a powerful, mass movement based on the principle of non-violence on a big scale through mobilization of people throughout the length and breadth of the country could rattle the British authority. The uniqueness of the Gandhian mass movement is underlined by the fact that thousands of women were able to take part in it in myriad forms. It would be difficult to appreciate the significance of women's participation in this movement without properly emphasizing the unique nature of the Gandhi-led mass movement, particularly because the national movement of India is the only movement in the world, which succeeded in overthrowing a semi-hegemonic state.

A major aspect of the national movement's strategy of building counter-hegemony was the constructive programme, which provided ample avenues for women's participation. And considering that the struggle for independence was a long-drawn battle in which open warfare had no role to play, the best way to establish close contacts with the masses was through constructive work on a large scale. The constructive programme as envisaged by Gandhi, had both inner and outer dimensions. At the inner level the workers were to be given moral and psychological training, while at the outer level the constructive programme meant the proper kind of economic and social activity. Mahatma Gandhi interpreted women's political participation as an extension of traditional and familial roles. He placed before the Indian women the example of Sita and encouraged them to emulate her self- sacrifice and devotion to Rama, her god-husband, as models for their behaviour in their conjugal families. He was of the firm conviction that "women had a greater capacity to resist the temptations of foreign rule, and to suffer non-violently for their beliefs. Through his

Satyagraha movements, Gandhi sought to instill non- violent courage in all Indians. For the Mahatma, therefore, women's participation in the nationalist movement was necessary for ideological reasons as well as for the practical reason that with women involved the national movement would be linked to every home in India".[1]

The Britishers tried to create norms, values, body of beliefs and attitudes in regard to what was good and what was bad, legal-illegal, right-wrong, etc. and thus succeeded in framing political, social and moral culture within the framework of which they could control, manipulate and establish their rule on a firm footing. It is in this context that Gandhi's role assumes great significance. He succeeded to a great extent in creating a counter-culture in the areas of politics, societies and morality.

The counter-culture of the Gandhi-led mass movement emphasized the feminine culture as opposed to the basic character of the British rule wherein the symbols of power, prestige, status and individual successes represented a masculine character. The feminine traits were simplicity, service, religion and dedication, which were not governed by the desire to secure benefits and favours from the colonial authority. The significant point is that the feminine traits represented passive resistance in which war or the use of brute force (which represented the masculine traits) had receded into the background. In this form of non-violent passive resistance, the masses firmly reject the oppressive, insensitive and immoral alien authority through withdrawal of support (without resorting to the use of force).

Gandhi has often been criticized because he had identified women with virtues of sacrifice, suffering and quiet, non-violent struggle and thus relegated them in the process to a somewhat inferior position in the male-dominated patriarchal

[1]Gail Minault, *The Extended Family: Women and Political Participation in India and Pakistan* (Chanakya Publications, New Delhi, 1981), pp. 10-11.

society. However, it would be fair to say that in extolling these feminine virtues Gandhi had not excluded men. In fact, he thought that the best way to counter 'male' symbolism (the British rule) was to project the alternative, feminine vision in opposition to individualism, competitive and aggressive self-development. Gandhi thought that women were much better placed at the moral, cultural and ideological levels to attempt the method of non-violent passive resistance. *Stree Dharma*, a women-oriented journal, reported in 1930: "Because the qualities which this new form of warfare is displaying are feminine rather than masculine, we may look on this life and death struggle to be free as the women's war."

II

Upsurge in Women's Politicization

The upsurge in women's politicization—as in the politicization of the entire Indian society—is associated with the Non-cooperation movement which saw the participation of women on a large scale in constructive programmes laid down by Gandhi like spinning and *khadi* work. According to Gail Pearson these were not mere extensions of "household activities",[2] but were intrinsic to the type of movement Gandhi had envisaged in which such constructive work performed by both men and women had an extremely valuable role to play. By the late 1920s women had started participating in increasing numbers in public bonfires of foreign cloth even in the mill areas at night, and by 1930, all-night *dharnas* consisting exclusively of women had begun to be organized. The myth of the drawing-room elite women fostered by the colonial bureaucracy had exploded by then. By the time the first phase of the Civil Disobedience movement ended in 1931-32,

[2]Gail Pearson, "Nationalism, Universalization, and the Extended Female Space in Bombay City", in Gail Minault, op. cit., Ch. 7.

women were firmly entrenched in the mass movement, which encompassed diverse sections of women—from the urban rich to the rural poor. The main body of women participants were not from the intelligentsia or even the big urban centres. Thousands of rural women took recourse to defiance of the law in forests and villages, where they stood with their children around them. Almost every house had become a sanctuary for the lawbreakers. Women selling the "salt of freedom" at every corner in the course of the Salt Satyagraha campaign universalized the concept.[3]

Before the appearance of Gandhi on the political scene of India, women from the elite classes had dominated the "women's movement" in India. Kamaladevi Chattopadhyay had characterized the Indian feminist women as inspired by Europe and within the bourgeois-capitalist framework.[4] While the Liberals and Radicals differed in their views in regard to the role of women in the freedom movement and the importance of tradition in their lives, they were unanimous in their opinion in so far as they viewed women within familial context. They both felt that women's main role lay at home and political participation by women was seen only as an extension of their familial roles. The idea of women's active political participation was just unimaginable. Even in the social reform movement women had a limited role to play because it regarded women as targets, and not instruments, of social reform. No serious effort had been made on a big scale to enlist the support of women.

With the formation of women's organizations at the national level like AIWC and WIA, women had begun to assume responsibility for their own education and for social reform. They also began to associate themselves

[3]Shashi Joshi, "Women and Indian Nationalism: A Theoretical Framework—Feminism, Mass Movement and Gandhian Ideology", paper presented at the Third National Conference on Women's Studies, Punjab University, Chandigarh, 1-4 October 1986.

[4]Ibid.

with political activity, though on a small scale.[5] Women leaders like Sarojini Naidu had already made their presence felt on the national scene. Some argue that it was the tide of nationalism which pushed women towards the path of progress. "The great leap forward made by the Indian women is one of the significant milestones in our national progress. Cramped by age-old customs, bound by mouldy traditions, they had lain languishing behind the four walls of their little domestic yard, seemingly untouched by the passing juggernaut of swift changes, until one day almost like a tornado the great gale of nationalism swept the land crashing down the ancient boundaries and setting into motion new currents, weaving new patterns of thought and living breaking through and across the deep-cuts of ancient usage".[6] But it was Gandhi who infused a new spirit and gave a new direction to the freedom movement and drew into it women in large numbers.[7]

Though no one can deny the influence exercised by Gandhi on women, particularly in regard to their participation in the national movement,[8] but at the same time there has been lots of criticism about the methods used by him to advance his movement.[9] The methods used by Gandhi generated a big controversy which led to the alienation of some leaders from his political ideology, prominent examples being Tilak and Bose; Godse too

[5]Aparna Basu, "The Role of Women in the Indian Struggle for Freedom", in B.R. Nanda, ed, *Indian Women: From Purdah to Modernity* (Vikas Publishing House, New Delhi, 1976), p. 20.

[6]Kamaladevi Chattopadhyay, *Indian Women's Battle for Freedom* (Delhi, 1983), p. 94; idem, "What Gandhiji has done for Women", in B.L. Rallia Ram, ed, *What Gandhiji has done for India* (Lahore, n.d.), p. 57.

[7]Aparna Basu, op. cit., p. 20.

[8]Geraldine Forbes, "The Indian Women's Movement: Struggle for Women's Rights or National Liberation", in Gail Minault, op. cit., Ch. 3.

[9]Ashis Nandy, "Final Encounter: The Politics of the Assassination of Gandhi", in idem, *At the Edge of Psychology* (OUP, New Delhi, 1980), pp. 70-98.

justified Gandhi's assassination on these grounds.[10] Besides, there were women too who were not in agreement with Gandhi's modus operandi, and therefore thought it prudent not to associate themselves with the Gandhian movement.[11] But the number of men and women who disagreed with him was marginal. Gandhi had the support of the majority. In fact, Gandhi was so deeply respected that even the guardians of women participants—fathers, husbands, and brothers—encouraged them to extend their wholehearted cooperation to Gandhi in his mission.[12] "Women were drawn to Gandhi by his magnetic personality, his unique naturalness and transparent sincerity".[13]

Apart form Gandhi's charismatic personality many other factors set him apart from other reformers and political leaders who had either preceded him or were his contemporaries. "It would be difficult to name a single modern Indian leader who stands apart from his province, caste or creed. We cannot think of Lokamanya Tilak without the historical traditions of the great Maratha race; we cannot picture Lala Lajpat Rai without the setting of the virile Arya Samaj. But the same cannot be said of Mahatma Gandhi.... Excepting the language, he has as much in common with the Gujaratis as with the sons of Madras and Bengal. He combines in himself the keen analytical faculty of Madrasee, the emotion of the Bangalee, the intrepidity of the Maratha, the directness and candour of the skin and the precision and tactfulness of a son of Gujarat".[14] He laid stress on self-reliance and the idea of seeking support from the government never appealed to him. He was of the firm belief that personal reform was to be given more importance than social reform, and social reform was to precede political independence. "To postpone

[10]Ibid., pp. 77-87.

[11]Aparna Basu, op. cit., p. 31.

[12]See interview with Sucheta Kripalani, Oral History Project, Nehru Memorial Museum and Library, New Delhi, 1968, p. 12.

[13]Aparna Basu, op. cit., p. 20.

[14]D.V. Athalye, *The Life of Mahatma Gandhi* (Swadeshi Publishing Company, Pune, 1923), pp. 1-2.

social reform till after attainment of Swaraj is not to know the meaning of Swaraj".[15] Also, women became targets as well as instruments of social reform. "Their historic role, therefore, was to lead the forces of social revolutions against inequality, exploitation and social justice—not only for women, but for all oppressed groups in society".[16] He believed that social transformation could take place only if efforts made for the uplift of all— particularly the Harijans and the women—led to the regeneration of the Indian society. One is inclined to submit that the Gandhian vision can be defined as a body of ethico-moral beliefs and social prescriptions urging radical overhaul of the existing political structure for the ultimate creation of an "ideal society".[17] According to Judith Brown: "He visualized a total renewal of society from its roots upwards so that it would grow into a true nation, characterized by harmony and sympathy instead of strife and suspicion, in which castes, communities and sexes would be equal, complementary and interdependent".[18] Gandhi thus encouraged women to take part in the freedom movement, apart from working for their emancipation at the social level.

Amrit Kaur, one of Gandhi's closest women associates remarked: "When he (i.e., Gandhi) called on Indians to join his army for the freedom fight he stressed that women would be just as acceptable to him, if not more so than men, because he needed moral courage far more than physical prowess. This was I felt an irresistible call to my sex and something which threw a new light...on how whilst fighting for freedom women would also, under his

[15]Charles Heimsath, *Indian Nationalism and Social Reform* (OUP, Mumbai, 1964), p. 343.

[16]Vina Mazumdar, "Another Development with Women: A View From Asia", in *Development Dialogue* (1982), p. 67.

[17]Rajan Mahan, *Women in Indian National Congress, 1921-1931* (Rawat Publications, Jaipur and New Delhi, 1999), p. 82.

[18]Judith M. Brown, *Gandhi, The Prisoner of Hope* (OUP, New Delhi, 1990), p. 213.

leadership, be able to fight against many of the excrescences (sic) that had crept into our society, including the subjugation of women. Indeed, political freedom for him was only the first step towards the building up a new order of society".[19] Gandhi's methods were thus in sharp contrast to those of his predecessors.[20] At Gandhi's call, "they came out in larger numbers from the shelter of their homes to take part in the struggle for India's freedom. Once the old shackles were removed, it was no longer possible to replace them in the same way. Attempts were no doubt made to go back, but they were bound to fail".[21]

III

Influences which Shaped Gandhi's Vision of Women

According to Gandhi, "... to call woman the weaker sex is a libel; it is man's injustice to woman. If by strength is meant brute strength, then indeed is a woman less brute than man. If by strength is meant moral power then woman is an immeasurably man's superior. Has she not great intuition, is she not more self-sacrificing, has she not great powers of endurance, has she not great courage? Without her, man could not be. If non-violence is the law our being, the future is with woman".[22] There are various factors behind Gandhi's motivation to support the cause of women and to involve them in the cause of the country's freedom. Some scholars attribute this to his upbringing and cultural background, or the influence of his deeply religious mother[23] and wife[24] or his

[19]Rajkumari Amrit Kaur, "Gandhi: The Man and His Appeal", in V. Grover and Ranjana Arora, ed, *Great Women of India* (Deep and Deep Publications, New Delhi, 1993), Vol. 5, pp. 281-82.

[20]Charles Heimsath, op. cit., p. 343.

[21]Jawaharlal Nehru's " Foreword" in Tara Ali Baig, ed, *Women of India* (Publications Division, New Delhi, 1958), p. vii.

[22]Aloo J. Dastur and Usha H. Mehta, *Gandhi's Contribution to the Emancipation of Women* (Popular Prakashan, Mumabi, 1991), p. 20.

effeminate character.[25] Perhaps "the most enduring influence which moulded Gandhi's thought and his attitude towards women was the profound impact of his mother, Putlibai Gandhi".[26] To quote Gandhi: "If you notice any purity in me, I have inherited it from my mother, and not from my father.... The only impression she ever left on my mind is that of saintliness".[27]

Gandhi's vision of women was also greatly influenced by his wife, Kasturba. While referring to his carnal desires, Gandhi candidly admits that he had inflicted innumerable tortures upon his wife "who bore them with remarkable forbearance and fortitude".[28] Gandhi further remarks: "Perhaps only a Hindu wife would tolerate these hardships, and that is why I have regarded woman as an incarnation of tolerance".[29] It may also be noted that during the course of his political career Gandhi had interacted with a large number of women who were his close associates, notable examples being Annie Besant, Oliver Schriener, Millie Graham Polock, Margaret Cousins, Madeline Slade (Mirabhen), Sarojini Naidu, Sarala Devi Chaudhurani, Amrit Kaur, Kamaladevi Chattopadhyay, Sushila Nayyar, and so on.[30] In their own humble ways, the women mentioned above did contribute to a certain extent in the framing of Gandhi's perception of women.

[23]P. Spratt, *Gandhism: An Analysis* (The Huxley Press, Madras, 1939), p. 8; Kamaladevi Chattopadhyay, op. cit., Lahore, n.d., p. 69; N. K. Bose, *My Days with Gandhi* (Calcutta, 1953), pp. 192-93, 202; M. K. Gandhi, *The Story of My Experiments with Truth* (Penguin, 1983), Preface.

[24]Kamaladevi Chattopadhyay, op. cit., Lahore, n.d., p. 69.

[25]N.K. Bose, op. cit., p. 2.

[26]Rajan Mahan, op. cit., p. 84.

[27]Quoted in Krishna Kripalani, *Gandhi: A Life* (NBT, New Delhi, 1968), p. 2.

[28]Rajan Mahan, op. cit., p. 85.

[29]M. K. Gandhi, *An Autobiography*, p. 17.

[30]Eleanor Morton, *Women Behind Mahatma Gandhi* (London, 1954) and idem, *The Women in Gandhi's Life* (New York, 1953).

Religion too played an important role in shaping Gandhi's vision of women. According to Athalye, Gandhi was mainly influenced by Vaishnavism, liberal Jainism and his deep respect for Christ.[31] Ganguli believes that it was Buddhism and Islam that had influenced Gandhi.[32] Basham opines that in supporting the cause of women in society, Gandhi was influenced by Western feminism.[33] Erikson says that since Gandhi had psychological problems in accepting the natural superiority of women in possessing such virtues as love, kindness, etc., he made efforts to become more maternal than the most motherly of mothers.[34] Even Gandhi's basic philosophy of Satyagraha is said to negate the aggressive, masculine stereotypes of human potential while incorporating the gentle, peaceful and communitarian aspects normally associated with women. But among the various influences which shaped Gandhi's vision of women, it seems that religion was the major factor which becomes evident from the fact that the ideals of womanhood emphasized by him were chiefly Sita, Savitri, Damyanti and Draupadi.

IV
Gandhi's Condemnation of Social Evils

Gandhi had ruthlessly condemned the various social evils which made the condition of women even more pathetic. He was very severe in his criticism of the preference for sons among the Indian families. To quote him: "I make no

[31]D.V. Athalye, *The Life of Mahatma Gandhi* (Swadeshi Publishing Company, Pune, 1923), p. 142.

[32]B.N. Ganguli, *Gandhi's Social Philosophy* (John Wiley and Sons, New York, 1973).

[33]A.L. Basham, "Traditional Influences on the Thought of Mahamta Gandhi", in R. Kumar, ed, *Essays in Gandhian Politics: The Rowlatt Act of 1919* (Oxford, London, 1971), pp. 41-42.

[34]Erik Erikson, *Gandhi's Truth* (W. Norton and Co., New York, 1969).

distinction between son and daughter. Such distinction is in my opinion invidious and wrong. The birth of a son or a daughter should be welcome alike".[35] Birth of a female child was not welcome mainly because of the inevitable weeding expenses and the "hateful system of dowry". Gandhi sharply criticized these abhorrent practices saying that even though women are the *ardhangini* or the better half, yet they are "reduced to the position of a mere chattel to be bought and sold".[36] Gandhi implored upon the educated youth to shun the despicable system of dowry. He was surprised that the educated youth did not dare to offer resistance to this unhealthy custom. He said: "How is it that so many boys and girls who have even passed through colleges, are found unable or unwilling to resist this manifestly evil custom (compulsory marriage with dowry paid and received) which affects their future so intimately"?[37] He went to the extent of saying that those young men who demanded dowry should be ex-communicated.[38]

Another social evil which deeply pained Gandhi was child-marriage, particularly ill-matched marriages in which young girls were married to men good enough to be their grandfather. Gandhi was so vehement in his criticism of child-marriage that he called it "an immoral and inhuman act", and he considered it "a crime against god and man to call the union of the children a married state...".[39] Gandhi was of the opinion that such a widespread evil could not be cured through mere legislation. He felt that the enlightened public opinion would be more effective.

[35]M.K. Gandhi, "The Marriage Ideal", in *Harijan*, 5 June 1937.

[36]*Collected Works of Mahatma Gandhi,* Vol. 39, 1928, p. 415.

[37]*Harijan,* 23 May 1936. Also see *Collected Works of Mahatma Gandhi,* Vol. LXII, pp. 435-36.

[38]*Young India,* 21 June 1928.

[39]*Young India*, 5 August 1926. Also see M.K. Gandhi, *The Role of Women*, edited by A.T. Hingorani (Bharatiya Vidya Bhawan, Mumbai, 1964).

> I am not opposed to legislation in such matters, but I do lay greater stress on cultivation of public opinion; the Madras case would have been impossible, if there had been a living public opinion against child-marriages. The young man in question is not an illiterate labourer, but an intelligent, educated typist. It would have been impossible for him to marry or touch the girl, if public opinion had been against the marriage or the consummation of the marriage of girls of tender age. Ordinarily, a girl under 18 years should never be given in marriage. This custom of child marriage is both a moral as well as physical evil. For it undermines our morals and induces physical degeneration. By countenancing such customs we recede from God as well as Swaraj. A man who has no thought of the tender age of a girl has none of God. And undergrown men have no capacity for fighting battles of freedom or having gained it.[40]

Gandhi was also deeply moved by the pathetic condition of child widows. He regarded prohibition of remarriage of child widows as senseless and cruel which ought to be abolished. He was extremely critical of the parents who committed the sin of marrying their infant daughters. He suggested that such parents should make amends by remarrying their daughters if they were widowed in their teens.[41] He also encouraged educated young men to marry girl widows.[42] However, in the case of older widows, Gandhi had a different point of view. He expressed the opinion that "voluntary enlightened widowhood is an invaluable social asset". According to him "a real Hindu widow is a treasure. She is one of the gifts of Hinduism to

[40] Aloo J. Dastur and Usha H. Mehta, op. cit., p. 73

[41] *Young India*, 7 October 1926 and 11 November 1926.

[42] Gandhi's speech addressed to the students of Pachiappa's College, Madras, *Young India*, 15 September 1927.

femininity". "Thus, a widow's life marked by self-control, sacrifice and service was an ornament, and benefit to religion and society and hence deserved reverence and veneration from Hindu society".[43]

In regard to the custom of *purdah*, Gandhi opined that it was a big obstacle to the growth of Indian women. To quote him:

> I thought of the wrong being done by men to the women of India by clinging to a barbarous custom which, whatever use it might have had when it was first introduced, had now become totally useless and doing incalculable harm to the country. All the education that we have been receiving for the past 100 years seems to have produced but little impression upon us, for I note that *purdah* is being retained even in educated households, not because the educated men believe in it themselves, but because they will not manfully resist the brutal custom and sweep it away at a stroke. I have the privilege of addressing hundreds of meetings of women attended by thousands. The din and the noise created at these meetings make it impossible to speak with any effect to the women who attend them. Nothing better is to be expected so long as they are caged and confined in their houses and little courtyards.[44]

Gandhi believed that the barbarous custom of *purdah* was causing immense harm to the country. He stressed: "Let us not live with one limb completely or partially paralyzed.... By seeking today to interfere with the free growth of the womanhood of India we are interfering with the growth of free and independent spirited men.... It (i.e., *purdah*) accounts for our own weakness, indecision,

[43]*Young India*, 19 August 1926.
[44]Aloo J. Dastur and Usha H. Mehta, op. cit., p. 75.

narrowness and helplessness. Let us then tear down the *purdah* with one mighty effort".[45]

In regard to the economic independence of women, a disciple of Gandhi had asked him about his attitude towards the modification of laws relating to the right of women to own property. Gandhi replied:

> I would answer the question by counter question: has not independence of man and his holding property led to the spread of immorality among men? If you answer 'yes' then let it be so also with women. And when women have rights of ownership and the rest like men, it would be found that the enjoyment of such rights is not responsible for their vices or their virtues. Morality, which depends upon the helpness of a man or woman, has not much to recommend it. Morality is rooted in the purity of our hearts.[46]

V
Traditional Role Differential between Man and Woman

As far as roles of men and women in society are concerned, Gandhi believed that there was the basic difference in the social roles and functions of man and woman. Though they were to play different roles, yet these were not contradictory. In the opinion Gandhi, a woman's place is in the home, while man is responsible for providing woman with the necessary means to enable her to run her home efficiently. In fact man is the bread-earner. Woman's first duty is towards her husband, then his family and finally the country. According to Gandhi, Sita personified the

[45]*Young India,* 3 February 1927. It is interesting to note that in December 1928, the All India Women's Social Conference passed a resolution condemning the custom of *purdah*. See *Stri Dharma,* Vol. 12, 1928-29, p. 123.

[46]Aloo J. Dastur and Usha H. Mehta, op. cit., p. 76.

spirit of sacrifice, fidelity, suffering and moral strength typical of Indian womanhood.

While emphasizing the complementary roles of men and women, Gandhi made it absolutely clear that women were in no way inferior to men. The very idea of calling woman the weaker sex was not acceptable to Gandhi.[47] He asserted that women were blessed with immense spiritual strength and they were not weak (*stree abala nahin hai*), though men were stronger at the physical level.[48] He went to the extent of arguing that those scriptures which look down upon women, should be condemned. "The ancient is, therefore, not sacrosanct to Gandhiji, if it has turned to dross. His heart bleeds for those who suffer under the burden of traditions".[49] Arguing that those scriptural injunctions which were in conflict with true morality should not be followed, Gandhi asserted that "all that is published in the name of scriptures will not be taken as the word of God". Gandhi even suggested the removal of all those injunctions in the Smritis which did not appeal to the moral sense.[50] He was of the opinion that men's lust for power and prestige had led to the subjugation of women and also to the degeneration of the society. Thus, while giving his consent to the traditional role differential between man and woman, he also wanted to break the traditional stereotypes. This he did by recommending equal rights for both, by emphasizing that women were in no way inferior to men and by encouraging women to fight for their rightful place in society.

However, Gandhi never thought of role modification or reversal of roles. His ideas on women's role were greatly influenced by his high-caste, middle-class Hindu upbringing within the patriarchal framework. The idea of transcending the constraints imposed by the patriarchal norms did not

[47]Ibid., p. 20.

[48]M.K. Gandhi, *Women and Social Injustice* (Navjivan, Ahmedabad, 1942), pp. v, 196.

[49]Kamaladevi Chattopadhyay, op. cit., Lahore, n.d., pp. 59-60.

[50]*Harijan*, 28 November 1936; *Collected Works of Mahatma Gandhi*, Vol. 67, p. 321.

appeal to him. Even where women were expected to take an active part in social reforms, this was merely considered as an extension of their familial roles. Perhaps this is the reason why the male guardians had no objections to women of their families taking part in Gandhi's constructive programmes. They felt secure that women would not try to transgress the boundaries of the male-dominated patriarchal framework.[51]

Gandhi had expressed the opinion that the entry of women into politics would purge the system of all corrupt practices and render the system clean. He thought that non-violence and passive resistance were basically feminine traits which women had imbibed as a result of long tradition of sacrifice and suffering within the home. It is for this reason he felt that women were ideally suited to participate in the national movement, the basic ideals of which were *ahimsa* and *satyagraha.* "According to Gandhi, progress in civilization consisted in the introduction into human life and social institutions of a large measure of the law of love or self-suffering which woman represented best in her own person. This was a profoundly transformed projection on the broad canvas of social life of an attitude, which had come into being in the privacy of his personal life".[52]

As already mentioned, Gandhi felt that the first duty of woman was towards her husband; the family and the country came later. Bringing up of children and taking care of the infirm and aged parents of the husband were the prime duties of woman. "It became my conviction that procreation and consequent care of children were inconsistent with public service.... If I wanted to devote myself to the service of the community... I must relinquish the desire for children and wealth and live the life of a *vanaprastha".*[53] Gandhi was thus of the opinion that it was

[51]Uma Rao and Meera Devi, "Glimpses: U.P. Women's Response to Gandhi, 1921-1930", paper presented at the Second National Conference on Women's Studies held at Trivandrum during 9-12 April 1984, Mimeographed, p. 8.

[52]N.K. Bose, op. cit., p. 203.

[53]M.K. Gandhi, op. cit., 1983, p. 196.

difficult for a woman to combine her duties at home with those outside the home. For those who were burdened with familial responsibilities, service to the country must come later. It is precisely for this reason that wife of Manidas was asked not to join the Dandi March.[54] Therefore, in Gandhi's scheme of things there could be no political participation for women at the cost of their familial responsibilities.[55]

Despite the views expressed above, Gandhi took up issues like Swadeshi[56] and prohibition and tried to motivate women to fight for them. He also expected women to play leadership roles.[57] He tried to capitalize on women's feminine traits and traditional qualities by extending their traditional roles into the political sphere.[58] How then did Gandhi strike a balance in his call to women to take part in the struggle for freedom? It may be reiterated that Gandhi gave priority to the familial responsibilities of women. They could take part in the freedom struggle only after fulfilling their responsibilities at home.

Another aspect of Gandhian ideology was that those men and women whose commitment towards the cause of the country's freedom was absolutely firm, should remain celibates (like Sushila Nayar); and if at all they married they should live like celibates. To quote Gandhi: "Without overcoming lust, man cannot hope to rule over self; without rule over self, there can be no Swaraj.... No worker who has not overcome lust, can hope to render any genuine service.... Great causes...cannot be served by intellectual equipment alone, they call for spiritual effort or

[54]M.K. Mehta, *Mahatma Gandhi and His Apostles* (Penguin, 1983), p. 51.

[55]Uma Rao and Meera Devi, op. cit., p. 6.

[56]Ibid., pp. 5-10 and pp. 18-20. Uma Rao and Meera Devi have given a detailed account of U.P. women's response to *swadeshi*, their active association with *prabhat pheris* and public demonstrations and the contributions made by women's journals and associations in making the Swadeshi movement popular.

[57]Ibid., p. 6.

[58]Gail Minault, op. cit., 1981, pp. 10-11.

soul force. Soul force comes only through God's grace and never descends upon a man who *is a slave to lust*".[59] He firmly believed that "without *Brahmacharya*, the *Satyagrahi* will have no lustre, no inner strength to stand unarmed against the whole world... his strength will fail him at the right moment".[60]

Gandhi is understood to have given advice to Vijaylakshmi Pandit and her husband to live like celibates at the time when he gave his blessings on the occasion of their wedding.[61] It is interesting to note that when the Kripalanis expressed their desire to marry, Gandhi discouraged Sucheta from marring J.B. Kripalani and he held the former responsible for J.B.'s straying away from the path.[62] It may thus be seen that though Gandhi did make efforts to demolish the traditional image of woman, yet he never tried to change the patriarchal system of Indian society.

In cases where women wanted to participate in the national movement but their husbands did not allow them to do so (despite their having fulfilled all their familial responsibilities), Gandhi advised such women to take the plunge and join the movement even if it meant defying their

[59]A newly married girl, Annapurana, was so much influenced by Gandhi that she started wearing *khadi* clothes from top to toe. Besides, she donated all her ornaments except the ones that signified her martial status. See *Collected Works of Mahatma Gandhi*, Vol. XIX, p. 413. Durgabai's first meeting with Gandhi brought about a radical transformation in her; she was inspired later to take part in the freedom struggle. See *Transcript of Durgabai Deshmukh Interview*, Nehru Memorial Museum and Library, Oral History Section.

[60]M. Venkatarangaiya, *The Freedom Struggle in Andhra Pradesh, 1921-31* (Hyderabad, 1965), p. 8.

[61]Vijaylakshmi Pandit, *The Scope of Happiness* (Vikas, New Delhi, 1979), p. 73. Also see Gandhi's letter to Naraindas Gandhi in *Collected Works of Mahatma Gandhi* (July-December 1930), Vol. XLIV (1971), p. 353.

[62]See interview with Sucheta Kripalani, Oral History Project, Nehru Memorial Museum and Library, 1968, p. 6; also see Sucheta Kripalani, *Unfinished Autobiography*, edited by K.N. Vaswani (Navjivan, Ahmedabad, 1978), p. 21.

husbands. In such cases, Gandhi put the blame on men for being selfish in not allowing their wives to fight for a noble cause. Gandhi even went to the extent of suggesting that, if necessary, women should not hesitate in using the civil disobedience based on *ahimsa* and truth against the unreasonable restrictions imposed within the home.[63]

It would be appropriate to point out here that in cases where women were actively involved in the national movement, it did lead to a certain amount of tension within their homes. Vijaylakshmi Pandit has pointed out in her autobiography that her mother Swarup Rani found it difficult to adjust to the new lifestyle which was brought about as a consequence of both her (Vijaylakshmi Pandit's) brother and father joining the Gandhian movement. Swarup Rani felt greatly disturbed at the constant encroachment on her privacy by the external world of politics.[64] She was just not prepared to sacrifice the interests of her family for the sake of the nation. Vijaylakshmi too had experienced great tension when she was put behind the bars and there was nobody to take care of her young daughter. She even expressed regrets for having taken part in the national movement at that point of time.[65] Another glaring example in this respect is that of Rajkumari Amrit Kaur who had developed strained relations with her brother because he resented her active involvement with the national movement. In his letters to Amrit Kaur, Gandhi had expressed his deep concern over this development and advised her to take urgent steps to sort out her differences with her brother. The stand taken by Gandhi was, however, inconsistent with his advice to women to actively involve themselves in the national movement even if it meant defying authority of their respective husbands and other family members.[66]

[63]M.K. Gandhi, *Women and Social Injustice*, op. cit., p. 202.

[64]Pandit, op. cit., pp. 64-70, 83.

[65]Ibid., pp. 109-10.

[66]M.K. Gandhi, *Letters to Rajkumari Amrit Kaur* (Navjivan, Ahmedabad, 1961), p. 85. Also see Barbara Ramusack, "Rajkumari Amrit Kaur : Feminist and Nationalist .....", Mimeographed, p. 6.

In regard to his relationship with his wife Kasturba, Gandhi says:

> Kasturba herself does not perhaps know whether she has any ideals independently of me. It is likely that many of my doings have not her approval even today. We never discuss them. I see no good in discussing them. For she was educated neither by her parents nor by me at the time when I ought to have done it. But she is blessed with one great quality... a quality which most Hindu wives possess in some measure. And it is this: willingly or unwillingly, consciously or unconsciously, she has considered herself blessed in following in my footsteps, and has never stood in the way of my endeavor to lead a life of restraint. Though, therefore, there is a wide difference between us intellectually, I have always had the feeling that ours is a life of contentment, happiness and progress.[67]

From the above quotation it becomes evident that Gandhi had attributed the intellectual difference between Kasturba and himself to her lack of education. Besides, Gandhi's perception of an ideal wife was governed by his own experience of a high-caste Hindu from Gujarat. Above all, he took it for granted that Kasturba had willingly agreed to play the traditional role and to stay in the background.[68] And whenever she assumed the mantle of leadership it was mostly when Gandhi when was in jail. Even in such times she appealed on behalf of Gandhi.[69]

[67]M.K. Gandhi, op.cit., 1983, pp. 256-57.

[68]Kamaladevi Chattopadhyay, however, was of a different opinion. She believed that Kasturba had her own independent views and never hesitated to differ from Gandhi. "She was not the wife who walked in his shadow, she was one who shed a light of her own". See Kamaladevi Chattopadhyay, op. cit., Lahore, n.d., p. 70.

[69]Ganpat Rai, *Gandhi and Kasturba: The Story of Their Life* (Kasturba Memorial Publications, Lahore, n.d.).

There can be no denying that Gandhi did succeed in the political mobilization of women on a mass scale, but the question is: Did he succeed in raising the consciousness of women to a level where they could start seeing the world from an altogether different perspective? It would be fair to comment that Gandhi did not succeed in this respect. In fact, he did not direct his attention to bringing about a change in women's level of consciousness. As already stated, in Gandhi's scheme of things radical change in the traditional framework based on the male-dominated patriarchal norms was never envisaged. Interestingly, the women political leaders who had worked in close association with Gandhi had tended to agree with Gandhi's framework of ideas and values. Even those women who were trying to better the lot of their fellow sisters did not question the system.[70] To quote Gail Minault:

> Sarojini Naidu, one of the best-known Congress women activists during the non-cooperation movement of 1920-22 and again during the Salt Satyagraha of 1930, emphasized traditional feminine models in a speech championing *swadeshi* before a gathering of women in 1921. They were the custodians of Indian culture, supreme in everyday affairs of life; only they could bring about a renewed pride in India. Swaraj had to begin in their homes, not by politics alone. She recalled the sacrifices of Sita, of Savitri, and the strength of Draupadi, and asked the women to give up all foreign clothing, to take up spinning, to wear only homespun saris, and in this way to resist foreign rule. Naidu thus emphasized the dual nature of women's roles, the self-sacrificing wife, the strong, self-sufficient mother.[71]

[70]Gail Minault, op. cit., 1981, p. 11.
[71]Ibid., pp. 10-11.

VI
Gandhi's Perception Compared to that of Nehru's

Just as Sita was Gandhi's cherished ideal of womanhood to be emulated, Jawaharlal Nehru's ideal woman was Chitrangada—the Manipuri princess portrayed in Rabindranath Tagore's celebrated lyrical drama. The image of Sita as depicted in the Ramayana served as the pivot around which gender constructions revolved through the century in the Indian civilization. Gandhi tried to capitalize on this powerful symbol in his efforts to mobilize the Indian women on a mass scale to participate in the national movement. However, this construction of gender relations (in which Sita has been identified with virtues like self-sacrifice, chastity, infinite capacity for suffering, power of endurance, etc.) has been criticized in the growing body of gender structures which have appeared in the last few years. The reason being that it did not cater to the basic needs of women, particularly in regard to their sexual needs and material requirements.[72]

But Rabindranath Tagore, by recasting the mythical image of Chitrangada, paved the way for a new gender construction that was more reasonable to women because it accommodated their needs within the family and in the area of work. The new image as portrayed by Tagore integrated woman's sexuality and her identity as man's equal partner in the sphere outside home. Nehru often saw the personality of Chitrangada—who believed in equality—reflecting through his wife Kamla, an ardent votary of gender equality. Kamla seemed to come to Nehru as Chitrangada herself, saying:

> I am Chitra. No Goddess to be worshipped, nor yet the object of common pity, to be brushed aside like a moth with indifference. If you deign to

[72]Jasodhara Bagchi, ed, *Indian Women: Myth and Reality* (1985).

> keep me by your side in the path of danger and daring, if you allow me to share the great duties of your life, then you will know my true self.[73]

Nehru and Kamla used to share in equal measure the common responsibility arising from a total participation in the national movement. This created a deep emotional bond between Kamla and Jawaharlal, which long spells of the latter's incarceration or phases of Kamla's illness could not shatter.

Nehru was greatly impressed by the enthusiasm shown by women while participating in the Civil Disobedience movement. This movement bound women from different backgrounds to a common cause and they took pride in their being co-sharers with their male counterparts to the cause of the country's liberation. Nehru, who was greatly inspired by the Russian model at the ideological level, said that the dynamism shown by women in taking part in the civil disobedience alongside men was much more appealing than the silent suffering of women in the Sita tradition. To quote him:

> Women had always been there of course, but now there was an avalanche of them, which took not only the British Government but their own men-folk by surprise. Here were these women, women of the upper or middle-classes, leading sheltered lives in their homes, peasant women, working-class women, rich women, poor women pouring out in their tens of thousands in defiance of government order and police *lathi*. It was not only that display of courage and daring, but what was even more surprising was the organizational power they showed.[74]

Gandhi did succeed in mobilizing women on a mass scale and in motivating them to fight for the country's liberation,

[73]Jawaharlal Nehru, *The Discovery of India* (New Delhi, 1984) p. 41.
[74]Ibid., p. 42.

but his perception and logic were different. He was quick to realize that by constantly holding out the example of Sita's power of endurance and silent suffering, he would be able to motivate women to join his movement which was based on the principles of non-violence and passive resistance. This type of movement was very much in keeping with the feminine traits of women. Gandhi was very clear about the role the women were supposed to play in the non-violent movement. He approved picketing, but did not like the idea of women joining the civil protestors. He did not want women to take part in any such protest, which was marked with violence. Gandhi's thinking on women and their sexuality was governed by his typical middle-class background. He thus restricted women's participation in the national movement within certain fixed social parameters. He was of the firm belief that woman's primary responsibility was taking care of her home and husband, and that there was a clear demarcating line between the roles of men and women. He declared: "In trying to ride the horse that man rides she brings herself and him down".[75] He thus discouraged those women from taking part in the national movement who were burdened with familial responsibilities. The idea of women becoming economically independent also did not appeal to Gandhi. He said, "I do not believe in women working for living or undertaking commercial enterprises".

Most men of those times agreed with Gandhian ideology vis-à-vis women because this did not challenge their dominant role within the patriarchal society. Some women, however, did not agree with Gandhi. Margaret Cousins wrote to Gandhi: "Division of sexes in a non-violent campaign seems unnatural and against all the awakened consciousness of the women of today... there can be no watertight compartments of service. Women ask that no marches, imprisonments (sic), demonstrations organized for

[75]M.K. Gandhi, *The Role of Women*, edited by A.T. Hingorani, op. cit.

the benefit of India should prohibit women from a share in them".[76]

Nehru, on the other hand, viewed women's role from a different perspective. Addressing the students of Mahila Vidyapeeth at Allahabad in 1928, Nehru said: "The future of India cannot consist of dolls and playthings and if you made half the population of a country a mere plaything of the other half, an encumbrance on others, how will you ever make progress".[77] Speaking at the same institution in 1934, Nehru said: "The habit of looking upon marriage as a profession almost and as the sole economic refuge for woman will have to go before woman can have any freedom. Freedom depends on economic conditions even more than political and if woman is not economically free and self-earning she will have to depend on her husband or someone else, and dependents are never free".[78]

Thus Nehru's approach was more realistic and practical as compared to that of Gandhi's. "This thinking was a part of his socialist philosophy, which through study and observation, and as a response of a sensitive and analytical mind, had fermented and crystallized in him over the years".[79] When Kamla got arrested on 1-1-1931, Nehru took pride in his wife's sacrifice for the sake of her country. He sent the following message to his daughter Indira: "... Mummie is thoroughly happy and contended.... It was a pleasant new year gift to me".[80] He further said: "She wanted to play her own part in the national struggle and not be merely a hanger-on and a shadow of her husband. She wanted to justify to her own self as well as to the world".[81]

[76]Quoted in Kamaladevi Chattopadhyay, *Indian Women's Battle for Freedom*, op. cit., 1983.

[77]*Selected Works of Jawaharlal Nehru*, Vol. III, p. 362.

[78]Ibid., Vol. VI, p. 220.

[79]Bimla Luthra, "Nehru and the Place of Women in Indian Society", in B.R. Nanda, ed, *Indian Women: From Purdah to Modernity* (Vikas, New Delhi, 1976), p. 5.

[80]Quoted in Promilla Kalhan, *Kamla Nehru: An Intimate Biography* (1990), p. 48.

[81]Jawaharlal Nehru, op. cit., p. 41.

Present studies on gender issues have shown that there is an attempt to recast women—both in the social reform movement of the 19th century and in the national movement —within the constraints of the patriarchal norms.[82] Some scholars argue that soft programmes like spinning which Gandhi had specially conceived for women had actually stereotyped women as domesticated subjects in a patriarchal society where men were supposed to play the role of bread-earners. Gandhi had also never spelt out women's role once the freedom struggle was over. To Nehru, however, the natural corollary to women's participation in the national movement was just the beginning of a greater struggle—a struggle which would give woman an independent identity and she would enjoy equal rights with men. He was one of the few leaders who wanted the women's movement to prosper. To quote him: "I have the greatest admiration... for the women of today. I have faith in them. I am not afraid to allow them freedom to grow because I am convinced that no amount of legal constraint can prevent society from going in a certain direction. And if you put too much legal constraint the structure breaks".[83]

At the time when the Karachi Congress passed a resolution on the fundamental rights in March 1931, Nehru made sure that due emphasis was given to women's rights. "One of the main points of the resolution was that in a planned society, woman's place 'shall be equal' to that of man; she was to have equal status, equal opportunities and equal respect. Women were not to be barred from any sphere of activity merely on grounds of their sex. Third, marriage was not to be a pre-condition to the enjoyment of full and equal civic status of social and economic rights by

[82]Kumkum Sangari and Sudesh Vaid, ed, *Recasting Women: Essays in Colonial History* (Kali for Women, New Delhi, 1989).

[83]Speech delivered during the debate on the Third Reading of the Hindu Marriage Bill, 5 May 1955, *Lok Sabha Debates*, Vol. IV, Pt. II (1955).

women. Fourth, the state was to consider the individual as the basic social unit and plan accordingly".[84]

Nehru was an ardent votary in respect of the identical standards of morality for men and women. In 1925, when Nehru was the president of the municipal committee of Allahabad, some members proposed that all prostitutes should operate in a certain area on the outskirts of the city. In this connection Nehru made the following observation: "The segregation of prostitutes, even if possible, would be objectionable precisely as the segregation of criminals would be objectionable. I do not believe in issuing a fiat that prostitutes must not live in any part of the city of Allahabad except a remote corner. If this is done I would think it equally reasonable to reserve another part of Allahabad for men who exploited women and because of whom prostitution flourishes".[85]

By highlighting the images of Sita-Savitri-Damyanti which provided the focal points of reference for virtues like self-sacrifice, chastity and moral power, the national leaders, including Gandhi, attempted to project the spiritual superiority of India over the Western scientific ideas in the material sphere. In the process they had created a "new patriarchy" for women.[86] Nehru, however, was opposed to the above ideas. He did accept that these "estimable ladies" had played an important role in the context of the times in which they lived, but at the same time he said that they had lived in a particular age and served certain social compulsions which were not applicable to the present-day modern world of science and technology. The silent suffering of Sita was certainly not the trait which Nehru wanted to see in women. He was of the firm conviction that a nation could not progress unless women were given their rightful place in society. While speaking at

[84]Bimla Luthra, op. cit.

[85]*Selected Works of Jawaharlal Nehru*, Vol. II, pp. 15-16.

[86]Partha Chatterjee, "The Nationalist Resolution to the Women's Question", in Kumkum Sangari and Sudesh Vaid, op. cit.

the centenary celebrations of Prof. Karve on 18 April 1958, Nehru made the following observation:

> It is more important, if there can be any comparison, for the women of a nation to be educated—than its men. I say it by way of emphasizing the importance of the mothers and daughters and sisters of a nation. One of the truest measures of a nation's advancement is the state of its women. For out of the women comes the new generation, and it is from their lips and from their laps that it begins to learn. Political revolution is important and economic revolution is still more important, but the most important of all is the social revolution in the people. It is in the measure that the social revolution succeeds that it provides the basis of the economic stability and progress. Women play the most important part in the social revolution.[87]

[87] *Jawaharlal Nehru's Speeches* (New Delhi, 1964), Vol. IV, p. 424.

CHAPTER III

NON-COOPERATION AND KHILAFAT CAMPAIGNS (1920-22), AND WOMEN'S MOBILIZATION

Gandhi's return to India around 1915 after his long-drawn struggle for the cause of the Indians settled in South Africa received a warm and big welcome from the Indian masses. His arrival in India was a turning point in India's struggle for freedom. He was venerated as a messiah, a harbinger of peace, and huge masses were drawn towards his charismatic personality from various sections of society irrespective of caste, creed and social status. The achievements registered by him in South Africa were well known to the Indian people. His simplicity, humility, simple dialect and down to earth style made his identification easier and spontaneous. Little wonder that when Gandhi made his Non-cooperation programme known to the masses, the response was overwhelming, with men and women from different sections of society extending their wholehearted support.

Though Gandhi had arrived in India from South Africa in 1915, the first political struggle was launched by him in 1919. After the end of World War I, when there were renewed demands for self-rule, the government passed the repressive Rowlatt Bills "at the beginning of 1919 prohibiting public protest and suspending civil liberties. This was when Gandhi began to develop a programme for women".[1] Gandhi formed a Satyagraha Sabha and announced that a *hartal* (closure of shops, offices and all public activity) would take place on 6 April. On this day, he addressed a gathering of women (representing different classes and communities) and impressed upon them the need to take part in the Satyagraha (peaceful resistance) movement.

On 13 April 1919, at the orders of General Dyer, hundreds of peaceful protestors were massacred at Jallianwala Bagh in Amritsar. "Men, women, and children were killed in this brutal massacre, unmasking forever Britain's civilizing mission".[2] The Hunter Enquiry Committee Report informed that as many as four hundred people were shot dead and twelve hundred were injured. This was not the end of it. There were various incidents where sufferings were inflicted upon women and their modesty was outraged. According to a statement made by twenty-three women: "We were called from our houses wherever we were and collected near the School. We were asked to remove our veils. We were abused and harassed to give out the name of Bhai Mool Singh as having lectured against the Government. This incident occurred at the end of Baisakhi last in the morning in Mr. Besworth Smith's presence. He spat at us and spoke many bad things. He beat some of us with sticks. We were made to stand in rows and to hold our ears. He abused us also saying: 'Flies what can you do, if I shoot you'"?[3]

In retaliation, there was an outbreak of violence in different parts of the country in the form of arson, looting and even assaults on Englishmen at the physical level. Gandhi felt greatly pained at these incidents, and on 18 April 1919 he called off his Satyagraha campaign. He

[1]Geraldine Forbes, *The New Cambridge History of India*, IV. 2: *Women in Modern India* (Cambridge University Press, 1996), p. 124.

[2]Ibid., pp. 124-25.

[3]Report on the Hunter Enquiry Committee, Indian National Congress, Statement 581, p. 868.

candidly admitted that his decision to launch the Satyagraha campaign was a "Himalayan miscalculation" because the masses were not prepared for this.[4] Though the campaign was called off, but it was very much clear that women had begun to actively associate themselves in the ongoing struggle for India's independence.

I
The Khilafat Question

Another important incident to have taken place around that time was the Khilafat question which had enormously agitated the Muslims of India. This issue was related to the Turkish Empire and the treatment meted out to the Khalifa who is held in high esteem by the Muslims by virtue of his being the temporal head of the Muslims all over the world. "The Khalifa, 'successor to the Prophet Muhammad, commander of the faithful, the shadow of God on earth'–these exalted titles convey the symbolic importance of the Khalifa to the community of Islam".[5]

During the period of war, the Prime Minister of England had given an assurance to the Muslims that no harm would be caused to the Turkish Empire. A deputation of the Muslim Khilafat Conference also paid a visit to England with the purpose of putting forward its point of view in regard to Turkey and the Khilafat. The British Government, however, turned down the requests of the Muslims. On 14 May 1920, a draft treaty called the Treaty of Sevres was published, setting aside all the assurances given to the Muslims by the British during the war period. This greatly annoyed the Muslims, and the Khilafat movement started assuming serious proportions during the 1919-20 winter.

[4]See "A Himalayan Miscalculation", in Gandhi, *The Story of My Experiments with Truth* (Navjivan, Ahmedabad, 1927), pp. 356-58, for a detailed account of the reasons for the withdrawal of Rowlatt Satyagraha.

[5]Gail Minault, *The Khilafat Movement: A Religious and Political Mobilization in India* (OUP, New Delhi, 1982), p. 1.

Gandhi saw this as a good opportunity for uniting the Hindus and the Muslims and for bringing the masses into the national mainstream. To quote him:

> I discovered the weapon of non-cooperation in the form we know while thinking about the Khilafat. I feel very much about this issue because I am a staunch Hindu. If I wish to see my religion protected against seven crores of Muslims, I must be ready even to die for the protection of their religion.... I do not believe that the Muslims will betray us once their end has been achieved. Those who believe in religion do not betray anyone. I do not know of a single instance in history of a great sacrifice by the Hindus having gone unrewarded. What was done before now was a kind of bargaining. There is no place whatever for bargaining in our dealings today. The Hindus should help the Muslims as a matter of duty and look to God for reward. They must not ask anything of the Muslims. I seldom mention the subject of cow-protection to the Ali Brothers. I have already published the conversation with Maulana Abdul Bari. He knows, all the same, that I have not concealed any hope of being able to melt the hearts of Muslims, by dying for them, if need be. It is my conviction that God always regards a good. My prayer is to God. I have sold myself to the Muslims without demanding a price and I ask each and every Hindu to do the same. This is no policy, but plain dealing. I would not have been ready to die for Muslims if their case had been weak. If knowing their case to be obviously just, I remained aloof through doubt or fear, my Hinduism would be disgraced and I would have failed in my duty as a neighbour.
>
> I know that the Khilafat agitation is not a political weapon. It is the duty of all Muslims to

> defend the Khilafat. It is a different matter that Hindus may not regard it as their duty as well. The Muslims will not accept cow-protection as a religious duty. But all Muslims know that for the Hindus it is so. In the same way, all Hindus must know that to defend the Khilafat is a religious duty for the Muslims. I have great respect for the devotion of the Ali Brothers to their religion. They would not have become fakirs just for the sake of political benefits. Of course, fighting for the Khilafat will increase the power of Islam. It is no crime to rejoice at this. The Muslims cannot but be glad; and, if we wish that people of other faiths should be happy at the awakening of a new spirit in Hinduism and its regeneration, we Hindus should also be glad at the regeneration of Islam.[6]

Gandhi sternly warned the government that if justice was denied to the Muslims, he would be left with no other option but to resume Satyagraha.[7]

Thus in September 1920, the Non-cooperation resolution was put forward before the Congress session at Calcutta. It was ratified at Nagpur in December 1920. In the first Non-cooperation agitation itself the participation of women became very much evident. In different parts of the country, women joined the processions, propagated the use of *khadi* and *charkha* and some of them even took the extreme step of leaving government schools and colleges. Urging the Hindu and Muslim women to adopt *swadeshi* goods and to start using the spinning-wheel, Gandhi wrote:

> It is plain that the Khilaft agitation will benefit the cause of *swadeshi*. But the resolve not to use

[6]Gandhi's views on Khilafat were published in *Navjivan*, 30 January 1921. Also see *Young India*, 25 August 1920.

[7]See Manmohan Kaur, *Women in India's Freedom Struggle* (Sterling, New Delhi, 1985), p. 140.

> articles made in Europe only so long as the Khilafat issue remained unsolved does not seem to me proper. Muslims ought not to use European goods even if they get full justice on the Khilafat question. It is, moreover, not enough to boycott European goods alone. No foreign goods, including Japanese goods, should be used. The Swadeshi movement is intended as a permanent change. No matter how justly Europe deals with us, it is our duty to use only *swadeshi* goods so that India may ever get perfect justice. The country, thus, can prosper only through the spinning-wheel and the handloom. Lakhs of Muslims have given up spinning and lakhs of Muslim weavers have given up weaving. If Hindu and Muslim women again take the spinning and Hindu and Muslim weavers to weaving, within a short time the country will be able to produce all the cloth it needs. I wish, therefore, to draw the attention of all.[8]

Women constituted a powerful group within the Khilafat movement. They extended their support to the movement both morally and financially by giving their ornaments in charity. A letter by Sir Harcourt Butler to Lord Hardinge aptly highlights the important role played by women in the movement. He writes: "The priests and women are the most important influences in India... and I am not very much afraid of the politicians until they play on these two".[9]

A woman who played an active role during the Non-cooperation movement was the indefatigable Ali matriarch Bi Amman. She was the mother of Ali brothers and commanded great respect in political circles. She was vehemently opposed to the idea of women remaining confined to their homes and not associating themselves

[8]*Navjivan*, 4-7-1920. Also see *Collected Works of Mahatma Gandhi* (hereinafter CWMG), Vol. XVIII, p. 8.

[9]Gail Minault, op. cit., 1982, p. 149.

with political activities. She had earlier been associated with women through meetings to support the work of the Anjuman-e-Khuddem-e-Ka'aba—collection of funds to maintain the house of the Ka'aba and other Muslim holy places, and to defend them against non-Muslim aggression, purposes which they emphasized were strictly religious, having nothing to do with politics.[10] "She then appeared on the national scene in 1917, at the age of sixty-seven, during the agitation to secure the release of Annie Besant and her own sons from their wartime internment. Annie Besant was released and elected President of the National Congress that year. Muhammad Ali was chosen to preside over the Muslim League in anticipation of his release which, however, did not occur. At the annual meeting of the League, Muhammed Ali's photograph occupied the presidential chair and Bi Amman spoke briefly on his behalf from behind the veil of her white *burqua*".[11] Perhaps, for the first time a Muslim woman addressed a political gathering in which both Hindus and Muslims were present. At the Congress session also she occupied a seat next to Annie Besant and Sarojini Naidu. This incident was extremely significant because it symbolized the growing participation of Indian women in the political field.

The Central Khilafat Committee started a women's branch in 1921 which organized women's meetings throughout the country during the Khilafat and Tilak Swaraj Fund raising campaigns. These meetings were addressed by Bi Amman, Begum Muhammad Ali and Begum Hazrat Mohani among others. They often joined forces with the Hindu women, prominent among them being Sarojini Naidu, Sarala Devi Chaudhurani and Basanti Devi, wife of C.R. Das of Calcutta. They addressed the

[10]Maitrayee Chaudhuri, *Indian Women's Movement: Reform and Revival* (Radiant Publishers, New Delhi, 1993), p. 129.

[11]Ibid., p. 30. Also see Gail Minault, ed, *The Extended Family: Women and Political Participation in India and Pakistan* (Chanakya Publishers, New Delhi, reprint, 1989), p. 13.

meetings held exclusively for women during the course of which "... they exhorted women to do their duty to God and their country by urging their men to support non-cooperation and by imbibing their children with religious faith and patriotism. They also called for contributions to the cause. Women responded with small gifts of cash and larger gifts of gold, bangles, anklets, and ear rings for the Khilafat and Tilak Swaraj Funds".[12]

At a meeting held in Delhi in May 1920, Akhtar Begum, an eminent local Shia woman, made a fervent appeal to the Muslim women to defend their religion by extending support to the Non-cooperation campaign. To quote her: "Are we not masters (Sir) in our homes? If we are, we can compel the men to observe the non-cooperation resolutions religiously. We should remain firm in our faith, ostracize all defaulters, and keep our men strictly in line. Our religion and resolve are on trial. If you wish to stand well in the eyes of God and the Prophet, and enter paradise in the retinue of Fatima, daughter of the Prophet, do not neglect your religious views".[13] Thus, support of the Khilafat cause and Non-cooperation were looked upon as religious duties.

Bi Amman continued to tour different parts of the country in support of the Khilafat cause even after the imprisonment of her sons again in late 1921. At a ladies' conference in Bombay which was attended by six thousand people, a resolution was passed urging women to come forward in large numbers. As President of the All India Ladies' Conference at the Ahmedabad Congress in December 1921, she appealed to the people to unite, for, "without cooperation among the different communities we can't liberate our country or live peaceful and honourable lives".[14] She also spoke about the way the British

[12]Maitrayee Chaudhuri, op. cit, p. 131. Also see Gail Pearson, "Nationalism, Universalization, and the Extended Female Space in Bombay", in Gail Minault, op. cit., p. 180.

[13]Jana Everett, *Women and Social Change in India* (Heritage, New Delhi, 1979), pp. 66-67.

[14]*Amrita Bazar Patrika*, 5 January 1922.

"had chained India in the twin fetters of slavery and eternal domination. The people had to choose whether to wear their chains or to work for their national and religious freedom".[15]

At a mass meeting in Punjab, she lifted the veil of her *burqa* while addressing a huge gathering and sought to justify this action of hers by saying that all the people present there were just like her sons and daughters. There was therefore no reason to follow the *purdah* custom in their presence. She further said that Swaraj was sure to come if women had "a heart to make sacrifices for the cause".[16]

By February 1922, she had visited Patna and Bhagalpur. At Bhagalpur, she was not given permission to see the political prisoners and as a mark of protest the prisoners and their relatives refused to see each other.[17] She managed to raise funds to the tune of Rs.60,000 from Darbhanga (Bihar) for the Khilafat Committee; and at Monghyr she was presented with a purse of Rs.20,000.[18] The Delhi branch of women's Khilafat Committee headed by Begum Ajmal Khan and Begum Ansari collected a sum of over Rs.20,000 (during Bi Amman's visit to Delhi).[19] It may thus be seen that these women leaders played a big role in raising funds and in aiding the *swadeshi* effort. They recognized the strength that women's traditional role in the family gave them and built upon that foundation. According to Gail Minault: "Indian woman for all her subordination to the male in society is queer in her own reality. She is the arbiter of words and instructor in basic religious observances and cultural attitudes. She is also viewed as vulnerable, needing to be protected and this too gives her a way of calling her men to duty to defend her honour and their own".[20]

[15]Maitrayee Chaudhuri, op. cit., p. 131.
[16]*Amrita Bazar Patrika*, 12 December 1922.
[17]Ibid., 5 February 1922.
[18]Ibid.
[19]Gail Minault, op. cit., 1982, p. 149.
[20]Ibid., p. 151.

The government did consider the idea of prosecuting Bi Amman for making objectionable speeches, but thought it prudent not to arrest her.[21] Mahatma Gandhi also had high regards for Bi Amman which is evident from the special message he sent to her at the time of his arrest in March 1922. He said: "Tell Bai Amman to pray for me and for all of us and to carry on the work which we have left behind. Her prayers and work will be quite sufficient to ensure our quick release and success".[22]

Thus from a stage when Bi Amman addressed basically religious meetings which were exclusively for women, she graduated to become a highly respected and popular mother figure of great eminence who had become confident enough to address gatherings unveiled before huge masses. She was the inspiring force behind the achievements of Ali Brothers, as is evident from the following quotation: "Don't give your old mother cause for grief, but confessing your faith, give up your life. Give your all in this home of trial, son, give your life for the Khilafat. Even had I had seven sons, God sacrifice them all for the Khilafat. This is the way of the faith of the Prophet, son, give your life for the Khilafat".[23]

Bi Amman continued to play an active role in the political field right till her demise in 1924. Gandhi paid a glowing tribute to her in the following words: "She realised that the freedom of India was impossible without Hindu-Muslim unity and Khaddar. She, therefore, ardently preached unity which had become an article of faith with her. She had discarded all her foreign or mill made clothing and taken to Khaddar....".[24]

[21]Home Political Proceedings, 1922, File No. 933, p. 1.
[22]*Amrita Bazar Patrika*, 21 March 1922.
[23]Gail Minault, op. cit., 1982, p. 13.
[24]*Amrita Bazar Patrika*, 23 May 1922.

II
Gandhi Launches the Non-cooperation Movement

Gandhi had always believed in following a policy of moderation and restraint[25] which became glaringly evident from his advice to the agitated delegates who had assembled in Amritsar : "I say, do not return madness with madness, but return madness with sanity and the whole situation will be yours".[26] However, two incidents which took place in May 1920 convinced Gandhi about the nefarious designs of the British. The first one was the publication of the text of the Treaty of Sevres on 15 May by the British Government "which verily signalled the complete dismemberment of the Turkish Empire".[27] The second one was the release of the findings of the Hunter Committee on 28 May which was appointed to examine the tragic incident connected with the Rowlatt Satyagraha. From the Report it became clear that the British had no intention of making amends for the violence unleashed by them in Amritsar. On the contrary, the British had every

[25]M. R. Jayakar, *The Story of My Life* (Bombay, 1958), Vol. I, p. 321.

[26]The Amritsar session was very significant for Gandhi's political career because Gandhi's close association with the Congress started with this. To quote him: "I must regard my participation in Congress proceedings at Amritsar as my real entrance into the Congress politics. My attendance at the previous Congresses was nothing more perhaps than an annual renewal of allegiance to the Congress". Gandhi, *The Story of My Experiments with Truth*, op. cit., 1927, p. 369.

[27]The text of the treaty with Turkey was published along with a message from the Viceroy to the Muslim people of India urging them to accept "Terms which I fear will be painful to all Muslims". This message is cited in the *Indian Annual Register*—1921, Vol. I.

intention of ignoring the criminal acts of its officials.[28] Realization then dawned upon Gandhi that every Indian was bound to participate in the Non-cooperation movement.

Gandhi felt justified in making a fervent plea to the Indian masses to adopt the path of Satyagraha with the ultimate purpose of removing a regime that showed scant regard to the basic principle of civilized governance. Writing in *Young India*, he made his views about the Non-cooperation movement very clear:

> We must voluntarily put up with the losses and inconveniences that arise from having to withdraw our support from a Government that is ruling against our will. Possession of power and riches is a crime under an unjust Government, poverty in that case is a virtue, says Thoreau. It may be that in the transition stage we may make mistakes, there may be avoidable suffering. These things are preferable to national emasculation.
>
> We must refuse to wait for the wrong to be righted till the wrong-doer has been roused to a sense of inequality. We must not, for fear of ourselves or others having to suffer, remain participators in it. But we must combat the wrong by ceasing to assist the wrong-doer directly or indirectly.[29]

On 23 July 1920 Gandhi made an announcement that the Non-cooperation movement would be inaugurated on 1 August 1920 which would be a day of fasting and prayer

[28]The findings of the Hunter Committee were so one-sided that it was not acceptable to the Indian members. The latter came out with a Minority Report which ruthlessly condemned the British authorities, military as well as civil. Gandhi condemned the Hunter Committee findings as "an attempt to condone official lawlessness" and said that it was "page after page of thinly disguised official whitewash". See *Young India*, 9 June 1920. Also see CWMG, Vol. XVIII, p. 482.

[29]*Young India*, 29 September 1921.

and the suspension of any kind of business. Tilak was firmly committed into extending his wholehearted support to the movement. But, unfortunately, he left for his heavenly abode before the dawn of 1 August. Gandhi, who was one of the pall bearers along with the Ali Brothers, Dr Saifuddin Kitchlew and many others, expressed his grief in the obituary note in the following words:

> My strongest bulwark is gone.... A giant among men has fallen. The roar of the lion is hushed.... For us he will go down to the generations yet unborn as a maker of modern India. They will revere his memory as a man who lived for them and died for them .... Let us erect for the only Lokamanya of India an imperishable movement by weaving into our own lives his bravery, his simplicity, wonderful industry and his love of his country.[30]

At the special session of the Indian National Congress held on 4 September in Calcutta the Congress decided to extend its full support to Gandhi's Non-cooperation campaign—a decision that was ratified at the annual session of the Congress held in December in Nagpur.[31] The stage was thus set for the first great struggle to be carried out in a purely non-violent manner against one of the mightiest imperial powers known to the history of mankind.

Barely a month and a half after the special session of the Congress which was held on 4 September 1920, Gandhi, while addressing a women's meeting at Dakor, made the following observation:

> This Government has taught us false ways. We have come to believe that foreign cloth adds to one's beauty. Even the clothes worn by you, in

[30]Cited in S.R.Bakshi, *Documents of Non-cooperation Movement* (New Delhi, 1989), p. 3.

[31]However, there were some opponents too, namely, C.R. Das, B.C. Pal, Madan Mohan Malaviya, Joseph Baptista, M.A. Jinha and Satyamurti.

this gathering, have the odour of foreign cloth. Even mill cloth is not *swadeshi*. The cloth produced by the mills is not sufficient to meet the needs of the country. You are not quite so poor. I have seen people who are poorer than you. I have seen men who have only a loin-cloth with which to clothe themselves and women who have not more than a torn skirt. We can set ourselves free this very day if India adopts *swadeshi,* if all women take to the good old spinning-wheel and if they put on clothes made only with yarn spun by themselves. To the women of the past, virtue was beauty. Wearing of foreign cloth makes a woman ugly. There is a touch of the harlot in a woman seeking loveliness by fine dressing. What is our image of Sita and Damayanti, whom we adore? Is it that of women clad in finery? We revere Damayanti who wandered in the forest, half-clad, and Sita who suffered *vanavasa* for fourteen years. In those days, people covered themselves with nothing more than leaves. To seek beauty by adorning oneself is to imitate the harlot. If you want to follow your *dharma*, you must first understand the *swadeshi dharma*. It consists in using cloth made with yarn spun by yourselves and woven by your menfolk, singing as they work. I am truly handsome, since the clothes I am wearing are made with yarn spun by women and lovingly woven by men. If you wish to deliver yourselves from *Ravanarajya* and establish *Ramarajya*, you must adopt *swadeshi* and introduce the spinning-wheel in your homes. There are many women now who will be able to teach you how to work it. Each one of you should spin for at least an hour daily, singing devotional songs all the while. Get the yarn, afterwards, woven into cloth.

You will no doubt find it difficult at first to use hand-spun cloth in place of foreign muslin. Some women in Bombay complained to me that their saris, which previously weighed less than forty *tolas* now exceeded seventy *tolas* in weight. I replied to them in figurative language, saying that, they had till now lowered their own weight by reducing the weight of their clothes. During pregnancy, women cheerfully carry their load for nine months and suffer the severe pains of child-birth with joy. This is the time for the birth of new India. Will you not be ready at least to carry the weight to heavy clothes at this hour? You can make India free only if you bear this burden. If you wish to give birth to a new India, every woman must bear this burden not merely for nine months but for nine years.

If you wish to be pure like Sita, if you would give up the many forms of subtle mental degradation of the kind I have described and make others give them up, if you wish to understand your true *dharma* rather than wickedness, then you must wholeheartedly join in the movement for Swaraj. Each one of us must be able to distinguish between true *dharma* and wickedness. Many fraudulent men will also come to you for contributions. I would ask you not to contribute to any of them. I hold out my hand to you only because I feel certain that you have trust in me. I shudder to introduce the corrupting influence of money in my work. Had I the strength and the *tapascharya* to be able to carry on my work without money, I would most certainly not ask for it. But I do not have such *tapascharya* and such strength. I also am a man of *Kaliyuga* and am full of failings, but I know that I am constantly striving to overcome these failings. So, if you

> trust me, contribute anything you wish to, from a pice onwards. The funds will be handled by the Swarajya Sabha.
>
> Finally, I request you to see that these few things I have placed before you do not go in at one ear and come out at the other. By adopting *swadeshi*, you will be able to save some money on clothes. You will be able to give your children milk and *ghee* out of this. At present, you spend on your children. I, too, want a small share from the amount you will save. But contribute only if you wish to. Even if you do not give money, you should at any rate follow the *dharma* of spinning which I have explained to you. We have today to wash off the pollution caused by the eclipse. The right way of doing so is to purify our hearts. If all of you take the name of Rama in good faith and pray for *Ramarajya* in place of *Ravanarajya*, I can assure you that you will find that Rama is the strength of the weak. May your hearts be ruled by God and may He set you free from all other forms of enslavement.[32]

Gandhi felt greatly satisfied that he had begun his Non-cooperation movement with women. The response which he got was indeed overwhelming. To quote him:

> I started begging for money at Dakor and, fortunately, I made a beginning with women. Among them, the sister who first gave me a piece of jewellery made a living by grinding flour for others. When she took off her ear-ring and handed it over to me, that same moment I was convinced that India's women had understood the holy nature of peaceful Non-cooperation. The experiences which followed were marvellous indeed. Girls in Ahmedabad parted with their

[32]*Navjivan*, 3-11-1920. Also see CWMG, Vol. XVIII, pp. 391-95.

bangles, rings and chains. In Poona, they literally showered jewellery on me. There were similar scenes in Belgaum, Dharwar and Hubli. Muslim women in Delhi, from behind their *purdah*, gave jewellery, currency notes and cash.

When the women in the country have woken up, who can hinder Swaraj? *Dharma* has always been preserved through women. Nations have won their independence because women had brave men for sons. By preserving purity of character, they have kept *dharma* alive. There have been women who sacrificed their all and saved the people. When women, who have done all this, have become alive to the suffering of the country, how long can that suffering last?

The women among whom I see this awakening cannot be described as educated, but they have understanding. They fully understand the obligations of *dharma*. What the educated classes take a long time to see, the women, with their gift of intuition, have understood at a mere hint. They have not taken long to realize that Swaraj means *Ramarajya*.

Everything has been put clearly before them. The nature of the [country's] suffering has been explained. They have also been told that the remedy for this suffering is Non-cooperation, and also what Non-cooperation means. They have realized their duty in helping to preserve Hindu-Muslim unity, while everyone understands and remains faithful to her own religion.

If women keep up what they have so wisely begun, I am sure we can provide education for the whole country with the help of the jewellery which they can spare. The women who have

> offered their ornaments have done so on the understanding that they will not ask them to be replaced before we have got Swaraj, but will do without them. Thus, with a little sacrifice of jewellery on women's part, we can arrange for the country's education and promote *swadeshi*. I hope, therefore, that they will continue the great *yajna* which commenced at Dakor and that the husbands or other relatives will not restrain any of them in this sacred effort.[33]

Thus, Gandhi was of the firm conviction that women had an important role to play in the national movement, and that they should consider it a religious duty to wear only *khadi* clothes.

> Mahatmaji appealed to the ladies not to neglect to do their part in the country's struggle for freedom. He urged them to exhort and encourage their husbands and sons to pursue the path of duty, and urged them to help vigorously and effectively in the building up of a free India by taking up *swadeshi*. In the days of Ravana's government even Sita Devi had to wear for fourteen years the rough garment made from the bark of the tree. Even so, today, when the adoption of *swadeshi* meant a long step in the path of freedom for India, the Indian ladies should make it a matter of religious duty with them not only to wear only *khaddar* clothes, both hand-spun and hand-woven, they must also devote one hour at least daily to hand-spinning and help in the hand-weaving of cloths. The women of India owed it as a duty of their country to discard fineries in clothes and to be simple in their dress.
>
> In *swadeshi* there is an effective way to Swaraj and redress of the Punjab and the Khilafat

[33] *Navjivan*, 28-11-1920. Also see CWMG, Vol. XIX, pp. 39-40.

> wrongs and vindication of the national honour. The main burden of the task of propagating *swadeshi* lay on the women of India and they must rise to the occasion.[34]

The women who had heard Gandhi's speech were so moved by his passionate pleas and the faith he reposed in India's woman power that they felt the least hesitant in giving their jewellery for the noble cause, and were greatly motivated to take the *swadeshi* vow.

The first Non-cooperation movement was a big success with women in different parts of the country joining the processions and propagating the use of *khadi* and *charkha*. Renuka Ray informs that she was so deeply inspired by the speeches made by Gandhi in Calcutta in 1920 that she, along with her other fellow students of the Diocesan College, offered their jewellery to Gandhi. "Many of these girls, including herself, gave up their studies and joined the Non-cooperation movement".[35]

Vijaylakshmi Pandit too came under the spell of Gandhi when he visited Allahabad and stayed at the historic Anand Bhawan. "I sat on the ground with my cousin and the little figure began to speak. He was quite incongruous.... He spoke very bad Hindi and yet the interesting thing was that none of these things seemed to matter after the first few minutes. He was saying something which was gripping everybody. He was compelling people to look at him, to listen to him.... And he ended by appealing to women to give him something".[36] In response to Gandhi's appeal, Mrs. Pandit donated her gold bangles, though she regretted that she did not give away more.[37]

[34]*The Bombay Chronicle*, 1-12-1920. Also see CWMG, Vol. XIX, pp. 44-45.

[35]Transcript of Interview with Smt. Renuka Ray, Oral History Section, Nehru Memorial Museum and Library, New Delhi.

[36]Cited in Aparna Basu, "The Role of Women in the Indian Struggle for Freedom", in B.R. Nanda, ed, *Indian Women: From Purdah to Modernity* (Vikas, New Delhi, 1976), p. 21.

[37]Transcript of Interview with Vijaylakshmi Pandit, Oral History Section, Nehru Memorial Museum and Library, New Delhi.

Punjab

In view of the consideration that the Amritsar tragedy was one of the main reasons behind the launching of the Non-cooperation campaign by Gandhi, it would be appropriate to consider the role played by women in this movement in the land of five rivers—Punjab. Though the women's participation was rather restricted, yet they had started taking part in the nationalist processions and in public meetings. Manmohini Sehgal has fond memories of a public meeting in Lahore during the period under reference. She says: "While the meeting was in progress, the police came and requested the women to leave the place so that they could lathi-charge the men. But the women refused to leave and later on the meeting dispersed, and men and women took out a procession.... It was the first time when women in Lahore participated in a political procession, raised slogans and walked in the streets together with men".[38]

Sarala Devi Chaudhurani had played a significant role in making the *charkha* and *khadi* popular among the women of Punjab. During 1919-22, Sarala Devi was so strongly influenced by the Gandhian ideology of Non-cooperation that she donated most of her jewellery for the nationalist cause. She even went to the extent of returning the prestigious Padmavati Gold Medal which had been awarded to her by the Calcutta University. She was the first woman to have been awarded with the Medal.[39] By learning to spin the *charkha* and by wearing a purely *khadi* dress, she became a Gandhian to the core. In a letter addressed to Gandhi she wrote that the *khadi* sarees worn by her greatly impressed her audiences, so much so that her songs and speeches did not draw much attention.[40]

[38]Transcript of Interview with Manmohini Seghal, Oral History Section, Nehru Memorial Museum and Library, New Delhi.

[39]Sukhbir Chowdhary, *Indian People Fight for National Liberation, 1920-22* (New Delhi, 1972), p. 85.

[40]CWMG, Vol. XVIII, p. 20. It is, however, interesting to note that even for a dedicated Gandhian like Sarala Devi, shifting over to *khadi* clothes in the initial stages was not very easy.

To make the Non-cooperation movement more popular, she organized and addressed several meetings in the Punjab region during the course of which she tried to inculcate among the Punjabi women the *swadeshi* fervour and nationalist feelings. Though she was based in Lahore, Sarala Devi travelled extensively in various parts of northern India in order to popularize the concepts of *charkha* and *khadi*. She was the spokeswoman of Gandhi in the true sense who felt that India's poverty could be countered only through *swadeshi:* "The hand that spun in India supplied the nation with food and comfort.... The revival and protection of a dead art, the remodelling of Indian homes, the reclothing of India by India's own hands —this is the Alpha and Omega of Swaraj".[41] Apart from Sarala Devi, other women who made significant contributions in mobilizing women in the Punjab region were Radha Devi, Parvati Devi[42] and Lado Rani Zutshi.

Thus in most of the women's meetings in Punjab the emphasis was on the propagation of Gandhi's view that poverty in India was due to the abandonment of *swadeshi* by the people. Gandhi had repeatedly asserted that: "We should use only such cloth as is produced here .... Our mothers should take the spinning-wheel into their homes. We should get cloth woven by our weavers and wear only that. I tell all my brothers and sisters of India: *swadeshi* is your duty. Wear *khaddar*: Non-cooperation consists in doing all this. Do not draw the sword. Sheathe it. The sword will only cut our own throats".[43]

In Lahore, the concept of *swadeshi* was sought to be made popular through the motto *shama se shama jaldi*

[41]Sarala Devi Chaudhurani, *At the Point of Spindle* (Ganesh and Company, Madras, 1922), p. 3.

[42]Radha Devi was the wife of Lala Lajpat Rai. Parvati Devi was a teacher in Amritsar who was firmly committed to propagating the Gandhian ideology of *swadeshi*. She was arrested in Meerut in December 1922 for her provocative speeches which the British found highly objectionable.

[43]See *Aaj*, 27 November 1920. Also see S.R. Bakshi, op. cit., 1989, p. 309.

hai which meant that those who had already accepted and imbibed the concepts of *charkha* and *khadi*, should try to convince at least ten other people into accepting the Gandhian ideology of *swadeshi* and wearing *khadi* clothes.[44] Thus the efforts made by Sarala Devi and other women of eminence in Punjab went a long way in binding the Punjabi women together at the emotional level. This can be gauged from the fact that "when Gandhi visited Jullunder in early 1921, the welcome address presented to him was printed on a piece of *khadi* supplied by the aged mother of a prominent lawyer of the city, Nazimuddin Shah".[45]

It is significant to note that the popularizing of the *swadeshi* concept did not remain confined to big cities only. In fact, its influence was felt in the smaller towns also. For example, in Karnal an exhibition to popularize *khadi* was organized and prizes were awarded to those *khadi* manufacturers who had done something substantial to make *khadi* popular. Also, as many as 3,000 women wearing *khadi* dresses "walked through the streets of Multan along with a cart full of *khadi* which they sold during the course of their unique march".[46] Above all, in auspicious occasions like marriages, people could be seen attending the functions attired in *khadi*. Expressing great satisfaction at the success of the Non-cooperation campaign among the women in Punjab, Gandhi made the following observation:

> It is my deep conviction that the women of the Punjab have understood my message. They have felt that *swadeshi* is not merely a means of protecting India's wealth but... that in it lies the country's best freedom.... I beg to state, deliberately and knowingly, that I do not believe the

[44]*The Tribune*, 22 March 1922.

[45]CWMG, Vol. XIX, p. 455. Also cited in Rajan Mahan, *Women in Indian National Congress, 1921-1931* (Rawat Publications, Jaipur and New Delhi, 1999), pp. 149-50.

[46]*The Tribune*, 1 October 1921 and 21 January 1922.

> profound feelings of the Punjabi women to be directed towards me personally. They are taken up with admiration for me because of the truth that they see in me and the simplicity of *swadeshi* which they have come to realize through me.[47]

Women began to participate in the Congress sessions in increasing numbers. At the annual session of the Congress held in Ahmedabad in December 1921, as many as seventeen women delegates represented Punjab, "which was the highest number for any province in the subcontinent".[48]

Gujarat

Gujarat was another region where the Non-cooperation campaign of Gandhi became immensely popular among women. Perhaps one important reason for this was that Gandhi himself hailed from Gujarat. Besides, many of his close women associates who were affiliated to his Ashram contributed a great deal to making the Non-cooperation movement popular in several towns, cities and villages of Gujarat.[49] Among the women of Gujarat who came into close contact with Gandhi during the early phases of the movement, the name of Anasuya Sarabhai stands out prominently.[50] She was the sister of Ambalal Sarabhai, a leading mill-owner of Ahmedabad. She had been rendering social service since 1914 through providing education both to the children of the workers and to the workers

[47]CWMG, Vol. XVII, pp. 31-32. Gandhi also expressed satisfaction at the enthusiasm shown by the women of Rawalpindi.

[48]H.N. Mitra, ed, *The Indian Annual Register, 1921-22*, Vol. I, Appendix I, pp. 12-13.

[49]Before the advent of Gandhi on the political scene of India, Gujarat had remained a politically backward area. See Mahadev Desai, *Day to Day with Gandhi* (Varanasi, 1968), Vol. III, p. 108.

[50]Anasuya Sarabhai ultimately divorced her husband, a rare thing in those times. She also studied in England where she got an opportunity to interact with George Bernard Shaw and Beatrice Webb. On her return to India, she opened a school for the children workers of Calico Mills owned by her family. She even opened crèches for the women workers of this mill.

themselves. "It was only natural that gradually a close association developed between Anasuya and Gandhi and it was mainly through their combined efforts that the Ahmedabad textile workers' strike in February-March 1918 (involving 16,000 weavers) was a big success. Later, Anasuya participated energetically during the Kheda Satyagraha and was also one of the first signatories of the 'Satyagraha pledge' evolved by Gandhi to oppose the Rowlatt Bills".[51]

During the course of the Non-cooperation movement, Gandhi toured many villages of Gujarat along with Kasturba, Anasuyabhen and some other "Ashramite sisters", and impressed upon women the need to spin the *charkha*, wear *khadi*, boycott government educational institutions, remove untouchability and promote Hindu-Muslim unity. This motivated women to take part in the constructive programmes. Under Gandhi's inspiration several girl students left government schools and colleges, prominent among them were Manibhen Patel and Miss Desai whose efforts were hailed by Gandhi in public.[52] In many of the women's meetings in Gujarat, women showed their generosity by donating jewellery and cash for the noble cause. Gandhi was so moved by such generous acts that after a meeting in Ahmedabad, he made the following statement: "This amount is more sacred than donations worth lakhs of rupees from millionaires. There is an aroma of the very soul of the women of Ahmedabad in every brass piece given here. Every coin is steeped with their devotion for the country.... It is on the basis of such sacred small coins that I will erect the edifice of Swaraj".[53]

Gandhi was ultimately convinced that in the programme of work for Swaraj, the contributions made by women were no less than those of men. He said: "I have marvelled at the awakening among the women of Gujarat. They have

[51]Rajan Mahan, op. cit., p. 155.

[52]See *Young India*, 29-9-1920.

[53]Gandhi said this during the course of his address to women at Kadivani in Ahmedabad on 3-10-1920. See Mahadev Desai, op. cit., p. 35.

great power in their hands. In the programme of work for Swaraj, the women's share is as great as, in fact greater than, the men's. I pray to God that the women of Gujarat may play their part to the full and win glory for themselves and for the name of Gujarat and of India".[54] It is important to note that the Congress session which was held in Ahmedabad in December 1921 was marked by a big historical event. For the first time in the history of the Congress, women performed their roles as volunteers. Under the leadership of Nandubhen Kanuga,[55] a total of 131 women volunteers was present on the occasion.

Bombay

In the metropolitan city of Bombay also women extended their wholehearted support to the Non-cooperation campaign. They imparted strength to the movement through a large number of meetings, emphasis on the importance of spinning, organization of *khadi melas* and, above all, through taking part in public programmes and demonstrations. Among the various women who played a key role in Bombay, the name of Avantikabai Gokhale deserves a special mention.[56] She played a leading part in the Champaran Satyagraha in 1917. Credit goes to her for writing the first biography of Mahatma Gandhi in 1918. She remained an active political worker during the period 1920-1946 and was imprisoned many times. She also worked for the uplift of Harijans and welfare of women, and started the Hind Mahila Sangh with the purpose of bringing about nationalist awareness among women.[57]

[54]*Navjivan*, 1-5-1921. Also see CWMG, Vol. XX, pp. 50-51.

[55]Nandubhen was the wife of Dr. Balvantrai Kanuga, a close associate of Vallabhai Patel. Gandhi felt extremely happy at the role played by women as volunteers at the Ahmedabad Congress. See CWMG, Vol. XXII, pp. 185-86.

[56]Avantikabai Gokhale was married to a Bombay engineer, Baban Gokhale. She was born in 1882.

[57]Usha Bala, *Indian Women Freedom Fighters, 1857-1947* (Manohar, New Delhi, 1986), pp. 98-99. Also see *Femina*, 23 October-7 November 1982.

Other eminent women who made efforts to popularize the constructive programme of *swadeshi* in Bombay were Perin and Goshibhen Captain,[58] the Petit women Jaiji Jehangir and Mithubhen,[59] the Faizi sisters,[60] women from the Tyabji family, Manekbai Bahadurji[61] and, above all, Sarojini Naidu.[62] These eminent women were closely associated with some of the established women's organizations of Bombay of those times like Bhagini Samaj, the Gujarati Hindu Stree Mandal and Hind Mahila Samaj. And by virtue of their close association with these organizations, these women were greatly facilitated in spreading Gandhi's Non-cooperation campaign. Some other women's organizations which came into being in 1921 in Bombay are: Shri Sarada Samaj of Dadar, the Ladies Khilafat Committee, and the Rashtriya Stree Sabha[63] which played the most prominent role because of its close association with the Congress. Also, a National Girls' School was established in 1921.[64] During the Satyagraha Week which was organized by the Congress during 6-13

[58]Grand-daughter of Dadabhai Naoroji, Perin Captain was born in 1888. She was married to D.S. Captain, a reputed lawyer. From 1920 she began to wear *khadi* clothes and play an active part in popularizing the *swadeshi* cause in association with her sisters, Goshibhen Captain and Khurshed Naoroji.

[59]They belonged to the highly respected family of the Petits. This name is well known in Bombay in the form of Petit Library, Petit Hospital and other charitable institutions. Mithubhen later shifted to Surat and was actively associated with the Bardoli Satyagraha.

[60]The Faizi sisters, namely, Atiya, Zohra and Nazli were the first women members to have gone abroad for education. They played a significant role in popularizing *khadi* among the Muslim women.

[61]Manekbai Bahadurji was the daughter of Dr. Atmaram. Under the inspiration of Gandhi, she had learned to spin personally and tried to propagate the concept of spinning through the Sevasadan.

[62]Sarojini Naidu was among the most devoted disciples of Gandhi who became the President of the Bombay Provincial Congress Committee and also of the Rashtriya Stree Sabha. She also became the President of the Indian National Congress in 1926.

[63]See Gail Minault, op. cit., 1989, p. 180.

[64]Ibid.

April 1921 in Bombay, Sarojini Naidu played a big role by addressing a number of meetings with the object of associating women in large numbers with the constructive programme of *swadeshi.* Significantly, on the last day of the week – 13 April – which happened to be the Jallianwala Bagh day, as many as 500 women were present to hear the speech of Sarojini Naidu.

There is no denying that the support extended by women in large numbers to the constructive programmes did make the Gandhian movement popular, but it would be fair to say that the household activities (like spinning, wearing *khadi*, etc.) "were not the only means of popularizing the nationalist movement". Two public events in which women of the extended female space participated had a great impact on public consciousness: a procession to oppose the visit of Prince of Wales to Bombay in November 1921 featured the participation of up to one thousand women. The procession received extensive publicity and was described as 'unique'. "The press also gave wide coverage to the participation of women in the public burning of foreign cloth in the mill areas at night. These events helped further to underwrite the legitimacy of the nationalist struggle. While the men of various factions argued among themselves, the women remained aloof from such politicking and worked for an idealized notion of Swaraj and national unity".[65]

The East Godavari Region of Andhra Pradesh

In the southern part of India, the East Godavari region of Andhra Pradesh deserves a special mention. Gandhi's visit to this region in connection with the All India Congress meeting at Vijayawada in 1921 was an important occasion in the political history of the district. His speeches in Andhra proved to be a big source of inspiration for women to participate in the struggle for freedom. In a speech delivered to women at Rajahmundry on 3 April 1921, Gandhi said:

[65]Ibid., pp. 180-81.

> You, my dear sisters, I want to warn you and to bring you to a sense of duty and religion. If there is a dancing girl amidst you, I ask you to make her life not one of shame. Take up the spinning-wheel and take the few pies that the work brings you, and it will bring pies and God into your house. Do you suppose that Rama and Sita would rest for a single moment if they knew a single woman might have to sell her honour for lust of men and for a mess of pottage? I ask you to discard all your fine garments and ornaments, if only for the protection of these dancing girls. Take up the spinning-wheel for their sake, if not for the sake of India. Take up the spinning-wheel for the sake of the purity of India. Take up the sari that the *charkha* can give you. Let the spotless sari of India be the protection of the virtue of man and woman in India. I ask you to consider that to wear fine foreign sarees is a sin.[66]

A prominent example is that of Subbamma who paid a visit to Vijayawada with a group of women to seek the blessings of Gandhi. Under the magnetic influence of Gandhi, she took the plunge notwithstanding the various social constraints prevalent in those times. She happened to be the first woman of the region to participate in the national movement, and to be sent behind the bars for the noble cause. She also succeeded in motivating other women of the region to participate in the freedom struggle. Her efforts were hailed by the local newspapers. *Sudarsini*, a local newspaper, gave the following report: "We congratualate Smt. Subbamma for her patriotism and courage to go to jail. We (the women) have greater tenacity of purpose than men. We hope that Andhra women will adopt *swadeshi* at least now that they have heard of the heroism and conviction of Subbamma".[67] Another local

[66]*The Hindu*, 8-4-1921. Also see CWMG, Vol. XIX, p. 509.

[67]*Sudarsini*, 16 July 1922. Cited in Leela Kasturi and Vina Mazumdar, ed, *Women and Indian Nationalism* (Vikas, New Delhi, 1994), p. 113.

publication made the following observation: "The District Collector of Godavari has acquired distinction in the policy of repression.... But what could the poor officers do? They have arrested the men, yet the movement did not stop. For women have taken the place of men and hoisted the banner of Swaraj...".[68]

However, in 1922, Gandhi called off the Non-cooperation campaign all of a sudden taking all concerned by surprise. But despite the suspension of the movement, "the atmosphere in the Godavari area remained charged, and women like Subbamma continued to conduct meetings to popularize *khadi* and the concept of the abolition of untouchability, the two most important items of Gandhi's constructive programme".[69]

Another woman of the Godavari district who was deeply influenced by Gandhi was Durgabai, who started her political career at the tender age of eleven. Gandhi's visit to the Godavari district brought a radical change in her thinking. Gandhi held a meeting at Rajahmundry on 6 April 1921. As a matter of chance Durgabai happened to be present in that city at that time in connection with the wedding of one of her close relatives. She made the best of her stay in Rajahmundry by attending Gandhi's meeting. Seeing the volunteers collecting money and other valuables for the Tilak Swaraj Fund, Durgabai too climbed the dais to offer her collection to Gandhi. Holding the little girl's arms Gandhi asked: "Why don't you contribute your golden bracelets too"? Durgabai readily parted with her bracelets for such a noble cause.[70]

The patriotic fervour shown by the women of Andhra did not go unnoticed in the fortnightly government reports, as is evident from the following observation: "One feature which was specially noticed in these reports was the

[68]Cited in Rajan Mahan, op. cit., p. 160.

[69]Leela Kasturi and Vina Mazumdar, op. cit., p. 113.

[70]Atluri Murali, "Changing Perceptions and Radicalism of the National Movement in Andhra, 1922-1934", *Social Scientist*, Vol. 16, No. 8, pp. 8-10.

active part played by women... in carrying on an active political agitation. Some of them like Duvvuru Subbamma, Ponakka Kanakamma and Unnava Lakshmibayamma excelled the men propogandists in their ability to sway large masses of people".[71] Thus, to a certain extent, credit for the success of the Non-cooperation movement in Andhra goes to women also. A recent study says that "if the Non-cooperation movement made relatively more progress in Andhra than in Madras Presidency, the credit goes partly to women".[72]

Bengal

In regard to the women's participation in Bengal in the Non-cooperation movement of Gandhi, Bharati Ray refers to three distinct features which are as follows:

> First, the identification of the freedom struggle with *deshpuja* and the invocation of *Shakti* continued, making women's entry into politics smooth.... Second, while Gandhi's views were not informed by a feminist perspective, they infused self-confidence into women. His assertion that women were morally better suited than men for the non-violent struggle removed the stigma of their inferiority vis-à-vis men.... Third, during the period under survey, Bengal produced political captains of national stature like C.R. Das and Bipin Chandra Pal, and politicized women with leadership abilities, such as Basanti Debi (b. 1880) and Hemaprabha Majumdar (b. 1884). These women leaders had access to the general body of women and helped to promote women's political and social awareness.[73]

[71]M.Venkatarangaiya, *The Freedom Struggle in Andhra Pradesh, 1921-31* (Hyderabad, 1965), Vol. III, p. 8.

[72]Cited in Rajan Mahan, op. cit., p. 160.

[73]Bharati Ray, "The Freedom Movement and Feminist Consciousness in Bengal, 1905-1929", in idem, *From the Seams of History: Essays on Indian Women* (OUP, New Delhi, 1995), pp. 193-94.

In Bengal, C.R. Das' wife Basanti Devi played a key role by giving the lead to women's demonstrations and picketing shops which sold foreign goods. On 7 December 1921 the police took her into custody for selling *khadi* in a public street in Calcutta. Urmila Devi and Suniti Devi, her close associates, were also taken into custody. Though the police released them within a few hours, yet this incident greatly agitated the public. To quote Urmila Devi : "We also had set an example to the rest of the women; our arrest had produced the desired effect".[74]

Basanti Devi became the President of the Bengal Provincial Congress during 1921-22 and presided over its session in Chittagong in 1922. Thus a Bengali woman, perhaps for the first time, came to occupy a prominent position in the political leadership of the country. She was very much conscious of the fact that unless the women at the grassroots level were involved the national movement would not succeed. Her concern for the grassroots level involvement becomes evident from the presidential speech of hers: "If we have to get back to the simple and best life of India of old days, we have also to revive the dormant villages .... We have to reconstruct our villages, to build up our village institutions under the conditions of modern life, but according to the genius of our national life".[75]

Bihar

Bihar too did not remain alienated from the Non-cooperation campaign of Gandhi. In 1921, Sarala Devi of Hazaribagh launched the movement. During her presidential address at the 16th Conference of Students of Hazaribagh in October 1921, she made a fervent appeal to them to boycott government schools and colleges and

[74]Cited in Bharati Ray, op. cit., p. 194, fn. 54 on the basis of personal interview with Kalyani Devi, daughter of Basanti Devi, on 19 April 1983.

[75]*Amrita Bazar Patrika*, 1922 (Report on the Native Newspapers of Bengal, West Bengal State Archives, Calcutta).

motivated them to register their strong protest against the Prince of Wales' visit to India.[76]

In Patna, it was Savitri Devi who played a significant role in making Gandhi's movement popular. In the later part of 1921, she presided over many meetings where she ruthlessly condemned the imperialist designs of the British. "At these meetings participants reiterated their resolve to continue their fight against the British. Women carried the message of non-violence from door to door. They appealed for the boycott of foreign goods, picketed liquor shops and popularized the spinning of *khadi* in rural and urban areas".[77]

Orissa

At the request of the Oriyan leaders like Gopabandhu Das, Gandhi visited Orissa for the first time on 23 March 1921. To introduce Gandhi to the people of Orissa, a big public meeting was held on the Kathjuri river bed at Cuttack.[78] Gopabandhu Das, the father of Orissa's freedom movement, introduced Gandhi to the people in the following words:

> Comrades! the Mahatma to whom you were all anxious to see is now present before you. He is known to every household and every individual in the country and it is superfluous for me to introduce him to you. Everyone in Orissa knows this great man. Orissa has not made sufficient advance in the political field but she is ahead of every other part of the country in all ages in the field of religion. All the great religious preachers of India have set their foot on the sacred soil of Orissa. Today another great man is here to preach the doctrine of political love. Orissa has attained glory through ages for religion. The

[76]Shiva Pujan Sahay, *Bihar Ki Mahilayen* (Mahila Charkha Samiti, Patna, 1962), p. 310.

[77]Leela Kasturi and Vina Mazumdar, op. cit., pp. 162-63.

[78]*Samaj*, 28 March 1921.

> Mahatma's politics is based on the very same foundation. I know that you are all anxious to follow the footsteps of the Mahatma. Orissa is famous for her catholicity. On the auspicious occasion of Mahatmaji's visit to Orissa, I appeal to you all to imbibe the message of Gandhiji in full recollection of the ancient glories and catholicity of the Oriya people.[79]

In order to involve women in his programmes, Gandhi thought it better to address women in separate meetings. Thus on the very first day of his visit to Orissa, Gandhi addressed a small gathering of women in the Binod Bihari building premises at Cuttack. Haimavati Devi made all arrangements for the meeting. Professor Mohini Mohan Senapati's wife sang a patriotic song on this great occasion.[80] About forty women were present in the first meeting, which goes to show that Gandhi had already started making inroads into the psyche of the Oriyan women.[81] Significantly, it was for the first time in the history of Orissa that the Oriyan women attended a public meeting. Even more significant was the fact that for the first time a leader of Gandhi's stature and eminence addressed women in Orissa in a separate meeting. "A small group of Oriya women who attended that meeting in *purdah* went on to become active political leaders of Orissa in the next ten years, being tremendously inspired by the charisma and oratory of Mahatma Gandhi".[82]

In a speech addressed to a meeting of Utkal Samillani, Madhusudan Das, an eminent freedom fighter of Orissa, said: "We are the foreigners. It must be in our hand. We

[79]Ibid.

[80]V. Rajendra Raju, *Role of Women in India's Freedom Struggle* (New Delhi, 1994), p. 29.

[81]Rama Devi, *Jeevan Pather* (in Oriya) (Cuttack, 1984), p. 53. Also see V. Rajendra Raju, op. cit., pp. 29-30.

[82]Cited in Bina Kumari Sarma, "Gandhian Movement and Women's Awakening in Orrisa", *The Indian Historical Review*, Vol. XXI, Nos 1 & 2, edited by Anup Taneja (ICHR and Motilal Banarsidass, Delhi, 1997), p. 82.

should use *charkha* and we should wear *khadi*".[83] Madhusudan Das' speech influenced his niece, Rama Devi, to such an extent that from that day onwards she started spinning the *charkha*. Gopabandhu Das also made fervent appeals to all sections of Orissa, particularly housewives,[84] to devote their leisure hours to spinning.

When the Government of Bihar and Orissa ordered that anybody found guilty of forcing people to boycott foreign clothes would be tried on the charge of criminal offences,[85] Kuntala Kumari Sabat retaliated by saying that: "Nation is our religion, *charkha* is our life. We will hold *charkha* in our hand and we will destroy all the conspiracy of the enemy".[86] Under the inspiration of Gandhi, she started creating a new awareness among women through her sapient pen. She appealed to the Oriya women to boycott the use of "foreign goods and to destroy the administrative machinery of the British authority".[87]

In 1922, Rama Devi, along with Padmavati Devi and Hiramani Devi, attended the annual session of the Indian National Congress held at Gaya.[88] This marked a significant breakthrough as they regularly attended the subsequent sessions of the Indian National Congress. Arousal of this political awareness among women during the Non-cooperation movement continued and became more manifest during the course of the freedom movement. Though initially the number of women who joined the movement was very small, yet a beginning was made and gradually it swelled. This small band of women leaders had great influence over the general body of women and this went a

[83]See V. Rajendra Raju, op.cit., p. 33.

[84]While emphasizing on the need to work on the *charkha* and spinning everyday on a regular basis, Gopabandhu Das said to women: "Devote at least six hours daily to spinning. It will keep your mind steady and pure. Mother India desires it from you". See *Samaj*, 27 August 1921.

[85]*Samaj*, 3 September 1921.

[86]See V. Rajendra Raju, op. cit., p. 42.

[87]Ibid., p. 36.

[88]R.C. Majumdar, *History of the Freedom Movement in India*, Vol. III, p. 178.

long way in rousing their political as well as social consciousness since 1922 onwards.[89]

III
Muslim Women's Participation in the Non-cooperation Movement

Gandhi also made special efforts to secure the Muslim women's participation in the Non-cooperation movement. To ensure this, he deftly avoided making references to Hindu mythology and scriptures which he generally employed to draw the Hindu women. When he appeared with Maulana Shaukat Ali to address a Muslim women's meeting at Patna, he deliberately avoided mentioning Rama, Sita, Ravana, Draupadi, and so on. He urged the Hindu and Muslim women to unite together in a spirit of harmony and to strengthen the movement by taking to *charkha* and spinning. In order to garner their wholehearted support, he told the Muslim women that "whatever was written in the holy Koran was all good and there was truth in all religions". The full text of the speech delivered by him at a meeting of Muslim women in Bombay on 19 July 1921 is quoted below:

> Mahatma Gandhi rose to address the meeting .... He said that he had long connections with Mussulmans and that the gentleman who took him to Africa for the first time was a Muslim friend. He regarded all those present to be his sisters. All their efforts for the attainment of Swaraj were meant for safeguarding their religion and there was no distinction whatsoever in his mind between the Hindus and the Muslims.
>
> The Mahatma said that, in his opinion, all religions were good. Sometimes mistakes crept into religion at the instance of some misguided followers.

[89]Cited in Bina Kumari Sarma, op. cit., p. 84.

Whatever was written in the holy Koran was all good, and there was truth in all religions. They all stood up for the cause of Islam and they did not want at all a Satanic raj in the world.

In the Satanic raj he could not do any good. He had received a telegram from Aligarh that afternoon intimating him that Mr. Sherwani had been sent to jail notwithstanding the fact that he was working for peace. There might arise an occasion when all good men might be sent to jail, and everybody should be ready for that occasion. In Africa, Hindus and Muslims, regardless of sex, went to jail and preserved the honour of their country. Those who were steeped in luxury would be unable to bear jail life where they would not get tea ten times a day and would not get fine clothes.

For the sake of your religion you should give up all luxury and begin to wear *khadi*. Until India gets Swaraj and the Khilafat and the Punjab wrongs are righted, everybody should regard foreign cloth as not permissible. When we get Swaraj, we would be able to prepare all kinds of *swadeshi* cloth and so you shall have to give up all luxury for six months.

He was very happy to hear of the spinning of Mrs. Haji Yousuf Sobhani. They should all keep the *charkha* near them as they kept their sons in their laps. Remembering God in their heart, they should spin on the *charkha* for the sake of Swaraj and Khilafat at least for some hours every day. By the *charkha* not only the honour of Indian womanhood would be preserved, but they would be in a position to earn an independent living within doors. They could do more for the cause of their country by the *charkha* than by the sword. Many Indians got about Rs. 8 to Rs.15 a month which was not quite sufficient for the maintenance of their families. In Bijapur, Bahen Ganga introduced two thousand *charkhas* into the homes of poor Indians, and as a result of this they were getting good and commendable hand-spun yarn from that place and they (the poor Indians) were earning thereby an independent living.

Continuing, the Mahatma said that they could manufacture the best Dacca muslin formerly, but owing to the present Government, their weavers were in a sorry plight and were quite unable to do their professional work. They should not go to Manchester for fine cloth. One Indian woman had given him an embroidered sari weighing about twelve seers and if they could wear saris of such weight, why could they not wear saris made of *khaddar*? Women could undergo greater pains and trouble than men and therefore nothing prevented them from the free use of the *khadi*. Mrs. Mazhar-ul-Huq gave him four bangles of diamond. Such a sacrifice showed that the Swaraj was coming nearer for women loved their ornaments very much. That woman was beautiful who had got in her heart the idea of God. They should give up all outward signs of beauty. They should not go to Japan, France and China for fine cloth. They should all pray for the success of Hindus and Muslims, but their prayers would be effective when they had pure hearts and bodies covered with *swadeshi* cloth. That was a difficult resolution. But if they once determined to resort to it, it would be very easy indeed.

Concluding, the Mahatma exhorted those present by saying that they either should burn foreign cloth or send it to Smyrna. He thanked them for inviting him and giving him a patient hearing.[90]

[90] *The Bombay Chronicle*, 20-7-1921. Also see CWMG, Vol. XX, pp. 396-98.

Gail Minault points out that in order to make the Khilafat and Non-cooperation movements popular among the Muslim women, religious items and anti-British sentiments were skilfully used. Indeed, Muslim women became "a powerful opinion group within the Khilafat movement, supporting it morally with their firm religious faith and financially with their ornaments".[91]

Apart from Gandhi, Bi Amman also made efforts to bring the Muslim women into the national mainstream. During the period 1920-22, as has already been pointed out, she toured different parts of the subcontinent to popularize the Khilafat issue. In an open letter written by her in 1920, Bi Amman made the following remark: "We had been sacrificing ourselves for our fathers, husbands and sons, but so long as this spirit of Indian womanhood is not lost, I, for one, feel that nothing which really matters is lost".[92] She was an ardent votary of Hindu-Muslim unity and was persevering in her efforts of propagating the *swadeshi* cause. Under the influence of Gandhi, she had herself started wearing *khadi* clothes. In her various speeches addressed to women, she exhorted women to take to spinning of the *charkha*.

Concluding Remarks

In conclusion we may say that although "women's participation in the first Non-cooperation movement was not on a mass scale and was mainly confined to those whose husbands, fathers, brothers or sons had already joined the struggle and were in jail",[93] there can be no denying that Indian women had made significant contributions both to the Khilafat cause and to the Non-cooperation campaign initiated by Gandhi. A Government of India publication observed that "... the growing interest displayed by upper and middle class women in political and

[91] Gail Minault, *The Khilafat Movement*, op. cit., 1981, pp. 149-50.
[92] *Amrita Bazar Patrika*, 9 January 1920.
[93] Aparna Basu, op. cit., p. 22.

social questions, their increasing prominence on the platform and in the press... must be taken as the dawn of a new era; and the fact that the number of women who take part in public life is still very small affords no reason for questioning its significance".[94] Margaret Cousins also pointed out that the Non-cooperation movement gave a big boost to the awakening of Indian women, and that "women's ardent desire for the freedom of their country has given them such personal freedom that they are now welcomed into the open street as volunteers, as pickets, as politicians.... They (i.e., women) do not naturally move towards fighting for their own freedom, but through throwing themselves into a 'cause' they achieve their own liberation.... The Indian National movement cannot progress without the aid of women; the liberation of women will be aided by their devotion to the national movement".[95]

[94]L.F. Rushbrook Williams, *India in 1922* (Calcutta), p. 222.

[95]M.E. Cousins, *The Awakening of Asian Womanhood* (Ganesh and Co., Madras, 1922), pp. 8 and 59-60.

CHAPTER IV

CIVIL DISOBEDIENCE MOVEMENT AND THE ROLE OF WOMEN

I

Bardoli Satyagraha and Women's Participation

The year 1928 proved to be a turning point in the national movement because it was in the February of this year that Simon and his colleagues arrived in India. Since this was an all-White Commission in which no Indian was represented, the Congress passed a resolution to boycott the Simon Commission at every stage and in every form. All important leaders and parties boycotted the Simon Commission and wherever Simon and his colleagues went, they were greeted by hostile crowds who exhorted them to go back. Women also did not lag behind. Hansa Mehta[1] was actively associated with the demonstration which took place in the metropolitan city of Bombay. Several women's associations criticized the Commission on two

[1]Born in 1897, and educated at Baroda, Hansa Mehta was married to Dr. J. Mehta in 1924. She was a prominent woman leader who had participated in the Simon Commission demonstration in 1928; the Civil Disobedience movement in 1930; and Bombay Pradesh Congress Committee in 1930. She was a member of the All India Congress Committee, 1931, and was imprisoned in 1930 and 1932. She was also the founder Vice-Chancellor of M.S. University of Baroda, 1949-58.

counts— non-inclusion of Indians and also of women from it. The women of Bombay held a meeting under the presidentship of Sarojini Naidu and passed a resolution for a vigorous struggle for complete Swaraj.

The British Government retaliated with utmost aggression, resorting to frequent *lathi* charges to curb the violent crowds. Leaders of the stature of Jawaharlal Nehru, Govind Ballabh Pant and Lala Lajpat Rai took the blows, but sadly, however, Lala Lajpat Rai, who was badly hit on his chest on 30 October, could not survive. The blows inflicted on his body proved to be so serious that he finally succumbed to his injuries on 17 November 1928.[2] Indeed, India had lost one of its most venerated leaders in extremely unfortunate circumstances. The hostility shown by the Indian leaders to the Simon Commission definitely gave a big boost to the ongoing nationalist struggle.

Another important event to have taken place in the year 1928 was the Bardoli Satyagraha. This was launched under the leadership of Sardar Patel with the basic purpose of correcting an economic injustice done to the peasants because of the sudden and steep rise of government demand for land revenue. "The Government of Bombay, contrary to the advice of the Joint Parliamentary Committee and contrary to the resolution of the Bombay Legislative Council of the Bombay Presidency in 1924, considerably enhanced the rate of rural taxation which was nominally 20 per cent but in actual application, in some instances, over 60 per cent. The public felt that the increase was unwarranted and that an impartial committee to hold enquiry be constituted. The government paid no heed".[3] When, in order to register their strong protest against this repressive measure, people stopped paying taxes, the government resorted to measures like *lathi* charge, imprisonment, fines, auction of land, etc. But none of these measures could change the people's resolve.

[2]It may be noted that the motivating factor in the assassination of Saunders in December 1928 was Lajpat Rai's death.

[3]Manmohan Kaur, *Women in India's Freedom Struggle* (Sterling, New Delhi, 1985), p. 151.

Women also participated in the no-tax campaign which was started at Bardoli. However, they lacked leadership. The women who made their presence felt during the Bardoli Satyagraha were Smt. Mithubhen Petit and Smt. Bhaktbhen Desai from Bombay. In order to stop the sale of land by the government, Sardar Patel had motivated Mithubhen, Bhaktbhen, Manibhen Patel[4] and other women to camp on those very lands by fixing their tents and huts on it. An unidentified woman donated an amount of Rs.200 and promised to make donations on a regular basis till such time the Satyagraha lasted.

Besides being an eye opener to the people, the Bardoli Satyagraha "created a cadre of women leadership and a band of volunteers and workers. It bridged the gulf between the elite and the common women.... Bardoli provided a spring board and the women and their organisations remained in the forefront of nationalist agitations both in 1930 and in 1942".[5] According to Mahadev Desai: "The heroism of the simple unsophisticated women of Bardoli...was an inspiration to all women outside Bardoli".[6]

Bardoli Satyagraha also gave an indication to Gandhi that perhaps time was ripe for launching the non-violent Satyagraha on a big scale. Judith Brown is of the opinion that Bardoli Satyagraha was a big motivating factor for Gandhi to re-consider his political strategy. In contrast to Gandhi's shattered hopes of 1922, "civil disobedience might now be properly used by Indians en masse as the sanction behind their demands".[7] Gandhi himself had

[4]Born in 1904 near Bombay, Manibhen Patel was the daughter of Sardar Vallabhbhai Patel. She received her early education at Queen Mary's High School and St. Joseph's Convent at Bombay. She later studied at Gujarat Vidyapith, Ahmedabad.

[5]Shirin Mehta, "The Role of Women in the Peasant Movement of Gujarat: A Study in Gandhian Phase", in N. Prasad, ed, *Problems and Issues in Gandhism* (Inter-India Publications, New Delhi, 1990), p. 67.

[6]Cited in Manmohan Kaur, op. cit., p. 152.

[7]Judith Brown, *Gandhi: Prisoner of Hope* (OUP, New Delhi, 1990), p. 221.

looked upon the Bardoli Satyagraha as a victory for truth and non-violence which had "almost restored the shattered faith in non-violence in the political field".[8]

In December 1928, the Congress, at its annual session held in Calcutta "accepted the Nehru Report's 'dominion status' objective as its immediate goal with the proviso that if the government did not accept a constitution based on dominion status by the end of the year, the Congress would not only adopt Poorna Swaraj (complete independence) as its goal but would also be free to launch a civil disobedience movement to attain that objective".[9] However, the failure of the government to consider the Nehru Report and the demand of the people left the Indian National Congress with no other option but to go ahead with its plans of launching Satyagraha as per its decision taken at its session in December 1928 at Calcutta. Thus the Congress session held at Lahore in December 1929 turned out to be among the most memorable sessions of the Congress. In this historic session which was presided over by Jawaharlal Nehru, Poorna Swaraj was adopted as the only viable goal for which the Indians would have to make gigantic efforts. Nehru asserted : "We have now an open conspiracy to free this country from foreign rule and you, comrades, and all our countrymen and country women are invited to join it".[10] Gandhi was also convinced that the launching of civil disobedience was the need of the hour. In the words of S. Gopal: "Civil Disobedience was the only means of challenging both British rule, which appeared to him 'a personification of violence', and the growing hatred towards the agents of this rule, which took the form of casual assassination".[11]

[8]Gandhi to C.F. Andrews, 24 August 1928, *Collected Works of Mahatma Gandhi* (hereinafter CWMG), Vol. 37, p. 200.

[9]Rajan Mahan, *Women in Indian National Congress, 1921-1931* (Rawat Publications, Jaipur and New Delhi, 1999), pp. 261-62.

[10]S. Gopal, ed, *Selected Works of Jawaharlal Nehru*, Vol. 4, p. 198.

[11]S. Gopal, *The Viceroyalty of Lord Irwin, 1926-1931* (Oxford, 1957), p. 55.

II

Breaking of Salt Laws

Gandhi was empowered to initiate the Civil Disobedience movement in any manner he thought appropriate. Since salt is one of the cheapest items used in every house as a matter or routine, Gandhi decided to capitalize on this by breaking the Salt Laws. Moreover, Gandhi thought that the issue of salt would also appeal to the imagination of Indian women. Thus from March 1930 a new phase of Satyagraha had begun. Gandhi's plan was to walk all the way from his ashram at Sabarmati to Dandi—a small village on the seashore situated at a distance of two hundred and forty-one miles from Sabarmati—and to make salt on the beach there. The idea was to defy the government monopoly in salt manufacture. Gandhi was of the opinion that since salt was a thing of common use, the government was not justified in imposing salt tax because this would put additional burden on the meagre, financial resources of the poor. H.F. Owen rightly remarks: "His (i.e., Gandhi's) manufacture of salt in illicit circumvention of the tax on this dietary staple was the most flamboyant example of his concern to increase material and social welfare, which included improvement in the status of women...".[12]

On 12 March 1930, Gandhi, accompanied by seventy-eight of his close associates, started his historic march from the Sabarmati Ashram. This march was a significant political event which appealed to the popular imagination. Dennis Dalton remarks: "The very notion of the march to Dandi exuded a 'come, join me' call for recruitment. Gandhi's methodical procedure of walking through dozens of villages, pausing regularly to hold public meetings, and covering the considerable distance of 241 miles in 24 days, may be seen, quite apart from the strength of the issue, as a massive political campaign".[13] As was expected, Gandhi was

[12]Cited in Rajan Mahan, op. cit., p. 266.

[13]Dennis Dalton, "The Dandi March", in B. R. Nanda, ed, *Essays in Modern Indian History* (OUP, New Delhi, 1980), p. 90.

taken into custody (on 6 April 1930) for violating the Salt Laws.[14] His arrest was the long-awaited signal and the campaign started with country-wide hartals.

Initially, Gandhi had begun his Dandi march by keeping women out of the Salt march. This was a big disappointment for women. Margaret Cousins wrote a strong letter of protest to Gandhi: "In these stirring, critical days of India's destiny there should be no water-tight compartments of service. Women asked that no conferences, congresses or commissions dealing with the welfare of India should be held without the presence of women. Similarly, women must ask that no marches, no imprisonments, no demonstrations organized for the welfare of India should prohibit women from a share in them".[15] Durgabai Deshmukh was also against the idea of excluding women from the Dandi march. In her letter of protest to Gandhi, she wrote that "we women should also be allowed to join".[16] Khurshedbhen, the grand-daughter of Dadabhai Naoroji, expressed her feelings of resentment to Gandhi, asking him as to why women were being prevented from breaking the Salt Laws.[17] Mridula Sarabhai, then a student at Gujarat Vidyapeeth, took the plunge in total defiance of the instruction of Principal Kaka Kalelkar not to do so.[18]

The main reason why Gandhi excluded women was his sense of chivalry.[19] Gandhi knew that if women were also

[14]P.G. Ghosh, *Mahatma Gandhi As I Saw Him* (S. Chand, New Delhi, 1968), p. 137.

[15]Aruna Asaf Ali, *The Resurgence of Indian Women* (Radiant Publishers, New Delhi, 1991), p. 100.

[16]Transcript of Interview with Durgabai Deshmukh, Nehru Memorial Museum and Library, New Delhi, p. 32.

[17]Usha Bhat, "Role of Women in the Freedom Struggle in Ahmedabad", unpublished Ph.D. thesis, Gujarat University. Cited in Aparna Basu, "The Role of Women in the Indian Struggle for Freedom", in B.R. Nanda, ed, *Indian Women: From Purdah to Modernity* (Vikas, New Delhi, 1976), p. 23.

[18]See Aparna Basu, ibid., p. 23.

[19]D.G. Tendulkar, *Life of Mahatma Gandhi* (K. Jhaveri and D.G. Tendulkar, Bombay, 1940), Vol. II, p. 20.

present in the march, the British Government would feel inhibited to attack the procession, unless there was a big provocation. He thought that the inclusion of women would defeat the very purpose of Satyagraha and men would be accused of hiding behind the skirts of women.[20] Gandhi explained: "Just as Hindus do not harm a cow, the British do not attack women as far as possible. For Hindus it would be cowardice to take a cow to the battlefield. In the same way it would be cowardice for us to have women accompany us".[21] But seeing the women in a defiant mood, he ultimately gave his consent to their participation in the Satyagraha.

Though no woman was present during Gandhi's historic march to Dandi, yet they were present everywhere on the way to greet him and to hear him speak. On reaching Dandi, Gandhi convened a Women's Conference in which he placed before women the special role he had envisaged for them.[22] Gandhi exhorted women to concentrate on activities like picketing of liquor and toddy shops and stores selling foreign cloth. He said: "Drink and drugs sap the moral well-being of those who are given to the habit. Foreign cloth undermines the economic foundations of the nation and throws millions out of employment. The distress in each case is felt in the home and therefore by women".[23] He further encouraged them to wear *khadi* and to ply the *charkha*. On the basis of his past experience, Gandhi had known that women had the necessary patience to perform these tasks, though to many these seemed secondary.[24]

The majority of women present in the Conference felt extremely enthusiastic about the roles assigned to them, and in order to accomplish this they formed an organization for

[20]Vijay Agnew, *Elite Women in Indian Politics* (New Delhi, 1979), p. 39.

[21]CWMG, Vol. 43, p. 12. Also see Rajan Mahan, op. cit., p. 268.

[22]See *Young India*, 10 April 1930.

[23]Ibid.

[24]Aparna Basu, op. cit., p. 24.

women in Gujarat. Mrs Tyabji and Mithubhen Petit became President and Secretary respectively of this new organization, the main task of which was picketing of liquor and toddy shops and making personal appeals to the shop-owners to keep their shops closed.

Gandhi also brought out a pamphlet titled "How to do the Picketing". As per the plan chalked out by Gandhi, the picketing team was to have nine women members and a leader. It was decided that before resorting to any actual picketing, the picketing team was to send a delegation to the owner requesting him to either close his shop (in case it was a liquor shop) or restrict sales, if it was a shop selling foreign cloth. And in case the owner refused to comply with their request, the women would start making appeals to potential customers. In the process of picketing, the women were required to wear a special uniform, carry banners and sing *bhajans*. Gandhi was very particular that the picketers should present themselves in a dignified manner, and the use of indecent language was to be strictly avoided. Men were to keep themselves away from this activity—the idea being to make sure that no violence took place. Those women who for some reasons could not actively participate in the picketing activity, were asked to contribute their services in other ways like encouraging their neighbours to spin and wear *khadi* clothes and distribute pamphlets, etc. to make the Gandhian programme popular among the masses. Gandhi was also very particular that proper accounts and vouchers in respect of money spent by the picketing team should be maintained.

The major resolutions adopted at the Gujarat Women's Conference held at Dandi on 13 April 1930 are as follows:

> 1. This Conference of the women of Gujarat assembled at Dandi on 13 April, 1930, and having heard Gandhiji, resolves that the women assembled will picket liquor and toddy shops of Gujarat, and appeal to the shopkeepers and the shop-goers to desist from plying their trade or

> drinking intoxicating liquors as the case may be, and will similarly picket foreign cloth shops and appeal to the dealers and the buyers to desist from the practice of dealing in or buying foreign cloth as the case may be.
>
> 2. This Conference is of the opinion that boycott of foreign cloth is possible only through *khadi* and therefore the women assembled resolve henceforth to use *khadi* only and will so far as possible spin regularly and will learn all the previous processes and preach the message of *khadi* among their neighbours, teach them the processes upto spinning, and encourage them to spin regularly.
>
> 3. This Conference hopes that women all over Gujarat and other provinces will take up the movement initiated at this Conference.[25]

III

Emergence of Women in the Civil Disobedience Era in Different Regions

The Civil Disobedience era occupies a very significant place in the history of women's role in the national movement because it was during the period 1930-34 that women started emerging in a big way as speakers, marchers, picketers, etc. In fact, women's active association with the ongoing freedom struggle had started from the very first day of the commencement of the Salt Satyagraha. Kamaladevi Chattopadhyay recalls:

> I still have before me the fantastic scene of Chowpatty Sands in Bombay, the first day, April 6, 1930, when the Salt Law was broken. Instead of the

[25]Rajan Mahan, op. cit., pp. 270-71. Also see *Young India*, 17 April 1930.

> tiny sands there was only a surging mass of humanity covering the sea face. The scene showed multitudinous women with water pots filled with salt water from the sea, little kids also carrying midget water pots, wending their way to their respective homes to make salt and defy the law .... Here was an unacceptable law being broken with purposeful deliberation throughout the country by men, women and children .... Above all, the revolt had now entered every home, nestled down in the very hearth. Women, like men, were getting the first taste of liberation; for throwing off the shackles of fear marks the birth of freedom.[26]

Gujarat

Shortly after the Women's Conference at Dandi, the Gujarati women, under the inspiration of Gandhi, made their intentions very clear. They wanted to be actively associated with the national movement. In a letter addressed to the Viceroy, the leading Gujarati women placed on record the following resolution: "We the undersigned women of Gujarat, have come to the conclusion that we may not keep ourselves aloof from the great national upheaval that is taking place. We are in full sympathy with the civil disobedience campaign".[27] They made untiring efforts to involve as many Gujarati women as possible in the picketing activities, and to organize the sale of contraband salt all over Gujarat.

Gandhi's confidence in women's participation can be gauged from the fact that he had specially nominated Sarojini Naidu to lead a raid upon Dharasana Salt Works[28] in May 1930. Exhuming utmost faith in women's abilities to

[26]K. Chattopadhyay, *Indian Women's Battle for Freedom* (Abhinav, New Delhi, 1983), pp. 106-07.

[27]Rajan Mahan, op. cit., p. 273.

[28]Dharasana Salt Works are situated at a distance of 150 miles north of Bombay.

do big deeds, Sarojini Naidu said: "The time has come in my opinion when women can no longer seek immunity behind the shelter of their sex, but must share equally with their men comrades all the perils and sacrifices for the liberation of the country".[29] However, in contrast to the confidence shown by Sarojini Naidu, a few Congressmen expressed apprehensions about Gandhi's decision to make the former the leader of the Salt Satyagraha at Dharasana. The enthusiasm of Sarojini Naidu became further evident from her statement made to the press:

> As is quite natural the sense of chivalry of my co-workers, particularly members of the Working Committee, was greatly perturbed at the idea of permitting me to undertake what by its very nature, must be an onerous task, but when on April 6th Mahatma Gandhi nominated me as one of his successors I accepted all the implications of the risks as well as of the responsibilities of that high privilege. The leaders assembled at Allahabad also felt that it was inadvisable for me to undertake this task in view of the fact that my presence was needed for other equally important work elsewhere specially in connection with the Hindu-Muslim problem, but I felt that I cannot break the word, I have given to Mahatma Gandhi.[30]

It was on 15 May 1930 that Sarojini Naidu carried out the instructions of Gandhi by raiding the Dharasana Salt Works. The police did arrest Naidu and her associates, but they were set free the same day. On 21 May 1930, Sarojini Naidu led another batch of 2,500 raiders upon the same Salt Works. When the volunteers reached the barbed wire stockade which was guarded by the police, they were ordered to disperse. The volunteers, however, remained adamant and refused to carry out the orders of the police. The

[29] *The Times of India*, 8 May 1930.
[30] *The Times of India*, 15 May 1930.

police then "rushed upon the advancing marchers and rained blows on their heads with their steel shaft *lathies*".[31] The injured men were removed, and when other volunteers came, they also were badly beaten by the police. The volunteers then changed their tactics and occupied seats on the ground near the salt pans.

This too was not acceptable to the police and they were again asked to disperse. The volunteers again gave a deaf ear to the orders, and this was provocation enough for the police to resort to savage kicking of the "seated men in the abdomen and testicles".[32] "The injured men writhed and squealed in agony, which seemed to inflame the fury of the police.... The police then began dragging the sitting men by the arms or feet, sometimes for a hundred yards and throwing them into ditches".[33] Webb Miller, an American journalist who was present on the occasion, was horrified at the sight of "unresisting men being methodically bashed into a bloody pulp" and said that "I have never seen such harrowing scenes as at Dharasana".[34]

Sarojini Naidu had anticipated that they would be beaten by the police, as can be seen from her following exhortation: "Gandhi's body is in jail but his soul is with you. India's prestige is in your hands. You must not use any violence under any circumstances. You will be beaten but you must not resist; you must not even raise a hand to ward off blows".[35] She was arrested the same day, that is, 21 May 1930. But this arrest did not dampen her spirits, as is evident from her message to her comrades: "Whatever happens, strictly adhere to the law of non-violence. Don't budge an inch from the place you have taken".[36] She also

[31]Quoted in Jack A. Homer, *The Gandhian Reader* (Bloomington, 1956), p. 252. Also cited in Manmohan Kaur, op. cit., p. 165.

[32]Ibid.

[33]Ibid.

[34]Cited in Rajan Mahan, op. cit., p. 274.

[35]Webb Miller, *I Found No Peace* (Simon and S. Chuster, New York, 1936), pp. 190-96.

[36]*Amrita Bazar Patrika*, 22 May 1930.

said: "I am making the most of this heaven-sent opportunity, I find something to bless, not to fear and regret".[37]

Mridula Sarabhai's Contribution: The Dharasana incident went a long way in the active association of women with the Civil Disobedience movement in Gujarat, where perhaps women's participation was the largest. In Sabarmati Ashram special classes were held to train women Satyagrahis. Mridula Sarabhai played an important role in popularizing the boycott of foreign cloth in Ahmedabad, where a Videshi Kapasa Bahishkar Samiti was formed whose President was Saraladevi Sarabhai and Secretary was Mridula Sarabhai. "It organized almost daily processions in which women wearing saffron coloured *khadi* sarees with volunteers' badges pinned on, singing patriotic songs, marched through the streets of Ahmedabad. They collected foreign cloth and made bonfires of them. They also distributed cyclostyled sheets throughout the city".[38]

The Rashtriya Stree Sabha launched an intensive campaign to make the concept of *swadeshi* popular. Volunteers paid personal visits to different homes with the purpose of securing signatures for their firm commitment to *swadeshi*. A picketing association was formed in Ahmedabad, the main centres of which were Maskati Market, Panchkuwa Market and Ratan Pole, whose shops sold foreign cloth. Even godowns where foreign cloth was stored were not spared from picketing.[39] Trucks carrying foreign cloth were not allowed to proceed. A conspicuous feature of these activities was that men and women from different social backgrounds took part, including women from the families of Congressmen. Young girls and boys also did not lag behind. They made their contribution by organizing *vanara senas* with the object of securing information about shops which were dealing in the sale of foreign cloth. The *vanara senas* also helped the

[37]See Naidu's statement in P. Sengupa, *Sarojini Naidu: A Biography* (Asia Publishing House, Bombay, 1966), p. 234.

[38]Aparna Basu, *Mridula Sarabhai: Rebel with a Cause* (OUP, New Delhi, 1996), p. 34.

[39]Ibid.

picketers by giving them prior information about the arrival of trucks carrying foreign cloth or of the police. Credit goes to Mridula for being the first one to organize a *vanara sena* of children in Ahmedabad.

> Children and women organized *praphat pheries* in the early mornings which moved round the city singing patriotic songs to the accompaniment of drums, bugles and *manjiras* (cymbals) and these became immensely popular. 'Dandi darya kinare Mohan mithun banave' (on the sea shores of Dandi, Mohan makes salt); 'Danko vagyo ladvaiya shura jagajo re' (the bell has sounded, brave warriors awake); 'Jan jaye to java dejo par tek no khojo re' (if you have to give up your life, do so, but do not give up the cause)—as these lines reverberated through the cities and villages of Gujarat, they brought a new political awakening, specially among women.[40]

Saraladevi Sarabhai, President of the picketing association, wanted to make sure that the programme of boycott of foreign cloth which was started with so much of enthusiasm did not come to an end. She thus sent a circular (letter) to all the mill-owners and traders, urging them to avoid the use of imported cotton yarn, artificial silk yarn or wool, and to sell only *swadeshi* cloth. Since shops selling *khadi* cloth were not in existence in those days, women carried bundles of *khadi* cloth for different residential areas on Sundays and holidays.

All over Gujarat, women were in high spirits, selling the contraband salt collected from Dandi and Dharasana, and singing in chorus, "we have broken the Salt Law which will wreck the British Empire".[41] They also raised slogans like "Holy Salt", "Gandhi Salt" and "salt that will free India, come and buy".[42] Salt from Dandi and Dholera was distributed among the volunteers, including Mridula and

[40]Ibid., p. 35.
[41]*The Tribune*, 9 April 1930 and 13 April 1930.
[42]*The Tribune*, 15 April 1930.

Khurshedbhen, each of whom got a packet of one *tola* which was sold often for Rs.500.[43]

Once in May 1930, when a procession of women carrying pitchers on their heads was going to give water to the Satyagrahis, the police in a most unbecoming manner did not allow them to move forward and give water to the Satyagrahis in spite of the scorching heat. The British authorities, in collaboration with Gholap, the District Magistrate, ordered the troops on horses to ask the women to go away. When the seven hundred women present there offered resistance, the mounted troops resorted to *lathi*-charge.[44]

The incidents mentioned above amply demonstrate the sense of devotion and commitment of women to the Civil Disobedience movement. It would be interesting to note that all the women who participated in the movement in Gujarat were not educated or sophisticated, the most glaring example being that of Gangabhen Vaidya who had become a widow at the young age of sixteen. She met Gandhi in Bombay and was advised to learn spinning. She was so greatly influenced by Gandhi that later on she decided to stay in Sabarmati Ashram on a permanent basis and dedicate her life to the ultimate goal of India's independence. On 21 January 1931, she led a procession of 1,200 women in Borsad. "The procession was *lathi*-charged, Gangabhen was severely beaten up and bled profusely, but she did not give up the tricolour she was carrying. She was in and out of jail till 1934, when she settled in Bochasan doing constructive work in the rural areas".[45] This incident was one of the worst outrages on women which clearly indicates that the British brutality had assumed such serious proportions that even women were not spared. In his letter of protest to the Viceroy, Gandhi stated: "On the 21st January a cruel, uncalled for and unchivalrous *lathi*-charge was made upon wholly innocent women and girls

[43]Mahadev Desai, *Diaries* (Ahmedabad, 1954), Vol. 13, p. 303.
[44]See Aparna Basu, *Mridula Sarabhai*, op. cit., 1996, p. 37.
[45]Cited in Aparna Basu, "The Role of Women", op. cit., 1976, p. 27.

who were forming a procession which was marching to a women's meeting that was to be held in order to protest against the brutal treatment of a girl 17 years old by a police official. Neither the procession nor the meeting was prohibited".[46]

The majority of women who took part in the procession of Borsad were affiliated to the Sabarmati Ashram. Gandhi eulogized the courage displayed by these women saying that "the Ashram women have immortalized themselves and the Ashram".[47] He even went to the extent of saying, during the course of the meeting of Women's Indian Council in London, that the heroic deeds of the Gujarati women had "converted the little town of Borsad into a Thermopylae".[48]

Bombay

Bombay was another region where women were actively involved during the Salt Satyagraha and the Civil Disobedience movement. Among the prominent women leaders who had played significant roles in Bombay were Sarojini Naidu, Kamaladevi Chattopadhyay, Lilavati Munshi, Hansa Mehta, the Captain sisters Perinbhen and Goshibhen, Jaishri Raiji, Avantikabai Gokhale, Jankidevi Bajaj, and several others associated with the Rashtriya Stree Sabha.

Kamaladevi Chattopadhyay was entrusted with the responsibility of leading the raid on the Wadala Salt Fields in the precints of Bombay. Initially, however, Kamaladevi was apprehensive about Gandhi's idea of breaking Salt Laws. She wondered "how this (civil disobedience) could be brought about by breaking the Salt Laws". She opened out her mind to Jawaharlal Nehru and

[46]The young girl was Lilavati while Gangabhen Vaidya was a widow, an inmate of Sabarmati Ashram. The latter received head injuries during the incident. See "Letter to Viceroy", 1 February 1931, in CWMG, Vol. 35, p. 137.

[47]Rajan Mahan, op. cit., p. 275.

[48]CWMG, Vol. 45, p. 152. See also "Speech at Meeting of Women's Indian Council" in London on 18-11-1931, in CWMG, Vol. 48, p. 312.

asked him if he could suggest some better method of carrying out civil disobedience. Nehru, however, had utmost faith in Gandhi's decision and told Kamaladevi: "Gandhiji is a very intuitive person and his instincts are always fruitful. We are not always able to see what he feels, what he is leading up to, but usually he is able to achieve something and therefore we shall have to act accordingly".[49] She had "visualised a mass raid embracing a large part of the city's two million population. I was sure that no force, not even machine-guns, could stop this raid".[50] However, the raid on Wadala Salt Fields could not take place because one day before the scheduled date, the British authorities arrested Kamaladevi. She recalls that when she was arrested she was represented by her little son of seven, "who proudly carried the banner and engaged in the drama of his first battle". "There were other freedom fighters of tender age. Johri of the Bombay Youth League organised youngsters into *vanar senas* (monkey brigades, named after the army that assisted the hero of the Ramayana epic), as twelve-year old Indira Nehru did in Allahabad. Girls of 10 or 12 would sell prohibited literature. Women would duplicate illegal news sheets in kitchen and barn, act as messengers, write on street walls the news of the day, and picket shops selling foreign cloth and liquor".[51]

Hansa Mehta,[52] Perin Captain[53] and Lilavati Munshi[54] played a prominent role in Bombay by going to different shop

[49]See Aruna Asaf Ali, op. cit., p. 101.

[50]Kamaladevi Chattopadhyay, "The Struggle for Freedom", in Tara Ali Baig, ed, *Women of India* (Publications Division, New Delhi, 1958), p. 21.

[51]Aruna Asaf Ali, op. cit., pp. 101-02.

[52]Hansa Mehta was an educationist and social reformer who was the first woman to be elected to the Bombay Legislative Council in 1931. She was also a member of the Constituenty Assembly, 1946.

[53]Perin Captain was the grand-daughter of Dadabhai Naoroji. She and her sister Goshibhen were close friends of Kamla Nehru.

[54]Lilavati Munshi, like her husband K.M. Munshi, was a leading writer in Gujarati. Both played an important role in the national movement. They were also known for their social reform activities.

dealers and urging them not to sell imported cloth. Besides, the Satyagrahis made fervent appeals to the customers to refrain from making purchases. The first ten months of 1930 saw as many as 17,000 convictions of women; the closing of shops was declared an unlawful act and shopkeepers violating this began to be arrested along with the picketers.

Kamaladevi herself was taken into police custody under the vagrancy law when she refused to give her address. She did not want her colleagues to be put into trouble. K. Natarajan, the Editor of the *Indian Social Reformer*, expressed his views forcefully when he came to know from his daughter about the inhuman treatment that was meted out to Kamaladevi in the prison. She was subsequently shifted to the 'B' class.

Kamaladevi and Aruna Asaf Ali, who came from affluent backgrounds, found life in jail a very rewarding and educative experience. This gave them a clear idea of the conditions in which the majority of women lived. Kamaladevi writes: "... a large number of women who were with me in prison came from very poor classes, poorer than the lower middle class.... I became more and more convinced how important it was to improve their economic life if their social life was to be improved – that it was not possible to think of merely trying to break caste, it was bound up with their poverty".[55]

Aruna Asaf Ali informs that the plight of prisoners in small towns and villages was much worse. "In the absence of toilets, the women would be marched out to the fields accompanied by male guards, outraging their sense of modesty".[56] In 1932, the police failed to draw a distinction between political prisoners and ordinary prisoners when they locked the political prisoners and the ordinary prisoners together in the same barrack in the Arthur Road Jail. The political prisoners registered their strong protest against this because several of the prisoners were

[55]Aruna Asaf Ali, op. cit., p. 102.
[56]Ibid.

prostitutes and this could be detrimental to the health of the political prisoners. They were then shifted to another barrack. The inhuman attitude of the police also becomes evident from the fact that only infants under the age of three were allowed to remain with their mothers in jail. Other children were left on the streets.[57] Expressing his concern about the inhuman treatment meted out to women prisoners in jail, Jawaharlal Nehru made the following observation:

> The lot of our womenfolk in prison was especially hard and painful to contemplate. They were mostly middle-class women, accustomed to a sheltered life, and suffering chiefly from the many repressions and customs produced by a society dominated to his own advantage, by man. The call of freedom had always a double meaning for them, and the enthusiasm and energy with which they threw themselves into the struggle had no doubt their springs in the vague and hardly conscious, but nevertheless intense, desire to rid themselves of domestic slavery also. Excepting a very few, they were classed as ordinary prisoners and placed with the most degraded of companions, and often under horrid conditions. I was once lodged in a barrack next to a female enclosure, a wall separating us. In that enclosure there were, besides other convicts, some women political prisoners, including the one who had been my hostess and in whose house I had once stayed. A high wall separated us, but it did not prevent me from listening in horror to the language and curses which our friends had to put up with from the women convict warders.[58]

Hansa Mehta and others formed the Desh Sevika Sangh which made noteworthy contributions by way of organizing

[57]Ibid.
[58]Jawaharlal Nehru, *An Autobiography*, p. 344.

picketing in different parts of Bombay. This work was carried out by highly committed Desh Sevikas, who were clad in saffron sarees and white blouses. In the true Gandhian spirit, they wore only *khadi* clothes and spent most of the time in spinning the *charkha*. The picketing activities of the Desh Sevikas were so effective that many foreign cloth merchants gave an undertaking not to sell foreign cloth till such time the country's honour and pride were restored. Seeing the dedicated manner in which the Desh Sevikas were carrying out their picketing activities, the government felt constrained to declare the Desh Sevika Sangh an illegal organization.[59]

The Desh Sevikas organized a number of demonstrations that found a wide coverage in the press and inspired women all over India. Forbes reports:

> Processions of one to two thousand women, accompanied by their children, were not unusual at this time. Even larger numbers came to listen to speeches about *swadeshi* and freedom. The largest crowd celebrated Gandhi's birthday and the release from prison of three of the most important women leaders: Lilavati Munshi, Perin Captain, and Mrs. Lukanji. A mile-long chain of women, led by *sevikas* dressed in orange saris and carrying placards, numbered more than 5,000. Crowds of 10,000 assembled at both ends of this parade. These numbers could not be matched in other areas of India, but patriotic women everywhere emulated the spirit.[60]

East Godavari District of Andhra Pradesh

The women in the East Godavari District of Andhra Pradesh also took part in the Salt Satyagraha and the

[59]Horace Alexander, *Gandhi Through Western Eyes* (Bombay, 1969), p. 64.

[60]Geraldine Forbes, *The New Cambridge History of India*, IV.2: *Women in Modern India* (Cambridge University Press, 1996), p. 135.

Civil Disobedience movement. Sambamurty, the district leader, initiated the Salt Satyagraha campaign in the East Godavari region. As a result of the inspiration provided by him, a number of women joined the procession to break the Salt Law at Chollangi, a coastal place in the district. The woman who played a prominent part in this campaign was Vedantam Kamaladevi of Kakinada, whose husband was very supportive and cooperative. Kamaladevi also encouraged her mother and young children to join the campaign as volunteers. She also visited other districts such as Vizagapatam with the purpose of motivating women to join the Salt Satyagraha. She was taken into police custody at Naupada in Vizagapatam district for violating the Salt Law and was imprisoned for six months. Her contribution was particularly commendable because despite having small kids, she was actively involved in the national movement.[61]

Madras

The Salt Satyagraha at Madras was conducted under the leadership of T. Prakasam. After his arrest, it was Durgabai who assumed leadership. She led fifty volunteers to the sea coast to conduct the campaign. In order to popularize the campaign she visited many places like Chittoor, Guditturam, Tiruttani, Prani and Arcot in May 1930. Her sincerity of purpose, total commitment and, above all, her fiery oratory impressed the audience so much that she became their beloved leader. Lord Cunninghan too hailed her as Sivamgi Durgabai – Durgabai, the lioness.[62] On 26 May 1930 she was arrested and sentenced to one year's imprisonment which she spent in the Central Jail for Women at Vellore.[63]

[61]Leela Kasturi and Vina Mazundar, ed, *Women and Indian Nationalism* (Vikas, New Delhi, 1994), p. 117.

[62]N. Seeta Devi, *Life History of Durgabai Deshmukh* (Madras, 1977), pp. 16-18.

[63]Transcript of interview with Smt. Durgabai Deshmukh, NMML, New Delhi.

George Slocombe of the *Daily Herald* wrote in his despatch on the Wadala Salt raid: "... One of the raiders carried out her mission with quiet dignity, very impressive to behold. It was a woman who emerged from the crowd, climbed through the barbed wire and approached the salt mound, as if it were an altar and filled her sari with salt as part of some unknown ritual".[64]

Orissa

In Orissa, the two important centres of Salt Satyagraha were Inchudi[65] in the Balasore district and Kujanga[66] in the Cuttack district. On 20 April 1930, the first batch of women Satyagrahis was led by Rama Devi and Malati Choudhury who went to Inchudi and openly manufactured salt there. Hundreds of women blowing conches followed them in a long procession in which volunteers from Gujarat and Bengal also participated.[67] As a result of the untiring efforts made by the women leaders in Orissa (who did door to door campaigning coaxing women to break Salt Laws), even illiterate women from the lower strata were drawn to their fold and came in large numbers. According to an estimate, as many as 1,500 rural women took part in the campaign.[68]

When the Satyagraha campaign at Kujanga received a setback because of the arrest of the prominent male leaders, women came out of the security of their homes and kept the movement alive. Displaying utmost courage, they toured the entire area "creating unbelievable enthusiasm among common men and Congress workers".[69] The movement was considerably strengthened when Rani

[64] *The Indian Annual Register*, Vol. I, January-June 1930, p.119.

[65] *Prajatantra*, 28 April 1930. Also see Bina Kumari Sarma, "Gandhian Movement and Women's Awakening in Orissa", *The Indian Historical Review*, Vol. XXI, Nos 1 & 2, edited by Anup Taneja (ICHR and Motilal Banarsidass, Delhi, 1997), p. 85.

[66] Home Political Proceedings (Home Pol.), File No. 5/62/1932.

[67] *Samaj*, 23 April 1930.

[68] *Young India*, 8 May 1930.

[69] Home Pol., File No. 251/1/1930.

Bhagyavati of Kujanga Raj family joined the Satyagraha in June 1930.[70] Following her example, about 500 women came forward to break the Salt Law. At Gandakipur, the Rani of Paradip extended her support to the Satyagrahis.[71] "Thus the presence of young and aristocratic women in processions, public meetings and the example of royal ladies manufacturing salt mobilized the masses to extend support to the movement. Rural women too discarded their *purdah* and welcomed the Satyagrahis passing through their villages".[72]

Kuntala Kumari Sabat, the celebrated poetess, social worker and freedom fighter from Orissa, made her contribution through writing books like *Sphulinga*, *Ahvana* and *Archana* which infused a revolutionary zeal and patriotic fervour among people.[73] Her poems became so popular that students began reciting them in public in order to motivate people to join the national movement in large numbers. Little wonder that the British Government decided to ban some of her works.[74]

The contributions made by the women of Orissa are all the more praiseworthy because they had to contend with the staunch opposition of their family members.[75] In her memoirs Rama Devi has mentioned the name of a widow named Susila of Rampur village who showed great courage in abandoning her home to join the Gandhian movement. To quote her: "... the courage of some spinsters was a matter of surprise and a fountain of hope that a country having such courageous women and girls could not be kept in

[70]See K.M. Patra, *Orissa Legislative and Freedom Struggle* (ICHR, New Delhi, 1979), p. 75.

[71]H.K. Mahatab, ed, *History of the Freedom Movement in Orissa* (Cuttack, 1957), Vol. V, p. 4.

[72]See Bina Kumari Sarma, op. cit., p. 86.

[73]Savitri Raut, *Pioneer Women in Oriya Literature* (New Delhi, 1971), p. 51.

[74]Chandradhar Mohapatra, *Kuntala Kumari Sabat* (in Oriya), pp. 123-29. Also see Bina Kumari Sarma, op. cit., p. 87.

[75]A.R. Desai, *Social Background of Indian Nationalism* (Popular Prakashan, Bombay, 1948), pp. 278-79.

bondage by any powers".[76] The women were so firm in their resolve that even the atrocities committed by the police did not deter them from moving ahead in their mission. The example of Satyagrahis who were returning from the Iram Salt Centre of Balasore aptly substantiates this. Seeing the Satyagrahis, the police allowed the men to go and "charged women (700) with *lathies* inflicting blows on their backs and legs. But the women remained firm".[77] Thus it would not be wrong to say that the nature of participation of Oriya women in the Salt Satyagraha became the most remarkable feature of the Gandhian movement in Orissa.[78]

During the course of the Civil Disobedience movement, Gandhi had chalked out an elaborate programme for picketing shops selling liquor and foreign cloth.[79] He preferred women for these activities because of their inherent trait of non-violence. Gandhi wrote: "Who can make more effective appeal to the heart than women"?[80] He believed that the Non-cooperation movement of 1921 could not register the desired impact because the job of picketing had been assigned to men who resorted to violence.[81]

Initially, seventeen women belonging to *purdahnashin* affluent families came forward as volunteers to organize the picketing of shops selling liquor and foreign cloth.[82] In Cuttack and Balasore, picketing was done mainly by women, "who stood in rows in front of liquor shops and pleaded with would-be purchasers to abstain from making purchases".[83] They urged the shopkeepers to give a written undertaking that they would not sell foreign cloth. The women picketed only those shops, the owners of

[76]Bina Kumari Sarma, op. cit.
[77]Home Pol., File No. 5/62/1932.
[78]Bina Kumari Sarma, op. cit.
[79]Home Pol., op. cit.
[80]*Young India*, 10 April 1930.
[81]Ibid.
[82]*Young India*, 8 May 1930.
[83]Home Pol., File No. 18/January 1931.

which refused to give undertakings. Thus, "women proved themselves indispensable as workers, organizers and actual fighters".[84]

> Oriya women from extremely traditional and conservative families who had never been out of *purdah* walked unveiled in public processions and also braved the concomitant discomforts of prison life. This gave them strength to give up both the *purdah* and their religious and caste prejudices. Some women who had participated in picketing came from a rich background and were accustomed to a life of leisure and comfort. Hitherto they had never visited such areas or left home unescorted. Their boldness therefore in visiting different places, approaching different people, facing *lathi* charge and imprisonment is highly commendable.[85]

In the Civil Disobedience campaign about fifty women had worked as volunteers.[86] Out of these, five, namely, Sarala Devi, Rama Devi, Malati Choudhury, Chandramani and Suryamani, courted arrest and were sent to the Bhagalpur, Vellore and Puri jails.[87] Government reports expressed grave concern at the boldness of women to picket despite the presence of police.[88] Gandhi was absolutely right when he said that if women had taken up constructive activities like picketing and specialized in them, they could have contributed more than men to the cause of the country's freedom.[89]

The opening session of the Karachi National Congress held in 1931 was a historic occasion for Oriya women.[90] This was addressed by Sarala Devi. About fourteen women

[84]Home Pol., File No.5/62/1932.
[85]See Bina Kumari Sarma, op. cit., p. 88.
[86]Home Pol., op. cit.
[87]Ibid.
[88]Home Pol., File No. 18/VII/1930.
[89]*Young India*, 20 April 1930; CWMG, Vol. XLIII, p. 220.
[90]*Orissa Review* (January 1987), p. 3.

delegates from Orissa graced the occasion by their presence and a poem titled "Tribute to Bhagat Singh" written by Kuntala Kumari Sabat was circulated among the members to instill in them the patriotic spirit.[91]

After the Civil Disobedience movement was called off, Gandhi remarked, "... the role women played in the freedom struggle should be written in letters of gold".

Bengal

The conspicuous feature of women's participation in Bengal was that their activities were more radical and revolutionary than those of women in other regions. This was mainly because of the revolutionary ideology of Subhas Chandra Bose which inspired many young girls to associate themselves with the revolutionary party. An annual report of the Police Administration observed: "Organized attempts, seldom successful, were made to hoist the Congress flag on Government buildings in the mofussil. An increasing share of the work was taken up by women, both because it was becoming more difficult to find male recruits and because the presence of women-folk was calculated to prove an embarrassment to the police".[92] This observation does not seem to be authentic for the reason that women did not join politics to embarrass the police. In fact, the police authorities never took a lenient attitude towards women for their nationalist activities.

In Bengal, the organizations through which women took part in the Civil Disobedience movement were: Nari Satyagraha Committee (NSC), Mahila Rashtriya Sangh and Ladies Picketing Board. The Mahila Rashtriya Sangh, which was established in 1928, was the first formal organization which started mobilizing women for taking part in political activities. At the instructions of Subhas Chandra Bose, Latika Ghosh—an Oxford educated teacher —founded this organization, which worked in close

[91]See Bina Kumari Sarma, op. cit.

[92]*Annual Report of Police Administration* (Bombay, 1932), p. xi.

coordination with the Congress. Though basically the NSC's ideological framework was radical-oriented, but in order to mobilize women, it emphasized the inherent religious nature of Indian women. Latika Ghosh tried to awaken the women's consciousness through writing articles. She told her readers that they were the embodiment of the Supreme Shakti and tried to infuse in them Divine Love for their motherland. She wrote: "Every one of you must be like a spark which will burn down all selfishness, all petty dreams—purified by fire, only the bright, golden love of the Motherland will remain".[93]

The women of Calcutta formed the Nari Satyagraha Samiti (NSS) in 1922 in response to the Congress call for women to prepare themselves for serving the nation. Urmila Devi and Jyotimoyee Ganguli were named the President and the Vice-President respectively of this organization. Santi Das and Bimal Protibha Devi were the Joint Secretaries. "This group had a core of fifteen to twenty women who were willing to picket and risk arrest. They were all Bengali women belonging to the three highest castes: brahmins, kayasthas, and vaidyas. They were educated, from professional families, and had all observed some form of *purdah*. They chose white *khaddar* saris as their uniform".[94]

During 1930 women took out their own processions in Calcutta and also led them and addressed meetings. Jyotimoyee Ganguli held one such meeting at Naughat in defiance of a prohibitory order. A ten year old boy, who was badly thrashed by the police, was lying unconscious on her lap. In order to associate herself wholeheartedly with the Civil Disobedience campaign she resigned from her government job. Nishtami Devi also addressed a meeting in Calcutta. As a result of these efforts, middle-class women, who normally remained confined within the four walls of their homes, came out in the open and appeared as Satyagrahis. Among them Bina Das was extremely

[93]Geraldine Forbes, op. cit., p. 137.
[94]Ibid.

popular. She was the one who fired a pistol at Governor Jackson. Bina's elder sister Kalyani and some other students formed the Chattri Sangha (Association for Female Studies). When Gandhi announced the commencement of Civil Disobedience in 1930, Kalyani played an active part by leading the Chattri Sangha girls in a demonstration outside Bethume College. When Nehru was arrested, these students demanded the closure of the College. When Mrs Das, the Principal, did not pay heed to their demand, they went on a strike.[95]

In 1931, when Kalyani was addressing a meeting at Hazra Park, she was arrested by the police and was "locked in an underground cell without saris, bedding, or a mosquito net, and given only three mugs of water per week".[96] Santi and Suniti, two school girls from Comilla, shot Magistrate Stevens to death on 14 December 1931. "From this date women crowded into unprecedented roles and actions in quick succession. Pritilata Waddedar led the attack on the Chittagong European Club, Kalpana Dutta jumped bail and disappeared underground with Surya Sen's band of absconders, Bina Das fired on the Bengal Governor Anderson at a Calcutta University convocation function".[97] Thus, in contrast to the earlier times when women had extended support to the revolutionaries indirectly (by collecting funds, providing them hiding and transport facilities, etc.), they now became directly involved in revolutionary activities. The women of Bengal were thus actively associated with the Civil Disobedience movement, though their *modus operandi* was somewhat different.

Bihar

At the time when the Satyagraha movement was commenced, Gandhi, in an open letter addressed to the

[95]Ibid., p. 139.
[96]Ibid., p. 140.
[97]Rajan Mahan, op. cit., p. 286.

women of India, asked them to contribute to the national movement through participation in the boycott of foreign cloth and intoxicants. This would in turn encourage the production of hand-made cloth. And Gandhi believed that this could be achieved if women started devoting "every available minute to the spinning of yarn".[98] He further said that in order to curb the Civil Disobedience movement the British authorities might go to any extent like inflicting bodily injuries, etc. Gandhi's advice therefore was that women should continue moving forward in their chosen path with utmost determination and be prepared for all eventualities. He said: "To suffer such insult and injury would be their pride. Such suffering it comes to them will hasten the end".[99] The women of Bihar responded well to Gandhi's call and came forward in considerable numbers to involve themselves in "breaking Salt Laws and forest laws, taking out *praphat pheris* and processions, picketing schools, colleges, legislative councils and clubs. These women who had already been feeling the pulse of a new life now came forward courageously in the world's broad field to share with men, the struggles, and joys in the country's battle for liberty".[100]

Shailabal Devi, wife of a Congress leader in Santhal Parganas district, made successful efforts to mobilize women at a meeting and made fervent appeals to them to violate the Salt Laws.[101] In Shahabad district, Mrs Rambahadur led a group of women to manufacture about a *chattak* of salt in front of the police station.[102]

In Bihar, women achieved remarkable success in picketing of both liquor and foreign cloth shops. Two women, namely, Mrs Hasan Imam and Vindhyavasini Devi, played a prominent part in this respect. Under the leadership of the former, a women's committee was formed in

[98] *Young India*, 10 April 1930.
[99] Ibid.
[100] See Leela Kasturi and Vina Mazumdar, op. cit., pp.164-65.
[101] Ibid., p. 165.
[102] Ibid.

Muzzafarpur for propagating the *swadeshi* concept through spinning activity.[103] In Patna, under the leadership of Mrs. Hasan Imam, women went "through the streets urging shopkeepers not to deal in foreign cloth".[104] Vindhyavasini Devi also took an active part in this campaign.

In order to curb the Civil Disobedience campaign, the government began taking repressive measures by arresting the Satyagrahis. In Bihar also several women were taken into police custody. "The first two women to be arrested were Saraswati Devi, the President of Hazaribagh District Congress Committee and Sadhana Devi, who was the daughter of a Professor of Physics in Hazaribagh. In July 1930, Mira Devi of Giridih subdivision was arrested for her participation in the movement. The daughter of a Professor in St. Columbus College at Hazaribagh, Mira Devi was the third woman to be arrested".[105]

Delhi

The success of Gandhi's appeal to women lay in the traditional idioms and images which he frequently used. This drew the masses towards him, and the response of women was particularly overwhelming during the Civil Disobedience movement. In Delhi, as elsewhere, picketing was one area of activity where women were drawn in large numbers.

A news item in *The Hindustan Times* read: "Lady Volunteers Parade Cloth Market—the lady volunteers paraded the Delhi cloth market today and warned the dealers that if they imported foreign cloth, they will do so at their own risk for in that case ladies would resort to picketing of their shops".[106] Picketing was not merely confined to shops selling foreign goods, foreign cloth and

[103]K.K. Datta, *History of the Freedom Movement in Bihar* (Patna, 1957), Vol. II, pp. 114-16.

[104]See Leela Kasturi and Vina Mazumdar, op. cit., p. 165.

[105]See K.K. Datta, op. cit., p.107.

[106]*The Hindustan Times*, 14 September 1930.

liquor but it was also directed towards the financial institutions which were aiding in the sale of foreign goods. A caption, "Picketing of Banks Campaign" contained the following elaboration: "Dr. Mrs. Vedi, Dictator of the Delhi Congress Committee, has in view of the representation made by various constituents of the three local European banks which are alleged to be furthering the sale of foreign cloth, decided to put off the picketing of these banks for some time. She considers the request of the depositors that they would withdraw their money at their earliest convenience from these banks as reasonable".[107]

Apart from the daily newspapers like *The Hindustan Times*, details about the foreign cloth picketing are also available in Delhi Satyagraha Report, 1930 and All India Congress Committee Papers, particularly the ones pertaining to Delhi Pradesh Congress. There were a number of cases where women volunteers bore the brunt of police *lathi* charge and were put behind the bars. Picketing in Delhi proved to be very effective in curbing the sale of foreign cloth. "On the whole, we can safely say that not a yard of foreign cloth is being sold openly in Delhi and every effort is being made to reduce leakage to the minimum".[108]

Very inspiring and provocative speeches were made by some of the women leaders in Delhi. In one of the public meetings held at Delhi grounds, various women leaders were arrested. The meeting began under the chairmanship of Dr. (Mrs.) Vedi. On a purely peaceful meeting the police indulged in repeated *lathi* charge and arrested all the women leaders who came to the dias to speak. In a very lucid and provocative speech, Mrs. Sen Gupta[109] said that the government was gloating over the alleged fact that the Civil Disobedience movement was weakening. She pointed towards the guardians of law and order and enquired whether the government's allegation was true;

[107] *The Hindustan Times*, 6 October 1930.

[108] *Delhi Satyagraha Report, 1930.*

[109] Wife of Shri J.M. Sen Gupta, she was convicted in a case in Delhi and lodged in Delhi Jail.

five hundred policemen armed with *lathis* and rifles had been sent to disperse a meeting of peaceful people.[110] In this meeting, some of the prominent leaders who were arrested were Mrs. Sen Gupta, Dr. (Mrs.) Vedi, Smt. Kausalya Devi (younger sister of Satyawati) and Raj Rani.[111] Police brutalities on the peaceful demonstrators took a very serious turn when a woman at Shamli who was beaten and arrested, had a miscarriage. To stifle public opinion arising from her case, police resorted to more brutalities. She was ill-treated in jail and was separately confined to induce her to apologize. Her complaint against the S.O. Shamli was shelved. She later on developed lunacy symptoms and was sent to Benaras Mental Prison.[112] Her case was brought to public attention by local newspapers.

In Delhi, the students of Indraprastha (I. P.) College also played an active part in the national movement. They participated in peaceful activities like hoisting the national flag in the college premises, and singing national songs.[113] I.P. College became a centre of controversy because its distinguished Principal was Miss Gminer, an Australian, who was a theosophist and an ardent follower of Annie Besant. The Chief Commissioner of Delhi threatened to withdraw the official grant to the Indraprastha Institution unless Miss Gminer put an end to her political activities. However, Babu Jugal Kishore, the founder of the institution, accepted the challenge and appealed to the public for

[110] *Delhi Satyagraha Report, 1930.*

[111] Born in 1904, resident of Delhi, wife of Dr. Yudhvir Singh, Raj Rani took part in the Civil Disobedience movement (1930) and the Quit India movement (1942). She was sentenced in 1930 to six months imprisonment for picketing wine shops. During the Quit India movement, her residence was the centre for the distribution of national literature. She was arrested along with Raghubir Singh Panch Hazari, and sentenced on 20 March 1944 to three months imprisonment in Central Jail, Delhi. Her husband Yudhvir Singh, one of the Congress leaders of Delhi, was also arrested and convicted a number of times.

[112] *Delhi Pradesh Congress Committee Report, 1931.*

[113] *The Hindustan Times*, 11 and 12 October 1930.

funds to make up for the loss resulting from withdrawal of government grant.[114]

Seeing the active involvement of women in the national movement, the British administration felt constrained to devise various strategies to curb the women agitators. In a letter to W.W. Emerson, Secretary to the Government of India, Home Department, a special officer of the Political Department wrote:

> Any measure which may have the effect of stopping women from participating in the next movement is strongly suggested by this government. Apart from the undesired effects politically of imprisoning women picketers or boycotters, there will be a difficulty in providing jail accommodation if their number is large. It is, therefore, in every way desirable that women participants in the movement should be fined and the fines should be recoverable from their husbands, parents or guardians.[115]

Thus, the British authorities were aware that the increasing involvement of women had the potential for creating serious problems in the future. They feared that they would arouse public sympathy both within and outside India, particularly if they continued resorting to inhuman and brutal tactics like *lathi* charge and beating of women, etc. Hence orders were passed by the Home Department to various provinces and all the local governments to avoid using force wherever possible, especially at places where women were assembled and to avoid taking any measure which would give opportunity for charges of indecent behaviour against government servants.[116]

The letter from the Chief Commissioner of Delhi, Sir John Thompson, to the Secretary of the Government of India, also reflects the seriousness of the problem:

[114]Babu Jugal Kishore Khanna, the founder of the I.P. School and College, was a nationalist to the core.

[115]Home Pol., File No. 14/4/1932.

[116]Ibid.

> The problem of dealing with the numbers of women demonstrators is a new one in India and an Indian government would be much qualified to deal with it than we are as they would be free from the odium which attaches to a foreign government when it employs what is called repression.... It has been suggested to me that one way in which this can be done is to get people of respectable position to visit the families from which women workers are likely to come and bring pressure and persuasion to bear on them. Another method which I've long been considering is to make use of the untouchables (females wherever possible) for dealing with women picketers. Picketing by women and the participation by women in demonstrations, I regard as a very grave menace unless some method of dealing with it is devised and I consider the experiment with the untouchables is well worth making.[117]

Wanting to kill two birds with one stone, he further wrote: "The Congress party with its professed affection and sympathy for this class can hardly raise objections. The depressed classes look to the government to champion their interests and the enlisting of their assistance in the maintenance of order would be a measure tending to their uplift".[118]

Women also played a very significant part in the propagation of *khadi*. Apart from paying house to house visits for securing temperance pledge, they also went to temples and Jamuna ghats where they successfully prevented people clad in foreign cloth from entering the temples and bathing in the holy river. They resorted to picketing at the famous Hanuman Mandir and allowed only *khadi*-clad people to enter the temple.[119] In 1930,

[117]Ibid.

[118]Ibid.

[119]*The Congress Bulletin* (New Delhi, June 1930), No. 23, in All India Congress Committee File (1930): 26 June 1930.

Delhi had more than 300 women volunteers affiliated to the Congress. Age did not seem to dampen the spirits of women who were committed to the nationalist cause. This is aptly demonstrated by the message given by Kamaladevi's aged mother:

> My hope has been fulfilled to see my dearest Kamla in prison as a result of her services in the cause of the country is the proudest privilege in my old age. Though age prevents me from entering the arena, the task will be completed and I feel confident that it will be done. I'm happy because the pretensions of the tyrant have been exposed as he has now come out in true colours by the persecution of women who love their country. Wherever I've travelled, I've witnessed an unprecedented upheaval. Everywhere one hears of liberty and liberty alone. All this portends the end of British rule in India.[120]

During the Civil Disobedience movement in the 1930s when most of the active male leaders were is jail, it were the women leaders of the Congress who kept the movement alive through speeches and organization work.[121] Notable examples are those of Mrs Kohli, Atma Devi[122] and Parbati Devi.[123]

[120]Ibid., 24 May 1930.

[121]Home Pol., File No. 18/VIII/July 1930.

[122]Born in 1890, resident of Delhi, wife of Shri Sahib Das Suri, Atma Devi was one of the leading organizers of Delhi women. She took part in the Civil Disobedience movement (1932-34) and the Quit India movement (1942) and was sentenced on 10 February 1932 to nine months Rigorous Imprisonment (R.I.) and on 20 October 1942 to four months R.I. in Central Jail, Delhi. She was transferred to Female Jail, Lahore, on 26 October 1942. Her son Shri Krishna Suri and daughter Satya were also arrested.

[123]Born in 1901, resident of Delhi, wife of Shri Chaturbhuj Didwania, social reformer, Parbati Devi was one of the prominent Congress members among Delhi Congress Mahila Sangh. She took part in the Civil Disobedience movement (1930) and the Quit India movement (1942) and was sentenced in 1930 to six months imprisonment. She was again arrested on 10 August 1942 and detained for two years under the Defence of India rules.

Satyawati's Contribution: Maternal grand-daughter of Swami Shraddhanand, Satyawati Devi (1907-45), played a significant role in the Civil Disobedience movement in Delhi during 1931-32.

At the time when Gandhi launched his Satyagraha campaign against the Rowlatt Bills in 1919, Delhi emerged as a crucial centre of nationalist politics. On 30-3-1919, Swami Shraddhanand exhibited great courage in countering the public bayonets and in challenging the soldiers to fire at him. The fortitude displayed by him made the police jittery and they soon retreated peacefully.[124] Hundreds of people who were present on the occasion were deeply impressed by the bold and unflinching attitude of Swami Shraddhanand. Also present among the crowd was a young girl of eleven, Satyawati, who was at that time a student of Indraprastha Girls' School which was already a centre of political activities in Delhi. Her mother's name was Ved Kumari. Like her maternal grandfather, Satyawati too was absolutely fearless.

Tall and slender, Satyawati with her charismatic personality and fiery oratory was able to mobilize and motivate women of Delhi to participate in the national movement, the most glaring example being that of Aruna Asaf Ali. To quote Aruna:

> Had it not been for Satyawati, I wonder if I would have ventured out of my sheltered domestic life, notwithstanding that my husband was a prominent Congressman who had already gone through the baptism of imprisonment in the non-cooperation movement of the twenties and was now again in the thick of the Civil Disobedience movement. I had just come out of a college run by foreign missionaries. With my Westernised habits I doubted whether I could adjust my way of life and my values to those expected of Satyagrahi. But

[124] *Young India*, 10 April 1930.

> Satyawati's burning zeal was infectious. I was drawn to her and could not stay away from the great fight.[125]

Students in particular, especially boys and girls of the Hindu College and the Indraprastha Girls' School, readily came forward to extend their support to Satyawati. Housewives, who had never before taken part in political activities, came out in the open at Satyawati's call. Memo Bai, a widow, also joined the movement. Gradually, she gained in confidence and became a constant companion of Satyawati. Soon Satyawati's name became a household word and women from orthodox families also jumped into the fray.[126] She organized many meetings in Delhi and among the prominent women who joined the movement at Satyawati's call were Saraswati Gadodia, Parvati Didmania, Damyanti Sahni, Chand Bibi, Chand Kohli and Aruna Asaf Ali.

During the Civil Disobedience movement leading Congressmen encouraged their wives, daughters and even mothers to involve themselves in the national movement. Swarup Rani, wife of Motilal Nehru, Vijaylakshmi Pandit, Kamla Nehru and her mother Rajpati Kaul, Lado Rani Zutshi and Manmohini Sehgal belonged to the families of prominent leaders.[127] In Delhi also, women from the families of well known Congressmen such as Professor Indra, Deshbandhu Gupta, K.D. Kohli, J.N. Sahni, Dr Yudhvir Singh, Jugal Kishore Khanna, Gopinath Aman, Ganda Mal Sharma, Nand Lal Mehta, Thakur Hukum Singh, Phool Chand Jain and Asaf Ali joined the national movement. Aruna Asaf Ali writes: "Women's participation

[125]Aruna Asaf Ali, op. cit., 1991, pp. 104-05.

[126]Upto 1930, women were assigned those tasks which they could do at home, such as practising *swadeshi* and spinning. Now, they were demanding a more active role. See Neera Ahuja, "Gandhi's Ideas on Women's Development: A Critical Analysis", unpublished Ph.D. thesis, University of Delhi, 1996, pp. 61-63, MSS Central Reference Library, University of Delhi.

[127]Aruna Asaf Ali, DPCC (File), 1985, DSA (Souvenir Record).

with men in India's mass movement is perhaps without a parallel in the world. I am convinced that had we women kept away from this exciting and crucial movement against imperialist rule, we would have remained backward".[128]

On 26 January 1930, at the time when Independence Day was being celebrated under the auspices of the Nav Jawan Bharat Sabha of Delhi, Satyawati, the Vice-President of the Sabha, her mother Ved Kumari, and Parbati Devi went from door to door with the purpose of mobilizing women. During February-March 1930, around sixty women's meetings were held in different wards of the city.[129] A special feature of these meetings was that they were organized by women and attended by women. Aruna Asaf Ali informs that during the launching of the Civil Disobedience movement, Chandni Chowk and the innumerable lanes and by-lanes around it "began to resound with patriotic songs and slogans raised by us during the *prabhat pheris* (early morning processions). As the day advanced, there would be picketing of shops selling foreign cloth and liquor, and street-corner meetings in defiance of prohibitory orders". She further says:

> Delhi being land-locked, Satyawati and some of us decided to break the salt law by assembling in a marshy vacant plot in Shahadara, a suburb where the sub-soil water had a high salt content. About 50 of us made illegal and muddy salt, of which we made packets for distribution rather like *prasad* (consecrated offering). This went on for 10 days, after which the police swung into action. The Satyagrahis were dispersed with *lathi* blows and tear-gas shells, and several were arrested. But each act of repression steeled us. When a fellow volunteer was arrested, we felt

[128]Oral Transcripts : Phool Chand Jain, Brij Kishan Chandiwala and Memo Bai, NMML, New Delhi.

[129]Aruna Asaf Ali, DPCC (File), 1985, DSA (Souvenir Record).

> thrilled and awaited our turn with eager anticipation.[130]

On 11 April 1930, a meeting of women was held in the Rang Mahal where it was resolved to picket shops selling foreign cloth. As many as seventy women belonging to respectable families offered their services as volunteers and took part in a procession to Chandni Chowk under the command of Satyawati. These women took their places outside the shops selling foreign cloth to the utter surprise of the shopkeepers. The enthusiasm shown by women volunteers popularized the movement so much that the next day the number of women volunteers swelled to two hundred. They marched through the city, picketing the centres of foreign cloth market. They could be seen on their posts of duty from 8 A.M. to 8 P.M. in the scorching heat. Picketing had become so popular that thousands of people would come daily to boost the spirits of the picketers.

On 13 April 1930, a meeting of women volunteers was held, where the following office-bearers were elected: Satyawati, Commander; Mrs. Vedi, President; Mrs Sahni and Mrs Rajpati Kaul, Vice-Presidents; Mrs Gadodia, Treasurer; and Mrs Kohli, Secretary.[131] The following women were appointed as Captains: Parbati Devi; Memo Bai; Jai Rani; Kanti Devi; Ved Kumari; Mrs Sahni; and Mrs Kohli.

After picketing the shops selling foreign cloth, the women now directed their attention to the picketing of liquor shops. A meeting presided over by Satyawati was held on 4 May 1930 during which it was decided to start the picketing of liquor shops from 5 May. The meeting was surrounded by a strong police contingent of about 200, carrying *lathis*. This was the first meeting which was

[130]Aruna Asaf Ali, op. cit., 1991, p.105.

[131]AICC File No. G-1/1931, NMML, New Delhi. Also see *The Hindustan Times*, 11 April 1930.

conducted under the strict surveillance of the police.[132] The women, however, remained undaunted and exhibited exemplary courage.

The 6th of May 1930 was a day of great importance for the women's movement in Delhi. A peaceful procession of no less than a lakh of people including five thousand women paraded the streets as a mark of protest against the arrest of Mahatma Gandhi. From Kashmiri Gate, a batch of two hundred women, young and old, led by Satyawati, went to the District Courts and demanded the immediate closure of the courts. After some time the police resorted to severe *lathi* charge inside Kashmiri Gate, which was followed by another *lathi* charge on the ladies present outside the courts. Mrs Sahni, Kaushalya Devi, Rajpati Kaul and Satyawati received injuries. Mary Campell, a temperance worker in India, described her amazed reaction in the *Manchester Guardian* as she watched picketing day after day: "The hefty policemen arrived with police vans and warned the women to go away. I thought that these delicate, sheltered women would give in now; they would never endure being touched by a policeman. But they did, and as fast as one relay was arrested another took its place. Altogether about sixteen hundred".[133]

Nowhere in India was Section 144 so openly violated as by the women of Delhi. Though as a result of frequent firing and *lathi* charge by the police the movement received a big setback, yet Satyawati continued working relentlessly for the noble cause. On 13 May 1930, she led a

[132]Ibid. Also see AICC File No. G-94/Pt.-1, 1930, NMML, Congress Bulletin, 3-6-1930. It was reported that most of the shopkeepers in Chandni Chowk were willing to close down their shops and lock their foreign cloth under the seal of the Congress.

[133]Communique issued by District Congress Committee, Delhi, AICC File No.18-21, of 1931, NMML. See also Home Pol. File No. 256/11/1930 & KW, Civil Disobedience movement in Delhi, for a copy of the Report of the Bar Association Sub-Committee, appointed to inquire into the incidents of 6 May 1930, which blamed the police for unprovoked firing on ladies' procession.

small procession of thirty women which paraded the city in total defiance of Section 144. The next day a mass meeting was organized in the Azad Park by the women. Four hundred policemen, *sawars*, riflemen and others helped by a dozen officers surrounded the meeting but the women remained unruffled and the proceedings were held with Satyawati in the Chair. When she was addressing the gathering of women, Senior Suptd., C.I.D., asked her: "Who is responsible for the meeting"? "I am responsible", Satyawati promptly replied. The women remained firm in their resolve and the police had to retreat. This open defiance of law by women under the leadership of Satyawati finally led to her arrest.

At her trial in Delhi, Satyawati remarked: "We have abandoned our homes and children to redeem our motherland from foreign bondage, and neither the threat of the dungeons nor of bullets and the merciless beatings can deter us from the duty which we owe to ourselves and the coming generation. I and thousands of my sisters are ready to suffer, but we must win India's freedom".[134] On 24 May 1930, Delhi witnessed a huge procession to bid farewell to Satyawati to the Kotwali. At the Clock Tower, thousands of people sang patriotic songs. She was sentenced to six months' simple imprisonment under Section 148. In a parting message she said: "So long there was even a single child she would not let the government rest, nor would she rest herself".[135] The written statement made by Satyawati after her arrest in the Court of Additional DM, Delhi, speaks volumes for her indomitable courage and firm resolve to secure freedom for her motherland:

> I am required to furnish security against seditious speeches. This is the telling indictment of the foreign domination which has compelled the traditionally meek and secluded womanhood of India to cast aside the habits and customs of ages.

[134] A.F. Brockway, *Indian Crisis* (London), p. 260.

[135] *Amrita Bazar Patrika*, 27 May 1930.

> And to join the ranks of those who are fighting for the birthright of India's toiling millions. I may be tried and cast aside into a nameless prison today but the foreign domination had already been tried at the bar of public opinion and the verdict has gone forth. In India, it is the first time since the days of Rani Laxmi Bai, our great woman warrior ancestor, that we have abandoned our home and children to redeem our motherland from foreign bondage and neither the threat of dangers nor of bullets and merciless beatings can deter us from the duty which we owe to ourselves and the coming generation. I and thousands of my sisters are ready to suffer but we must win India's freedom.[136]

Her arrest inspired new life in Delhi, especially among the women, who made the Delhi Jail their place of daily pilgrimage as long as their leader was there. Hundreds of women, young and old, rich and poor, came out in the open and expressed their willingness to follow the example of Satyawati.[137]

On 26 November 1930, Satyawati was released after serving a term of six months and was given a unique reception in the city. Her mother, Ved Kumari, and thirteen other ladies were also released in the same week and rejoined the movement.[138] In 1932, Satyawati became immensely popular in the political circles of Delhi through various activities like enrolling lady volunteers, distributing posters, and organizing the Swadeshi league. She continued

[136]*Congress Bulletin*, 28 May 1930, in *All India Congress Committee Reports* (1930)

[137]AICC, File No. G-1/1931, NMML. See also Brij Kishan Chandiwala Private Papers, NMML. See Campell in H.Z.E. Zakaria, *Renascent India from Ram Mohan Roy to Mohan Das Gandhi* (London, 1930).

[138]Brij Kishan Chandiwala, 75th Birth Anniversary article on Satyawati, Private Papers of Chandiwala, MSS Section, NMML, New Delhi.

helping the Congress secretly and assumed Congress leadership in Delhi. She had also been helping the revolutionaries financially and arranged for the publication of a leaflect titled "The Memorial Day of the Brave Sardar Bhagat Singh". She was again sent to prison on 21-4-1932 for leading a procession on the Jallianwala Bagh Day and released in September 1933. She resumed her work through her association with the Achut Sevak Sangh and Dalit Sudhar Sabha, Delhi. She was also actively associated with Navjawan Bharat Sabha, Jatindra Das Union, Gandhi Ashram, Riyasi Praja Mandal, Students Harijan League and Bharat Mitra Mandal.[139] Besides, she was also involved in the organization of two political bodies—The Matri Mandal and Mahila Hindustani Seva Dal. She was again convicted on 26-1-1934 for being a member of an illegal assembly. She was released on 10 February 1934. In the same year, she became an important member of the Congress Socialist Party, Delhi, and was elected Propaganda Secretary of the District Social League, Delhi; President, Delhi Congress Committee; and presided over the Provincial Congress of the Socialist Party.[140] Satyawati was the Chairman of the Reception Committee when the Congress Socialist Party held its annual conference at Meerut, near Delhi, in 1936. Kamaladevi Chattopadhyay, who presided, was greatly impressed by her. She remarked: "The thing I remembered the most about the session is Satyawati".[141]

However, her frequent arrests and the hard life that she led both within the jail and outside, took their toll and she fell victim to tuberculosis. She left for her heavenly abode on

[139]History Sheet of Satyawati, op.cit. A CID report states: "Satyawati of Delhi is equally interested in the activities of revolutionaries and she has promised to help such young men. She wishes to publish a series of leaflets against the capitalists". Delhi Police CID (Special Branch), File No. 59/1934-39, III Inst. NMML.

[140]A CID source AZIZ, dated 11-7-34, states that nearly all women interested in the Congress are in the Socialist group, File No.11/1934, Delhi Police CID.

[141]Oral History Transcript, NMML, New Delhi.

21-10-1945. Paying tributes to the departed soul, Jawaharlal Nehru said during a speech in Delhi on 3-11-1945: "With feeling I refer to the death of Shrimati Satyawati. Her image is before my eyes. I had despaired of her life, when I saw her in the hospital. I want the people of Delhi to erect a befitting memorial in her honour. I am not in favour of a memorial of stone. I am in favour of earmarking a good amount out of the purse presented to me for Shrimati Satyawati's memorial".[142]

The important role played by Satyawati for the emancipation of the country and in mobilizing women, students, workers and peasants of Delhi shall always remain fresh in the minds of the Indian people. Her firm commitment and dedication become evident from the following statement made by her barely nine months before her demise: "Brothers and comrades; you should take a vow that you will make every possible sacrifice for the emancipation of our poor country—that no oppression or tyranny may severe us from our path; and that we may continue our struggle till our country is completely free".[143] Among the nationalist women of Delhi, Satyawati occupies a unique position because she was the one who provided dynamic leadership to women and infused in them the patriotic spirit. In one of the Congress bulletins it has been reported: "In recent years Delhi has not produced a greater leader and organizer of women, she was inspiration personified and all the praise Mahatma Gandhi lavished on Delhi in the matter of boycott of foreign cloth was entirely due to her .... Young in years, she had an inexhaustible fund of enthusiasm and energy and even capable men fighters for India's freedom will find in her example a fit object of envy".[144]

[142]Cited in Aruna Asaf Ali, op. cit., 1991, p.106.

[143]File No.10/2-44 SB, dt. 14 Janaury 1945, National Archives of India.

[144]Congress Bulletin, 24 May 1930, All India Congress Committee Reports (1930).

Memo Bai's Contribution: Memo Bai, an eminent Gandhian freedom fighter, whose name figured quite often in the columns of *The Hindustan Times* of 1930s, got herself enrolled as a Congress worker in 1930.[145] Repeated references to her arrest during the Civil Disobedience days when picketing of foreign cloth was in full swing, point to her active involvement in the national movement. She was often referred to as Captain of lady volunteers.[146]

Memo Bai was born in an affluent family of Delhi and was married at an early age of ten. Barely a few years after her marriage her husband died and she came back to her parents' home, where she spent the rest of her life. All her family members joined the Congress in 1919. She was influenced a great deal by Satyawati's lecture in her colony (*katra*). She got around one hundred pledges for *swadeshi* filled up. She was also associated with the Hindustani Seva Dal. Memo Bai actively participated in the Civil Disobedience movements of 1930 and 1932-34, during the course of which she was imprisoned several times. She was in-charge of Delhi Cloth Market and conducted the picketing activities there. Some other women of Delhi who worked in cooperation with her were Gori Bai, Lacho Bai, Mrs. Hardayan Singh and Chameli Devi from Karol Bagh and Dr. Sharda. She also mentioned names of some shops of Delhi where picketing was done: Pandit Brothers, Mohan Brothers, Parmeshwari Das and Gujju Mal Nikku Mal.[147] In Delhi, there were some pockets from which a large number of women participated during the Civil Disobedience movement. Memo Bai informs that the main pockets were : Katra Neel, Bazar Sita Ram, Subzi Mandi and Karol Bagh.[148] She also testifies to the participation of the students and teachers of Indrapratha School in the Civil Disobedience movements. Two

[145]*The Hindustan Times*, 13 September 1930.

[146]*The Hindustan Times*, 15 and 16 October 1930.

[147]Interview recorded by Dr Hari Dev Sharma in Oral History Section, NMML, on 30-1-1970.

[148]Ibid.

permanent students of the School, Chameli and Shakuntala, who were the sisters of Raghunandan Saran, played an active part in the movement after the arrest of Gandhi in 1933. In Lahore Jail, Memo Bai along with Satyawati and other women unfurled the national flag and sang patriotic songs. Memo Bai informs that around one hundred women in the entire Delhi were jailed in 1930 during the course of liquor and foreign cloth picketing.[149] Some of the Muslim women who were active in the movement were Mrs Kidwai, Sardari Bano and Mrs Anes Kidwai.

Subhadra Joshi's Contribution: Another woman of Delhi in the Gandhian mould was Subhadra Joshi.[150] Born in 1919 in an affluent family, she spent her earlier days in Punjab. At the time of her birth, her father was Inspector General of Police. She was greatly inspired by her father who took an active part in the movement of foreign goods. As the Civil Disobedience movement gained in momentum, he left his job and went to Sialkot in Punjab. Because of his active association with the Civil Disobedience movement, he was arrested and sent to jail for some time. After his release, he tried his hand in business but could not succeed. He again joined the police as Superintendent in Jaipur.

After a few years of initial schooling, both Subhadra Joshi and her elder sister Kaushalya were sent to Lahore for studies. It was in Lahore that Subhadra and her sister got involved in politics. Her sister was a student of Class IX of Lady Mcladen's School when she started taking part in processions and demonstrations of the Congress. When the Principal of the school came to know about her sister's activities, she was called and questioned. Interestingly, this news about the Principal questioning a young girl was

[149]Ibid., p. 16.

[150]The information provided here about Subhadra Joshi is based on interview conducted by Ruchi Seth. See idem, "Women's Response to the Freedom Movement: A Case Study of Delhi", unpublished dissertation, Master of Philosophy, University of Delhi, 1991.

reported in local newspapers and created quite a stir. After a few days, the girls of Class VI, of which Subhadra was one of the students, gheraoed their English teacher and raised the slogan: *Todi Bacha Hai Hai.* That day Subhadra Joshi became a victim of the Principal's wrath and was punished. This news also found coverage in the press with an exaggerated version of the ill-treatment of girls by the Principal. To register their resentment, the Congress Sevika Dal resorted to picketing outside the school's premises. The main picketers were Lado Rani Zutshi and her sister Manmohini Sehgal. To express their solidarity with the Congress Sevika Dal, the girls of the school too expressed their resentment by wearing saffron coloured sarees and slippers.

This incident was a provocation enough which finally led to the expulsion of Subhadra and her sister along with some other girls from the school. Her sister took admission in some other school in Lahore because she had to appear in her matriculation examination. Subhadra Joshi was sent to the Jullunder National School. Being a national school, revolutionaries like Sushila Mohan, Durga Devi, and so on, used to visit this. Thus the school's atmosphere was conducive to nationalist activities. In the school there was an abundance of revolutionary literature, some of which Subhadra Joshi took home for her brothers. Fearing that her active association with the national movement might lead to her arrest, her father brought her back from Jullunder and got her admitted in the Maharaja Girls School in Jaipur from where she passed her matriculation. After finishing her studies in Jaipur, her father sent her to Lahore where she completed her studies up to the post- graduate level at Forman Christian College. In Lahore, she and her sister stayed in a rented room. In the late 1930s, she actively participated in the Congress meetings, and was an ardent supporter of *khadi* and delivered fiery speeches. She was also associated with the students' organization which was affiliated to the Communist movement. Along with her secret involvement with the students' organization, she continued to participate in Congress meetings. At Lahore, she, along with her friend, bought a photostating machine from Khadi Bhandar and learnt cyclostyling. They xeroxed the underground revolutionary papers and distributed them among various sections of society.

After completing her M.A. in 1942, she became a lecturer in Queen Mary's College, Lahore. Though most students in the College came from aristocratic backgrounds (belonging to princely families), Subhadra Joshi did inspire them and had a lot of influence on them. Drawing inspiration from her talks, the students expressed their desire to do *hartal* in the college. However, since the Principal came to know about it, the idea had to be abandoned. When her activities in Lahore increased manifold, the CID officials told her sister that if she did not mend her ways, she would be arrested. She then came over to Delhi and joined a private school as a teacher.

In Delhi (1942-47), she actively participated in the freedom movement as well as in the trade union activities. She worked with a group of people whom she came to know through a teacher in the school. They were Brahm Prakash, B.D. Joshi and Raj Singh Rana. They opened Harijan schools in various localities for adult education with the idea of making the freedom movement popular. They also brought out an underground newspaper "Hamara Sangram" which was a secret publication (it was started by Brahm Prakash). Subhadra Joshi used to do the translation work from Hindi to English. She had to leave this private school as her activities became known and joined another missionary school. She was put in jail while participating in the flag hoisting ceremony. She was also an active worker of the Trade Union movement and was associated with the Textile Union of Delhi Cloth Mill, which was formed by B.D. Joshi whom she later married (in 1948). She worked during the riots of 1947 in Delhi when she stayed in a mess together with Brahm Prakash, Raj Singh Rana, B.D. Joshi and T. K. Nayar. At that time, some other women who were actively associated with the freedom movement in Delhi were: Choti Devi (Birla Mills worker), Munni Devi and Mrs. Anand.

Aruna Asaf Ali's Contribution: Another woman from Delhi who played a significant role in the Civil Disobedience movement was Aruna Asaf Ali. Aruna hailed from a Brahmo Samaj family of Bengal. After marriage, her parents, Mr. and Mrs. Gangulee, did not remain for long in Bengal. They spent most of their years at Kalka where Mr. Gangulee was in-charge of the Kalka railway refreshment room. Aruna and her younger sister Purnima received their early education at the convent of Sacred Heart at Lahore. However, Aruna was soon removed from the Catholic atmosphere when her parents came to know about her impractical ideas (of renouncing the world and becoming a nun) and sent her to a Protestant school at Nainital where Mr. Gangulee by that time had opened a hotel. She thus finished her education at Nainital. Her English education had filled her mind with Western ideas and after meeting Asaf Ali at her sister's place in Allahabad and falling in love with him—despite their big age difference (Asaf Ali was 41 and Aruna 18) and difference in religion (Asaf Ali was a Muslim and Aruna, a Hindu)—she married him. Her parents, however, did not approve of the marriage. During the wedding ceremony, only two relatives of Aruna and a few common friends were present. This inter-provincial and inter-communal marriage proved to be a great success. In Aruna's own words: "No man could be more generous and liberal than Asaf Ali".[151] After their marriage they shifted to Delhi.

It was with the launching of the Salt Satyagraha that Aruna Asaf Ali started taking a keen interest in politics. The arrest of her husband Asaf Ali proved to be a big motivating factor in her active involvement with politics. She started her political career by delivering a fiery speech about the revolt of 1857. She went about addressing

[151]*Fragments from the Past – Selected Writings and Speeches of Aruna Asaf Ali* (New Delhi, 1989), Introduction, p. 3.

meetings, preparing salt and also led processions. The Chief Commissioner of Delhi viewed with serious concern her political activities. This led to her prosecution, not on the charges of sedition, "but for being a vagrant having no ostensible means of livelihood".[152]

> She was asked to furnish security for good behaviour, which she refused. Aruna was arrested and was sentenced to one year's imprisonment. A few months later most of the political prisoners were released under the Gandhi-Irwin Truce. The government, however, did not think advisable to release Aruna who was in Lahore jail. Her women co-prisoners refused to leave on the ground that unless Aruna was released they would not move. Gandhiji had to intervene and the prisoners left Aruna in jail. Later, in response to a strong public agitation, Aruna was released after a few days.[153]

Aruna was arrested again in 1932 and was asked to pay a fine of Rs.200. In those days, as has already been pointed out, political prisoners were treated very badly. As a mark of protest against this, Aruna went on a hunger strike. Though the authorities did concede to the demand of the political prisoners, yet Aruna was made to suffer heavily. She was later transferred to Ambala jail and kept there in solitary confinement.[154] After the term of her imprisonment was over, she returned to Delhi and for the next ten years, she completely withdrew from politics.

When Aruna, along with Satyawati, was arrested for breaking the Salt Law in a marshy vacant land in Shahadra, Delhi, she found the life in jail a very rewarding experience. This was because she came from a very well-to-do family. She writes:

[152]Cited in Manmohan Kaur, op. cit., p. 219. Also see *The Tribune*, 18 February 1946.

[153]Manmohan Kaur, op. cit., p. 219.

[154]*The Tribune*, 18 February 1946.

> In prison we led a self-disciplined life, plying the *charkha*, singing patriotic songs in defiance of the jail rules, conducting literacy classes for non-literate inmates of the jail, and improving our own understanding of politics and economics by reading books (many of them smuggled in, like V.D. Savarkar's). Distinctions of community, caste and sub-caste crumbled in the shared community life of the prison house. No more for us the rituals associated in orthodox homes with cooking and eating. All of us shared the daily chores of scrubbing the floor, cleaning and peeling vegetables, washing utensils and minding the *chulah* (fireplace). But the cooking was reserved for the experts among us. We fought for and got rations issued instead of cooked food. Pooling our rations helped us to vary the fare of *roti* (bread), *dal* (pulses) and vegetables. Visitors from our families, who were allowed once a fortnight, brought welcome additions to our larder in the form of fruits, spicy papad and pickles. Jail, which was intended by the alien rulers to isolate and to demoralise us, turned out to be a university of life where we learnt to rise above our former self-centred existence.[155]

IV
The Non-Gandhian Women

Though the majority of the women who took part in the national movement were inspired by Gandhi, yet there were a few to whom Gandhi's ideology of non-violence was not acceptable. The revolutionary organizations came into being in 1930s and were particularly active in Bengal, with "Dacca, Comilla and Chittagong being the storm centres. Young college girls joined these secret societies. Kalpana

[155]Aruna Asaf Ali, op. cit., 1991, p. 105.

Joshi nee Dutt and Preeti Waddadar were associated with the Chittagong Armoury raid. Preeti led a raid on the Pahartali Railway Officers' Club, as a result of which one European lady was shot. Preeti took potassium cyanide and killed herself. Kalpana, often dressed in male attire, was very active in this area. She was arrested in connection with the Chittagong armoury supplementary trials and was sentenced to transportation for life".[156]

The *modus operandi* of the non-Gandhian women was very much different from that of Gandhian women. Women in the revolutionary mould were full of hatred for the British. They were highly emotional and impulsive and by virtue of their constant association with revolutionaries and their literature, they came to believe that individual acts of heroism—and not building up of a mass movement—were more potent instruments for fighting the British imperialism.

Durgadevi Vohra's Contribution

Among the non-Gandhian women from Delhi, the name of Durgadevi Vohra, wife of Bhagwati Charan Vohra, stands out prominently. She was part of the Young India movement of the 1930s. Her husband was a close associate of Bhagat Singh, Rajguru and Sukhdev. Durgadevi too worked in association with them and played a very important part in rescuing Bhagat Singh by taking him away from Lahore to Calcutta after Saunder's assassination.

Durgadevi was born in 1907 in a religious Gujarati family settled in Ahmedabad. Her mother died when she was barely ten months old. She was brought up by her widowed paternal aunt (*bua*). Since she was married at a tender age of eleven, she acquired most of her education after marriage. In fact, she appeared in her matriculation examination after her release from prison. Her father-in-law was conferred with the title of Rai Saheb by the British because of which she and her husband were often suspected by their associates.

[156]Aparna Basu, "The Role of Women", op. cit., 1976, p. 31.

Durgadevi was a teacher in the Lahore Girls School and she had started taking part in revolutionary activities at a time when her son was barely three and needed her maximum attention. After her husband's death in a bomb blast in 1929, she got even more actively involved in revolutionary activities. She worked in the defence committee for Bhagat Singh's case. When the police issued warrants against her name after the raiding of the bomb factory in a house at Lahore, she came to Delhi in a *burqa*. In Delhi, she worked in association with revolutionaries like Dhanvantri,[157] Professor N. K. Nigam,[158] Chandrashekhar Azad[159] and Vaishampayan.[160] In Bombay, she along with Sukhdev[161] and Prithvi Singh[162] shot at two Englishmen at Hamilton Road. She also helped the

[157]Born in 1902, resident of Delhi, son of Shri Durga Dutt; participated in the freedom struggle; one of the accused in Delhi Conspiracy Case; sentenced to seven years R.1. in 1933 in Delhi and later transferred to Port Blair Jail (Andaman).

[158]Born in 1906, lecturer with an M.A. degree, who took an active part in the revolutionary movement (1929-35) and the Quit India movement (1942).

[159]Associated with the secret organization of North India, the Hindustan Republican Association, Chandrashekhar Azad was involved in Kakori Conspiracy Case (1925) in September 1928. He became the top leader of Hindustan Socialist Republican Army and the Commander of the Military Division. He was associated with the attempt to blow up the Viceroy's train, the Assembly bomb incident, the Delhi Conspiracy Case, the shooting of Saunders at Lahore and the Second Lahore Conspiracy.

[160]A close associate of Bhagwati Charan Vohra, Vaishampayan actively participated in the freedom movement.

[161]Born at Lyallpur in Punjab, Sukhdev was a close associate of Chandrashekhar Azad and Bhagat Singh. He took a leading part in the reorganization of the revolutionary party into Hindustan Socialist Republication Army in September 1928 and looked after its activities in Punjab and U.P. He planned the shooting of Saunders in December 1928 and the Bomb Outrage in the Central Legislative Assembly in April 1929. He was tried as a principal accused in the Lahore Conspiracy Case and received death punishment along with Bhagat Singh and Rajguru.

[162]Prithvi Singh had participated in the freedom struggle and took an active part in the Civil Disobedience movement in Delhi.

revolutionaries through delivery of bombs, money and pistols which she carried from one place to another.

In 1932 she was imprisoned for nine months and for three years she was kept confined within the boundaries of Lahore. In 1938 she was elected the President of Delhi Provincial Congress Committee[163] and in 1940 she started the Lucknow Montessori School. Durgadevi's revolutionary ideas were greatly influenced by her leftist husband and Russian literature including the writings of Gorky and Tolstoy.

Roopvati Jain's Contribution

In Delhi, Roopvati Jain at the age of seventeen was in-charge of a bomb factory during the 1930 movement under Chandershekhar Azad. "This factory at Qutab Road, run in the name of 'Himalayan Toilets' produced picric acid, nitro glycerine, gun-cotton and other ingredients for bombs. Mrs. Jain was an expert in washing picric acid which left yellow, easily detectable stains on the skin".[164]

Sushila Devi's Contribution

"Sushila Devi, another revolutionary worker, cut her finger and placed mark of blood as *tilak* on the foreheads of the revolutionaries, Bhagat Singh and Batukeshwar Dutt on 9 April 1929. Because of her association with Bhagat Singh to whom she sent letters, *rakhi* and food, she was arrested and imprisoned. She was declared an absconder in the Delhi and Lahore Conspiracy cases and served a number of jail terms".[165]

Prakashvati Pal's Contribution

Another revolutionary woman who was actively associated with the national movement was Prakashvati Pal, wife of the noted Hindi writer and freedom fighter, Yaspal. Her memoirs were published in the June 1988 issue of the

[163]*The Hindustan Times*, 15 August 1972.
[164]Aparna Basu, op. cit., 1976, p. 33.
[165]Ibid.

Ganga magazine. The account given below in based on her memoirs.[166]

Born and brought up in Lahore, she left her home at a very early age. From childhood, she had strong inclination towards revolutionary activities. In school, her teacher Premvati who was associated with Yashpal, Bhagwati Charan Vohra and Durgadevi Vohra encouraged her and other girls to do their best for the revolutionaries. In her memoirs,[167] Prakashvati also refers to her friend Swadesh Kumari, daughter of Lala Pindidas; Rukmini, daughter of Dr. Gopal Chand Bhargava, a Congress leader of Punjab; and Vimla who were working for the revolutionaries. Money was needed in large amount to fight the court cases by revolutionaries. At one place, Prakashvati confesses that many times she stole gold and money from her own house to donate for the cause of the revolutionaries. She even gave away her gold chain and pendant. As a child, she actively participated in the movement for boycott of foreign goods.

Her contacts with Yashpal and other revolutionaries coupled with her strong inclination to work actively in the freedom movement made her realize that she could work better if she was not confined to her house. She worked as a volunteer in the Lahore Congress in 1929. In April 1930, the day of her engagement, she left her house. That day her brother had read the letter addressed to her by some revolutionary. In the letter, the writer had inquired about the date of her joining the party. After hearing it, her father lost temper and shouted at her in front of all the guests. He told her to leave the house and go wherever she wanted. Being very independent minded she could not take the insult and immediately took the decision to leave the house. At a time when women were mainly confined to the four walls of their homes—and even if they stepped out, it was with the consent of the male members of the

[166]See June 1988 issue of *Ganga* magazine. The details given here are based on Ruchi Seth, op. cit.

[167]Ibid.

family—Prakashvati's decision bears ample testimony to her bold and courageous attitude. After 1930, there was no going back for her and she kept working for the revolutionary party in the true spirit of patriotism. She worked just as hard as the men in the party did. She travelled along with the revolutionaries to Delhi, Kanpur, Lucknow and Dehradun. While going through her memoirs one can hardly get the feeling that it is a young girl that we are reading about. It was indeed a remarkable decision by a young girl to leave her home and stay with revolutionaries. In the context of gender relations, it speaks volumes for her independent and liberal outlook.

Prakashvati always used to keep a pistol with her.[168] She, along with Vatsyayan[169] and Yashpal, made bomb *masala* at a home in Delhi. Being a true revolutionary, she was often required to shift to other places. At Dehradun, she was known by the name of Shakuntala and worked there in a school as a teacher. It is highly creditable that despite her active involvement with revolutionary activities, she carried on with her studies. She passed the *Prabhakar* examination from Punjab University while she was in Karachi in 1933. The following year she appeared in the High School examination from Banaras and then did a two-year diploma course from Dental College, Karachi. She happened to be the only woman student in the college.

In her memoirs,[170] she has been frank and forthright enough to describe her relationship with Yashpal which later culminated in marriage. She candidly admits that it was love at first sight. Their marriage took place in jail—a very unconventional thing indeed! She also informs that her marriage in jail was the first and the last one. After her marriage, a law was passed according to which marriages in jail were forbidden. When seen in the context of the social structure in India of 1930s, Prakashvati

[168]Ibid.

[169]He was a close associate of Yashpal.

[170]See Ruchi Seth, op. cit.

stands apart as a dynamic and liberated woman with radical ideas. And she was not alone in her revolutionary activities. In her memoirs she time and again refers to her women associates such as Durgadevi Vohra, Rukmini, Sushila didi, and so on.

Prakashvati had also expressed her disagreement with the Gandhian ideology based on the principle of non-violence. Gandhi's criticism of the activities of the revolutionaries and his refusal to protest against the death sentence of Bhagat Singh generated an anti-Gandhi wave among the leftists and Prakashvati Pal was no exception. From her memoirs it becomes clear that the sacrifices made by the revolutionaries carried more weight than the Non-cooperation movement of Gandhi in the restoration of the country's independence.

It may thus be seen that the *modus operandi* of the revolutionary women was much different from that of the Gandhian women. Though the number of women nationalists who drew inspiration from Gandhi was much more than those associated with revolutionary activities, but at the same time due credit has also to be given to the revolutionary women who made noteworthy contributions to the cause of the country's independence.

Conclusion

By 1934, the Civil Disobedience movement that had started with the Salt Satyagraha came to an end. Indeed this movement was a turning point in the emergence of Indian women from their traditional seclusion. In the past the role of women was confined only to those from elite classes who were highly educated. But now women from all classes and categories came forward in large numbers in different parts of the country with utmost patriotic zeal and fervour. Women marched in processions; organized picketing of shops selling foreign cloth and liquor; addressed public meetings; and played a much more dominant role. What is more praiseworthy is that they stuck to their task desipte all sorts of atrocities perpetrated against them by the British authorities. The contribution of women was no less than that of men. In a resolution passed by the Indian National Congress on 26-1-1931, it was stated: "We record our homage and deep admiration for the womanhood of India who in the hour of peril for the motherland forsook the shelter of their homes and with unfailing courage and endurance stood shoulder to shoulder with their menfolk in the front line of India's National Army to share with them the sacrifices and triumphs of the struggle".[171]

A significant feature of the Civil Disobedience era was that in various provinces and districts of the country, women became the 'dictators' to run the Congress movement and the remarkable organizational skills shown by them was a big revelation. All this went a long way in bringing a radical transformation in the self-perception of many women. Besides, it also contributed a great deal to the women's improved status in Indian society. It gave them a new sense of power, self-confidence and a new self-view. To quote Jawaharlal Nehru:

> Most of us menfolk were in prison. And then a remarkable thing happened. Our women came to the front and took charge of the struggle. Women had always been there of course, but now there was an avalanche of them, which took not only the British Government but their own menfolk by surprise. Here were these women, women of the upper middle classes, leading sheltered lives in their homes—peasant women, working-class women, rich women—pouring out in their tens of thousands in defiance of government order and police *lathi*. It was not only that display of courage and daring, but what was even more surprising was the organisational power they showed.[172]

[171]Cited in Aloo J. Dastur and Usha H. Mehta, *Gandhi's Contribution to the Emancipation of Women* (Popular Prakashan, Bombay, 1991), p. 48.

[172]Jawaharlal Nehru, *The Discovery of India* (London, 1960), pp. 27-28.

CHAPTER V

WOMEN AND THE CONGRESS MOVEMENTS, 1935-47

I

The 1937 Elections

The passing of the Govt. of India Act of 1935 was a big occasion for the Indian women because it paved the way for them to be elected to the State Legislatures and also to become administrators. It also gave voting rights to women above twenty-one years of age "who qualified because they owned property or had attained a certain level of education".[1]

However, it was only after a long deliberation over a period of time that the act of 1935 was promulgated. In the first entry of his Indian Diary, Edwin Montagu recorded: "I received a letter from Jaipur in the vernacular and the request for an interview from the women of India".[2] This was in fact a reference to a letter signed by four members of the Senate of the Indian Women's University. A deputation of fourteen women led by Sarojini Naidu had demanded in December 1917 that as far as franchise was concerned women should be treated on a par with men. Women's Indian Association held a number of meetings in

[1]Geraldine Forbes, *The New Cambridge History of India*, IV. 2: *Women in Modern India* (Cambridge University Press, 1996), p. 191.

[2]Edwin Montagu, *An Indian Diary* (London, 1930), p. 5.

support of Franchise Committee (of which Lord Southborough was the President), demanding that women be granted the right to vote "on the same property qualifications as for men, or to at least women graduates".[3] Annie Besant, Sarojini Naidu, Hirabai Tata and Mithan Tata also supported this issue. At a special session of the Congress held in August 1918, Sarojini Naidu spoke on behalf of women's suffrage. During the course of her speech, she tried to impress upon the audience that there was an urgent need to extend the franchise to women that was "rational, scientifically and politically sound, compatible with tradition, and consistent with human rights".[4] She also tried to convince her audience that politics did not affect women's femininity adversely as was generally believed. To quote her:

> Never, never, for we realize that men and women have their separate goals, separate destinies and that just as man can never fulfill (sic) the responsibility of the destiny of a woman, a woman cannot fulfill (sic) the responsibility of man.... We ask for the vote, not that we might interfere with you in your official functions, your civic duties, your public place and power, but rather that we might lay the foundation of national character in the souls of the children that we hold upon our laps, and instill into them the ideals of national life.[5]

In 1918, the Indian National Congress also passed a unanimous resolution, supporting the voting rights of women.

During the course of the Franchise Committee's visit to Bombay, Indian women placed before it a petition signed by as many as 800 women. Similar requests were also made

[3]Aparna Basu, "The Role of Women in the Indian Freedom Struggle", in B.R. Nanda, ed, *Indian Women: From Purdah to Modernity* (Vikas, New Delhi, 1976), p. 34.

[4]Ibid.

[5]*Report of the Indian Franchise Committee* (1919), pp. 4-5.

by the Women Graduates, University of Bombay, the branches of the Indian Women's Association, the women's branch of the Home Rule League and other women's associations.[6]

The Southborough Committee, however, expressed the opinion that the prevalent social conditions of India were such that the extension of freedom to women was not considered appropriate.[7] However, the Govt. of India Act of 1919 provided that the provinces should decide the issue of franchise for women. Thus, one after another, the provincial legislators began enfranchising women on the same terms as men. The first province to take the initiative was Madras, which also had the "distinction of having the first Indian woman legislator, namely, Dr. S. Muthulakshmi Reddy, who was chosen Dy. Speaker of the Madras Legislative Council". Though a nominated member, she resigned her seat in protest against Gandhi's arrest in 1930. The first woman to have taken the bold step of risking election was Kamaladevi Chattopadhyay. She stood as an independent candidate from South Kanara in 1926. Even though Margaret Cousins was actively involved in her election campaign, yet she got defeated by a margin of 515 votes.[8] As far as election to the provincial legislatures was concerned, by 1926 women began to be treated on an equal footing with men in all the provinces. The Govt. of India Act of 1935 enabled six million Indian women to exercise their franchise, a remarkable improvement in the figure of 315,000 under the Act of 1919. It would, however, be significant to note that though the number of women voters increased considerably, yet only two and a half per cent of adult women had received the right to vote.

Above all, the Congress did not seem particularly inclined to support aspiring women politicians as

[6]"One who Knows" (Dr. S. Muthulakshmi Reddy), *Mrs Margaret Cousins and Her Work in India* (Madras, 1956), p. 63.

[7]A.B. Keith, *A Constitutional History of India, 1600-1935* (Allahabad, 1961), p. 359.

[8]*Report of the Indian Franchise Committee* (1932), Vol. I, p. 166.

candidates. After the passing of the Act of 1935, the Congress, which had earlier focussed entirely on its anti-imperialist fight, began emerging as a political party showing preference for propertied men. Sumit Sarkar makes the following observation: "Despite its national multi-class ideals, the Congress as a ruling party found it almost impossible to go on pleasing Hindus and Muslims, landlords and peasants, or businessmen and workers at the same time. A steady shift to the Right, occasionally veiled by 'Left' rhetoric increasingly characterized the functioning of the Congress ministries as well as of the party High Command between 1937 and 1939".[9]

Nehru and Gandhi too who were ardent votaries of the women's cause did not seem to favour the idea of women's involvement in politics and the "promises of civil disobedience campaign had been set aside in favour of realpolitik".[10] The Congress did, however, support the view that women should be considered for reserved seats. But Dr. Muthulakshmi Reddy did not favour the idea of separate seats for women.[11] At the same time the majority of women interested in politics preferred uncontested seats; the idea of political campaign was not palatable to them.

Radhabai Subbarayan, one of the rare cases where a woman came forward to fight for a general seat in Madras, was betrayed by the Congress. To start with, the Chairman of the Madras Provincial Congress Reception Committee decided to support her, but when a man expressed his desire to fight for the same seat, the Congress backed out from its earlier decision of supporting Subbarayan. When Subbarayan questioned C. Rajagopalachari about this, he replied that her refusal to sign the Congress pledge was not appreciated by the Congress, and hence the betrayal.

[9]Sumit Sarkar, *Modern India, 1885-1947* (Macmillan India, New Delhi, 1983), pp. 350-51.

[10]Geraldine Forbes, op. cit., p. 193.

[11]"Against Separate Electorates", Speech by Dr S. Muthulakshmi Reddy, DRP, File No. 11, cited in Forbes, op. cit., p. 193.

Rajagopalachari told her that the Congress could not make the seat available "merely because it was a woman candidate that was seeking to be elected.... I do not believe that (the) advanced type of women politicians want political favours because they are women".[12] This incident "demonstrates the insincerity of much of Congress sympathy with the aspirations of women, and proves that the Congress party is no better than others in its treatment of women candidates. Women are useful to head disobedience processions but scarcely good enough to sit with the Party in the Assembly".[13]

Women, however, had something to cheer about when the results of 1937 elections were declared. Eight women were elected from general constituencies and forty-two from the reserved constituencies. Six women became ministers when the provincial cabinets were formed. Vijaylakshmi Pandit became Minister for Local Self-Government and Public Health in UP; and later Anasuyabai Kale of Central Provinces, and Sippi Milani of Sind were appointed Dy. Speakers in Madhya Pradesh and Sind respectively. Hansa Mehta and Begum Shah Nawaz took office as Parliamentary Secretaries in Bombay and Punjab respectively. Three women—Mrs Subbarayan, Begum Shah Nawaz and Sarojini Naidu—attended the Round Table Conference during 1931-32. This victory greatly encouraged women's organizations and they recommended the nomination of women to commissions, boards and councils. They believed that women were better placed to understand the problems faced by women and children.[14]

But despite some success registered by women in the political field, election politics had remained male-dominated. Women had hopes that they would be rewarded for the support extended by them to the Congress both in the Non-cooperation movement of 1920-21 and the Civil Disobedience movement of 1930-32. This, however, did not happen.

[12]Ibid., p. 194.
[13]Ibid.
[14]*WIA Report, 1936-38*, p. 27.

II
Individual Satyagraha

The year 1939 saw the beginning of the Second World War in Europe. On 3 September 1939 England declared war on German Reich, "professedly in defence of democracy and the weak nations".[15] Ironically though Britain was against the idea of granting freedom to India which was her dependency. Lord Linlithgow, the then Governor-General of India, without consulting the leaders of the Congress and members of the Indian Legislative Assembly or the Provincial Governments, declared India to be at war the same day, that is, 3 September 1939.

Gandhi and Nehru, together with other like-minded leaders, strongly felt that India should not participate in the war. In fact, way back in 1936, the Indian National Congress had made it clear in its election manifesto about its "opposition to the participation of India in an independent war".[16] The Working Committee of the Indian National Congress which met in September 1939 had also made its stand absolutely clear. The Working Committee observed that the "declared wishes of the Indian people ... have been deliberately ignored by the British Government"; and while the Committee "unhesitatingly condemns the latest aggression of the Nazi Government in Germany against Poland... the issue of war and peace for India must be decided by the Indian people".[17]

However, India was ready to consider giving help to the British Government in the war period provided it made a firm commitment that independence would be granted to India. The British Government, on the other hand, was not prepared to concede to this. This was what provoked Gandhi to launch his Individual Satyagraha campaign and to

[15]Manmohan Kaur, *Women in India's Freedom Struggle* (Sterling, New Delhi, 1985), p. 197.

[16]Jawaharlal Nehru, *The Unity of India, Collected Writings – 1937-40* (London, 1941), p. 407.

[17]Idem, *Toward Freedom* (New York, 1941), p. 432.

openly pursue the anti-war propaganda. The Congress decided to "carry on non-violently and openly anti-war propaganda" and "to preach non-cooperation with the government in their war efforts".[18]

This campaign was opened by Vinoba Bhave on 17 October 1940, which was sanctioned by Gandhi in the beginning of October 1940. "Individual Satyagrahis, in the beginning people personally chosen by him, made public anti-war speeches in defiance of emergency orders. One by one Congress leaders declared themselves opposed to the government, were arrested and imprisoned. Altogether four hundred Congressmen and women were jailed in 1940. By June 1941, almost 20,000 had gone to jail but the movement declined after that".[19] The campaign continued till the end of the year when the government felt constrained to release the political prisoners in view of the disturbed political situation of the country.

Women in different parts of the country took part in the Individual Satyagraha campaign. In Orissa, the Provincial Satyagraha Committee nominated forty-eight people for taking part in this campaign in the first batch.[20] This list was then sent to Gandhi, who selected twenty-seven names for the campaign in Orissa. The campaign in Orissa was inaugurated by H.K. Mahatab on 1 December 1940. He delivered a fiery speech in a meeting near Balasore and was arrested.[21] Smt. Sarala Devi was the first woman who took part in the Individual Satyagraha in the first batch along with H.K. Mahatab.[22]

In Cuttack also Individual Satyagraha started with full vigour in different places. Gandhi gave permission to Smt.

[18]R.R. Diwakar, *Satyagraha in Action* (Signet Press, Calcutta), p. 96.

[19]G. Forbes, op. cit., pp. 203-04.

[20]Confidential D.O. No. 9114-C, Cuttack, 4 December 1940. File No. 18-12-1940, Home Pol. (N.A.I.).

[21]Ghanshyam Das, ed, *History of the Freedom Movement in Orissa* (Cuttack, 1957), Vol. IV, p. 63.

[22]Susil Ch. De, *Diary of Political Events in Orissa* (Cuttack, 1964), p. 34.

Priyambada Devi[23] to start Satyagraha at Cuttack. Malati Choudhary also sought permission from Gandhi to participate in the Satyagraha, but he declined – the reason being that at that time her daughter was only one year old.[24]

In the Ganjam district of Orissa, Satyagraha started at different places. On 4 December 1940, Smt. A Lakshmibai expressed desire to take part in the campaign at the Congress Committee office verandah and delivered an anti-war speech in a grand meeting held at Berhampur. The police, however, immediately took her into custody.[25]

In Rasalkonda (Bhanjanagar), Smt. Champa Devi carried out her Individual Satyagraha campaign right in front of the police.[26] Also, Smt. Taramani Acharya,[27] an extremist leader, took part in the Individual Satyagraha campaign at Anarkali Bazar in Lahore on 18 August 1941. She was kept in the prison for seven months at Lahore Jail.[28]

The women of Bihar also did not lag behind. The women who took an active part in the Individual Satyagraha campaign in Bihar were Priyambada Devi, Janki Devi and Jagatrani Devi. They were arrested in Gaya and sentenced to an imprisonment of four months in addition of a fine of Rs. 200 each.[29] However, some women who took part in the Individual Satyagraha in Santhal Parganas were not arrested.[30] An announcement was made that a public meeting would be held (in Dhumka in Santhal Parganas) in

[23]Priyambada Devi, wife of Bhagirathi Das, of Village Anandpur.

[24]See V. Rajendra Raju, *Role of Women in India's Freedom Struggle* (New Delhi, 1994), p. 77.

[25]*Nabeen*, 19 December 1940.

[26]*Dainik Asha*, 15 August 1990.

[27]Smt. Taramani Acharya is the wife of the late Pandit Kirtan Bihari Acharya of Baragadia district of Cuttack. She wrote a number of books in Oriya and Hindi.

[28]See V. Rajendra Raju, op. cit., p. 77.

[29]Niroj Sinha, "Women and Indian Nationalism: The Case of Bihar", in Leela Kasturi and Vina Mazumdar, ed, *Women in Indian Nationalism* (Vikas, New Delhi, 1994), p. 169.

[30]R.R. Diwakar, op. cit., p. 96.

February 1941 in which Mrs. Mahadevi Kejariwal—the wife of the President of Santhal Parganas Congress Committee—would take part in the Individual Satyagraha campaign. Mrs. Kejariwal met the Dy. Commissioner at his residence on 26 February in order to give him prior information about her plans. The written notice which she gave him contained the following message: "This is not a war of India, therefore it is a sin to give support to the British either through money or through individuals. We should oppose the armed battle through Satyagraha".[31] As per the plans, Mrs. Kejariwal did offer Satyagraha after giving the notice, but the Dy. Commissioner did not pass orders for her arrest.[32]

In the East Godavari District of Andhra Pradesh, "the only woman who took part in the campaign was Vedantam Kamala Devi".[33]

Other eminent Congress women who took part in Individual Satyagraha were: Vijaylakshmi Pandit, Sarojini Naidu and Sucheta Kripalani. Vijaylakshmi Pandit was jailed for four months.[34] Sarojini Naidu was arrested on 3 December 1940, but she fell ill and had to be released on 11 December 1940. Sucheta Kripalani who had been in-charge of the women's department of the A.I.C.C. since 1939, also courted arrest.

Among the women of Delhi, Satyawati, along with Ved Kumari, Hans Kaur and Siddheshwari Devi,[35] took part in the Individual Satyagraha. Satyawati was jailed for one year and released in 1941. Aruna Asaf Ali too, along with her

[31]Cited in Niroj Sinha, op. cit., p. 169.

[32]Shiva Pujan Sahay, *Bihar Ki Mahilayen* (Mahila Charkha Samiti, Patna, 1962), p. 319.

[33]Sreeranjani Subba Rao, "Women and Indian Nationalism: A Case Study of Prominent Freedom fighters of the East Godavari District of Andhra Pradesh", in Leela Kasturi and Vina Mazumdar, op. cit., p. 121.

[34]Padmini Sengupta, *Pioneer Women of India*, p. 156.

[35]C.K. Nair, "Behan Satyawati—As I knew Her", in Jayant Vachaspati, ed, *Dilli-ki-Joan of Arc, Behan Satyawati* (New Delhi, 1977), pp. 2-3.

husband, was chosen by Gandhi to participate in Individual Satyagraha. To quote Aruna: "On the Viceroy rejecting the Congress offer, renewed in July 1940, to support the war effort if a provisional national government was formed with the promise of independence at the end of the hostilities, the Congress launched a Satyagraha campaign. But it was confined to token civil disobedience... in order not to embarrass the British during 'the perils and dangers of war'. Imprisonment was courted by individuals chosen by Gandhiji. Jawaharlal was arrested in October 1940; my husband and I were soon added to the honours list".[36]

According to Gandhi: "The Congress never organized a movement more glorious... than the Individual Satyagraha campaign from October 1940 to December 1941, for no Civil Disobedience movement was more civil, more distinguished by dissociation from indiscipline and violence than this campaign".[37] However, Congress leaders were not happy with the Individual Satyagraha campaign. In the words of Sumit Sarkar, this campaign was "among the weakest and least effective of all the Gandhian national campaigns".[38]

III
Quit India Movement

The visit of Sir S. Cripps to India, instead of creating goodwill and an amicable solution, left feelings of ill-will and bitterness among the Indian people. The failure of the Cripps Mission and the further reverses suffered by the British forces in the World War made Gandhi very apprehensive. He feared that India might go the way of Malaya and Burma if the British did not quit. In an

[36]Aruna Asaf Ali, *Resurgence of Indian Women* (Radiant Publishers, New Delhi, 1991), p. 135.

[37]M.N. Das, ed, *A Centenary History of the Indian National Congress*, Vol. III, 1935-1944 (New Delhi, 1985), p. 395.

[38]Sumit Sarkar, op. cit., pp. 381-83.

interview to an American journal, Gandhi made the following observation:

> Hundreds, if not thousands, on their way from Burma perished without food and drink, and the wretched discrimination stared even these miserable people in the face. One route for the whites, another for the blacks! And discrimination even on their arrival in India! India is being ground down to dust and humiliated.... And so one fine morning I came to the decision to make this honest demand: 'For Heaven's sake leave India alone. Let us breathe the air of freedom. It may choke us, suffocate us, as it did the slaves on their emancipation. But I want the present sham to end'.[39]

In its meeting held at Wardha on 14 July 1942, the Congress Working Committee passed a resolution, calling for the immediate withdrawal of British rule from India. The All India Congress Committee, which met at Bombay on 7th and 8th August 1942, reiterated this decision. The operative portion of the resolution said:

> The Committee resolves, therefore, to sanction for the vindication of India's inalienable right to freedom and independence, the starting of a mass struggle on non-violent lines on the widest possible scale...such a struggle must inevitably be under the leadership of Gandhiji and the Committee requests him to take the lead and guide the nation in the steps to be taken.
>
> The Committee appeals to the people of India to...carry out his instructions as disciplined soldiers of Indian freedom.... A time may come when it may not be possible to issue instructions or for instructions to reach our people, and when no

[39]*The Collected Works of Mahatma Gandhi* (hereinafter CWMG), Vol. LXXVI, pp. 195-96.

> Congress Committee can function. When this happens, every man and woman, who is participating in this movement must function of himself or herself within the four corners of the general instructions issued. Every Indian who desires freedom and strives for it must be his own guide urging him on along the hard road where there is no resting place and which leads ultimately to the independence and deliverance of India.[40]

On 8 August, Gandhi concluded his speech with the following remarks: "The Congress will do or die .... I shall make every effort to see the Viceroy or address a letter to him and wait for his reply before starting the struggle. It may take a week or a fortnight or three weeks". Maulana Azad, the Congress President, announced that the copies of the resolution would be sent to President Roosevelt, to the Chinese Government and to the Soviet Ambassador in London. Gandhi wrote later: "The movement was not started by the resolution of 8 August. Before I could function, they arrested not only me, who was to lead and guide the movement if negotiations failed, but principal Congressmen all over India. Thus it was not I but the government who started the movement".[41]

Gandhi was arrested on 9 August 1942. Aruna Asaf Ali informs that Gandhi and his colleagues had no inkling whatsoever that they would be taken into police custody within a few hours. "Some of us, however, knew that the arrests were coming. My husband and I had told the leaders about the government's plan before the A.I.C.C. meeting began, but they would not believe".[42]

Gandhi's message "Do or Die" became a motto for the millions, which brought about mass awakening among the Indians. Even the government employees started supporting those who were fighting for the country's freedom.

[40] Aruna Asaf Ali, op. cit., pp. 136-37.
[41] Ibid., p. 137.
[42] Ibid.

Jugal Kishore Khanna, the then General Secretary of the Delhi Pradesh Congress Committee, informs that he had come to know through a friend in the Home Department about the Top-Secret circular to the Bombay Government, the Railways and other concerned authorities about plans of the arrest of Gandhi and other Congress leaders immediately after the adoption of the Quit India resolution.

> I sent the information through Asaf Ali to Bombay. He left on 3 August 1942 in the morning by the Frontier Mail and gave the information to the Working Committee at its first meeting. But, as I was told later on in Bombay on the 6th or the 7th, Sarojini Naidu and others laughed it away saying: 'These Delhi people always bring all sorts of news'. On the 7th, the information was confirmed by a Bombay Secretariat source. On the 8th, the proceedings (of the AICC) went on till 10.30 p.m. Mahatma Gandhi for the first time made a very long speech, for about one-and-a-half hours instead of the usual 15 or 20 minutes, on 'Do or Die', the final struggle. Maulana Azad asked us to meet him at Birla House (where he was staying) at 7.30 the next morning for proceeding to the flag-hoisting ceremony at Gowalia Tank Maidan. I laughed at the idea.[43]

When informed of the secret plans about the impending arrests, Sarojini Naidu "called it the wild talk of opium workers at a Chandukhana in Delhi".[44] "My husband and I were not in the least surprised when, in the early hours of 9 August, the police knocked on the door at the flat where we were staying. When they announced Asaf Saheb's arrest, I asked 'What about me?' 'There is no warrant for you, madam', I was told".[45]

[43]Oral History Transcript, NMML, New Delhi.
[44]Aruna Asaf Ali, op. cit., p. 138.
[45]Ibid.

The news of Gandhi's arrest on 9 August 1942 led to hartals in Bombay, Ahmedabad and Poona. By 11 August the movement assumed threatening proportions, with people taking out processions, holding meetings and demonstrations. Industrial labour went on a strike in Ahmedabad, Bombay, Kanpur, Indore, Bangalore and Mysore.[46]

The movement soon spread to other places as well "where peasants rebelled against landowners and the agents of British authority".[47] At several places people declared independence and took charge of the police stations. Flags were hoisted on Secretariat buildings, courts and other government offices. The government machinery was in complete shambles in several districts in Bihar, Central Provinces, Andhra, Uttar Pradesh, Gujarat, Karnataka, Assam, Orissa and parts of Bengal. In order to bring the situation under control, the government enacted "The Penalties Enhancement Ordinance, Collective Fine Ordinance, the Special Court Ordinance, the Whipping Ordinance".[48]

Women too played a prominent part in the Quit India movement in different parts of the country, particularly in the absence of male leaders who were arrested in the first round. Apart from taking out processions and holding demonstrations, women also organized training camps in which "they were given training in civic duties, and first aid, educated on democracy and Indian Constitution. Training in *lathi* and drill was also imparted in the camps".[49] The women also organized Political Prisoner's Relief Fund and collected a large amount of money. Some women went underground and directed the movement from there.

[46]"August Struggle Report", Part II – Report prepared under the patronage of All India Satyagraha Council, U.P. Branch, All India Congress Committee Office, New Delhi, p. 5.

[47]G. Forbes, op. cit., p. 204.

[48]Cited in Manmohan Kaur, op. cit., p. 199.

[49]*Hindustan Standard*, 27 July 1942.

Aruna Asaf Ali's Contribution

Aruna Asaf Ali played a significant role in the Quit India movement. She remained underground for four years, evading arrest. She brought out a number of bulletins and edited in collaboration with Ram Manohar Lohia, the *Inquilab*. The British authorities had announced a reward of Rs.5,000 to anyone who could tell about her whereabouts. Indeed "the heroine of 1857 was the Rani of Jhansi, that of the 1942 revolution was undoubtedly Aruna Asaf Ali".[50]

Aruna Asaf Ali was of the opinion that the reign of Akbar and the Mughal period should be our guide, and not Ram Raj. Though she was an ardent Gandhian to start with, but her ideological beliefs underwent a change when she came into contact with the likes of Jayaprakash Narayan, Achyut Patwardhan and Ram Manohar Lohia. Her inclination to follow the path of Socialism becomes evident from the following statement of hers: "Towards Socialism, I shall march".[51] In 1940, when Gandhi launched the Individual Satyagraha campaign, Aruna Asaf Ali took part in it and was arrested in Delhi.

In 1942, when Aruna went with her husband to attend the 45th Session of the Congress at Bombay and unfurled the national flag at Gowalia Tank Maidan, the police released gas to disperse the crowd. The sight of the white Sergeant trampling over the national flag that Aruna had unfurled a few minutes back, was a big motivating factor in her decision to channelize all her energies to the cause of the country's freedom. To quote Aruna:

> A white Sergeant gave two minutes for the crowd to disperse. I quickly scrambled up to the dais, announced to the people the arrest of the leaders, and pulled the cord to hoist the national flag. Few knew my identity; some thought that the girl with plaited hair was a college student

[50] *The Tribune*, 18 February 1946.

[51] *Fragments from the Past – Selected Writings and Speeches of Aruna Asaf Ali* (New Delhi, 1989), p. 10.

> from Delhi. Hardly had the flag been unfurled when the police lobbed tear-gas shells into the crowd. The men and women ran helter-skelter with tears streaming from their eyes. Among them was Indira Gandhi, though I was not aware of it at the time.... The experience of that morning made me decide that I would not again tamely enter jail by offering Satyagraha. The people were indignant at the arrest of the leaders and the indignation should find organized expression in such a forceful manner that the alien rulers would have no option but to quit India.[52]

Apart from Aruna Asaf Ali, some other delegates who had come to attend the A.I.C.C. session of Delhi were Deshbandhu Gupta and Jugal Kishore Khanna. The three of them decided to go to Delhi quietly and organize the movement there, staying underground. In Delhi, she had a large number of friends who were prepared to provide shelter to her. A police officer who had made frantic efforts to trace Aruna reported to his senior officer: "As against nine of us who are searching for her, there are nine lakhs in Delhi alone to offer her protection and quarter. It is an uneven game and you cannot blame us if we don't succeed".[53]

In the beginning of her underground life in Delhi, Aruna was looked after by Nirmala and Uma, the daughters of Dr. N.C. Joshi, eminent surgeon of Karol Bagh, west Delhi. He was a patriot to the core and believed in the lofty ideal of secularism. During the partition riots, he saved the lives of many Hindus and Muslims. Unfortunately, however, he was later killed by a Muslim fanatic.[54]

There are a number of stories connected with Aruna's underground life. Once she was warned that the place where

[52]Aruna Asaf Ali, op. cit., 1991, pp. 138-39. Also see *Remembered Moments* (Indira Gandhi Memorial Trust, New Delhi, 1987).
[53]*Fragments from the Past*, op. cit., 1989, p. 14.
[54]Aruna Asaf Ali, op. cit., 1991, p. 139.

she was putting up was no longer safe and that she should shift to some other place immediately. The notice was so short that she was at a loss to decide as to where she should go. Fortunately, she remembered reading an advertisement in the morning paper that an English family wanted a European paying-guest. Aruna got into a taxi and dashed to the address advertised. The good old English lady was so captivated by Aruna's charming personality that she decided to wave aside her stipulations in favour of a European boarder and accepted Aruna as her paying guest. When the police arrived in great triumph to arrest her, they found that the mysterious bird had slipped out of their hands once again.[55]

Many eminent leaders began to feel that mere flocking into the jails would not be a fitting response to the reign of terror which had been unleashed by the British authorities. Socialists like Jayaprakash Narayan, Ram Manohar Lohia, Achyut Patwardhan and Aruna Asaf Ali and also staunch Gandhians like R.R. Diwakar and Sucheta Kripalani felt that there was an urgent need to plan an organized movement on the lines of anti-Fascist resistance in Occupied Europe.

All the committed Socialists, including Aruna Asaf Ali, went underground with the purpose of effectively organizing people's resistance to the British authorities and to dislocate the war effort. Aruna Asaf Ali informs:

> The only Left group to stand apart, and even to oppose us, were the Indian communists. They believed that Hitler's attack on the Soviet Union in June 1941 had transformed the hostilities into a people's war. We felt differently. While we deeply sympathised with the Soviet people and admired their heroic resistance to Hitler's hordes, we were of the view that they were fighting for their freedom and we for ours and there was no contradiction between the two struggles.[56]

[55]*Fragments from the Past*, op. cit., pp. 14, 15.
[56]Aruna Asaf Ali, op. cit.

While underground, Aruna Asaf Ali rendered useful services to her countrymen in a variety of ways. She and her colleagues toured the famine stricken areas often and tried to help the poor villagers by looking after their needs. It would be interesting to note that it was the pilot Biju Patnaik (who later became the Chief Minister of Orissa), who in a plane requisitioned for military purposes facilitated Aruna's visits to many remote districts and rural areas.[57] However, the hard underground life to which Aruna was not accustomed to took its toll and her health started deteriorating. But the help and cooperation which was given to her by many of her friends in different parts of the country enabled her to regain her lost health. Aruna writes:

> Much has been made of my own part in the movement. I was but a splinter of the lava thrown up by the volcanic eruption of a people's indignation. It is true that during my underground existence for three-and-a-half years, the incessant travel, unaccustomed living conditions, food at irregular hours, and the constant tension told on my health. But so many other comrades in the movement suffered similar or greater hardship.
>
> If I had often to undergo discomfort, there were interludes when I was affectionately taken care of by sympathisers of the cause of freedom. They belonged to all sections of Indian society including the patriotic bourgeoisie. I remember how Mridula Sarabhai, after she came to know that I was in Bombay and was ill, located me and drove me to the palatial home of her wealthy kin, who took me into their care despite the harm that could come to them for harbouring a fugitive for whose capture the police had announced a reward.

[57]Vijay Agnew, *Elite Women in Indian Politics* (New Delhi, 1979), pp. 69-73.

> There were similar, kindly hosts in Delhi and Calcutta and elsewhere who not only helped me to recover my health with medication and nourishing food but supplied me with the rich silks and fancy goggles of a society lady which I used as disguise, in place of my accustomed wear of grey and printed *khadi.*[58]

Though Aruna was a great admirer of Gandhi, she had her own independent thinking and chose to follow a different path during the Quit India days. She writes: "But for Gandhiji's innumerable campaigns which drew together the masses as no other movement did, we could not have availed ourselves of the opportunities for revolutionary action which suddenly opened up when war came in 1939".[59] Gandhi's repeated advice (to her) to surrender was not acceptable to her and she continued leading a life of a fugitive revolutionary. She said: "It was under these circumstances that we took a resolve that as long as there is breath in us we shall not shut up in the prisons of the enemy".[60]

Some Gandhians like Sucheta Kripalani were of the opinion that sabotaging the war effort which Aruna Asaf Ali and other Socialists were organizing was against the Gandhian ideals of non-violence. This was somewhat surprising because in the illegally circulated pamphlets, the Socialists had made it very clear that the strategy of planned dislocation of Britain's imperialist war effort did not mean senseless destruction of life and property. Through sabotage they wanted to bring about a mass uprising. But even though some ardent Gandhians severed their links with Aruna for her alleged violent activities, neither Gandhi nor Nehru disowned her. In fact, Gandhi wrote to Aruna on 9 June 1944: "I have been filled with admiration for your courage and heroism. I have sent you

[58]Aruna Asaf Ali, op. cit., p. 140.
[59]*Fragments from the Past*, op. cit., p. 190.
[60]Ibid., p. 32.

messages that you must not die underground. You are reduced to a skeleton. Do come out and surrender yourself and win the prize offered for your arrest. Reserve the prize money for the Harijan cause".[61]

Nehru also, while speaking at Almora on 16 June 1945, made the following observation in regard to Aruna Asaf Ali:

> I pay homage to those who are playing with their lives and those who are now at the door of death. Among them, it is only in the fitness of things that I must take the name of one of India's brave women, Aruna Asaf Ali. If my voice can reach her, I want to send her my love and esteem. I want to tell her that whatever she has done shall not be wasted and will bear fruit. It will leave its impression on her countrymen.[62]

Aruna also differed with Nehru on the question of tricolour flag flying on the Red Fort. She said:

> This Red Fort is the constant reminder of our national humiliation. Every stone of this evil and monstrous structure serves us with a daily reminder of humiliation of Bahadur Shah. It was in this building that the last of our independent ruler was presented with the heads of his sons.... Such being the ugly memories of this Red Fort, how can we tolerate even for a second the sight of this murder house where hundreds of our patriots have been done to death.[63]

She further declared that "the national flag should be hoisted not on the Red Fort but on the Imperial Secretariat where ordinances after ordinances were manufactured in 1942 to suppress the rising of the people of India when their leaders were in Ahmadnagar Jail".[64]

[61]CWMG, Vol. LXXVII, p. 306.

[62]*Selected Works of Jawaharlal Nehru*, Vol. 14, pp. 1-2.

[63]*Fragments from the Past*, op. cit., p. 33.

[64]Ibid.

Usha Mehta's Contribution

Born on 24 March 1920 at Satara district, Surat, Usha Mehta was the witness to the important resolution of the Quit India movement. To make this resolution a success, she wanted to do something different and more challenging than mere picketing of foreign cloth and liquor shops. When some of her friends placed before her the idea of running a secret transmitting station, she felt greatly interested. To quote her: "It appealed to me immensely and I jumped at the idea and plunged into the movement in spite of staunch opposition from my father who being a government servant did not approve of my idea and who wanted me to finish my education".[65] Though her father—a government servant—was very much against this idea, yet Usha remained adamant and firmly committed to her plans.

It was from 9 August 1942 when most of the important leaders were in jail that Usha started making preparations for setting up a radio in the name of "Voice of Freedom".[66] A transmitter was necessary for the success of the project. Babubhai Khakar and Usha Mehta were the pioneers of this project. But they did not have the necessary funds. A women relative of Usha came forward to offer her jewellery but Usha did not think it proper to accept this offer. Ultimately, Babubhai Khakar managed to pool the funds, which enabled the setting up of the transmitter.[67] The Congress Radio had its own transmitter, transmitting station, recording station, its own call sign and last, but not the least, a distinct wave-length. It started broadcasting on 14 August 1942. "This is the Congress Radio calling on 42.84 metres from somewhere in India".[68]

In order to make sure that the police was kept at bay, they frequently kept changing their abode. According to Usha:

[65]Cited in Manmohan Kaur, op. cit., p. 213.
[66]Ibid.
[67]Ibid.
[68]Ibid.

> Fortunately for us, one uncle from upcountry or our sister or some other relative would come to our rescue. Uncle wanted a flat for one month. One of his nephews would go and hire it, take all the luggage there and would anxiously wait for him. But by the time uncle was expected another flat would have to be hired for some other fictitious purpose. Every time the process was to go from the broadcasting station to the railway station and from there again to the new transmitting station. This had to be done every fortnight or so. Once Babubhai and I found a very good place; quite safe according to us. We were extremely happy at the idea that we would be able to carry on at least for a month or two. We went to the owner to pay the rent. A queer apparatus was lying there. We said 'Sethji, what is this supposed to be?' 'A detecting machine to catch the illegal radios', came the reply. 'Detecting machine', I exclaimed in my mind, but I took care to see that the face did not betray the expressions. Babubhai cleverly joined him in abusing all those who did such illegal acts and we were off. We thanked our stars for having been cautioned in time. The first words of Babubhai were 'Behn, we are saved from the tiger's jaws'.[69]

The main job of Usha was to broadcast news and give talks in Hindustani. Credit goes to this broadcasting station for being the first one to relay the news of Chittagong bomb raid, Jamshedpur strike and the atrocities committed in Ashti Chimur. The speeches were basically meant to highlight the Congress stand both from the national and international points of view. In regard to the Quit India movement, the following comments were relayed: "So far we were conducting a movement, but now we are conducting a revolution. In a revolution, there is victory or

[69] Ibid., pp. 213-14.

defeat. This revolution is not of one party or community, but of the whole of India, we hope you will not rest content till the British Empire is burnt to ashes".[70]

Aruna Asaf Ali opined that the transmission made by the Congress radio was of considerable help in making the movement successful. She wrote:

> We had cooperation, too, from young entrepreneurs and technologists with whose help a Congress Radio came up in Bombay and managed to function for more than four months. Babubhai Khakhar and Vithalbhai K. Jhaveri procured the money and the materials for the transmitter as well as the technical experts. The chief announcer was Usha Mehta, who was working for her Master's degree and was one of the tens of thousands of students all over the country who joined the 1942 movement. 'The only political activity that she had so far been involved in', says Vijay Agnew, 'was meeting with fellow students interested in promoting the use of Hindi as a national language'. The Congress Radio operated from 20 August 1942 till the end of December, with Dr. Rammanohar Lohia as a frequent speaker. The station countered the alien rulers' propaganda disseminated by 'anti-India Radio', as we called the British-controlled All India Radio. The clandestine radio station, announcing itself as broadcasting from 'somewhere in India', would play every day Iqbal's *Sare Jahan se Achha Hindustan Hamara as well as Bande Mataram.*[71]

However, this radio received a big setback when the government came to know of it and raided the place on the night of 12 November 1942. Babubhai and Usha were arrested in the Radio Conspiracy Case. The police made all possible efforts to get the details from Usha Mehta but she

[70]Ibid., p. 214.

[71]Aruna Asaf Ali, op. cit., 1991, pp.140-41.

did not budge an inch. Describing her life in the police custody, she informs: "The lock up period is perhaps the most trying time in the life of a prisoner. During the day you have to face the policemen and at night your only possible activity could be either to kill the bugs or to kill time. Again it is humanly impossible to sleep in a cell full of filth, dirt and nauseating smell".[72] "In spite of six months continuous interrogation, the police could not get any information from her and finally charged her with agreeing in conspiring among and between ourselves and others, to do or cause to be done illegal acts like possessing, establishing, maintaining and working illegal wireless telegraph without lawful... authority or excuse prejudicial acts and spreading prejudicial reports".[73]

Usha Mehta was finally sentenced to four years imprisonment. She remained in jail till April 1946.

A secret letter dated 27th January 1943, from the Home Department (Special), Bombay, to Sir Richard Tottenham, Additional Secretary to the Government of India, forwarded a report by the Commissioner of Police, Bombay, on the Congress Radio case. The report contained a note on Miss Usha Mehta who made several of the records used in the broadcast and also operated the transmitter. The report referred to her as "an ardent Congress woman".[74]

Satyawati's Contribution

Satyawati also played a prominent role in the Quit India movement. She was, however, of the view that by remaining underground she would be able to organize the movement in a much better way. For the Delhi region, Satyawati, Premjas Rai and Jugal Kishore Khanna were leading the movement secretly. Satyawati moved around in a car with tainted glasses along with Aruna Asaf Ali urging people to extend their wholehearted cooperation to the Quit India

[72]Manmohan Kaur, op. cit., p. 215.

[73]Ibid.

[74]Home Political, 1943, 3/44/43-Poll (1).

movement, after the arrest of Gandhi and other leaders.[75] She was also in regular touch with the Students' Federation and motivated the student community to come forward in support of the movement. Besides, she also gave the lead to a number of workers' associations and labour unions. For their active involvement in the Quit India movement, Satyawati, along with her son Krishan Kumar, mother Ved Kumari and sister Kaushalya and her elder daughter Kusum were taken into police custody. But soon Satyawati fell ill and she and her mother Ved Kumari were sent to a sanatorium in the hills. Ved Kumari was expected to take care of her during her illness.[76]

Satyawati faced another tragedy when her younger daughter Munna took seriously ill, due to separation from her mother, and subsequently died. Surprisingly, the British authorities did not convey the message about Munna's serious illness to Satyawati. Nor, for that matter, did they allow Satyawati to come to Delhi. It was sad indeed that the dying child was deprived a meeting with her mother during her last moments. To register her protest against her internment, Satyawati conveyed the following message to the Governor of Punjab and to the Chief Commissioner of Delhi: "As a non-violent fighter, I have to resist all evil forces of the world to save human rights and it is my effort to liberate human society from cruelty, exploitation and tyrannies of imperialism and fascism".[77]

Satyawati passed away on 21 October 1945. Thousands of tearful mourners came to pay homage to the departed leader who had played an important role in mobilizing women, students, workers and peasants in Delhi.

The Quit India movement soon spread to many areas, particularly in parts of Bihar and eastern provinces and in some pockets of Bengal, Orissa, Karnataka and

[75]C.K. Nair, op. cit., pp. 2-3.

[76]Brij Kishan Chandiwala, Urdu Diary, Private Papers of B.K. Chandiwala, File No. 9, NMML, New Delhi.

[77]File No. 10/2-44 SB, dt. 14 January 1945, NAI.

Maharashtra. The peasantry played a big role in this movement. Some areas were even liberated for some time.

Orissa

The Gandhian ideology of non-violence had always had a special appeal to the Oriya temperament.[78] Therefore, the Oriyas took an active part in the movement with utmost enthusiasm in large numbers. At the historic session of the Congress held at Bombay on 8 August 1942, many Oriya Congress workers, including Malati Choudhury, were present. On 9 August 1942, the police arrested almost all the eminent Congress leaders of Orissa. While some leaders, including Rama Devi—a staunch Gandhian—voluntarily courted arrest,[79] there were others like Malati Choudhury and S.N. Dwivedi,[80] who managed to hoodwink the police and came to Cuttack via Bhubaneswar.

Malati Choudhury encountered great difficulty during her journey from Bombay to Cuttack. At the Bhubaneswar station the police had maintained a strict vigil. She, therefore, ventured to walk all the way to Cuttack. It was midnight; the Kathjoli river was flooded and the Kathjoli bridge was guarded by the police. But she managed to overcome these obstacles: with the help of a broken boot[81]

[78]Bhupen Qanungo, "The Quit India Movement 1942", in M.N. Das, ed, *A Centenary History of the Indian National Congress, 1885-1985*, Vol. III, p. 543.

[79]*The Indian Historical Review*, Vol. XXI, Nos 1 & 2, edited by Anup Taneja (ICHR and Motilal Banarsidass, Delhi, 1997), p. 89.

[80]Surendra Natha Dwivedi, a staunch follower of Gandhi, was also a top-ranking Congress leader of that time. On Gandhi's arrest, he and Malati Choudhury came back to Orissa with the following message of Gandhi: "Our country is independent from today. Follow the peaceful method. Praise the Government, you yourself become a leader. This is the last struggle. In it there is no compromise". S.N. Dwivedi, *August Biplab* (August Revolution) (Cuttack), p. 13.

[81]V. Rajendra Raju, op. cit., p. 79.

and singing the song of poet Nijarul,[82] she crossed the flooded river. Thus risking her life she reached Cuttack and laid the foundation of the "August Revolution" in Orissa.[83]

Gandhi had wanted the Quit India movement to be vastly different from the traditional Satyagraha. He wanted this movement to be imbued with the spirit of "do or die" wherein there should be open defiance of law and refusal to pay taxes. In Orissa, under the leadership of Malati Choudhury and S.N. Dwivedi, a large number of women actively involved themselves with the Quit India movement. At Malati's instructions, railway lines were tampered with and telephone wires were disconnected—the idea was to help the Congress workers to accomplish their mission without any obstacles.[84] At the same time there were strikes, protest meetings and open defiance of law. People even went to the extent of looting banks and government treasury. Thus within a few days, the situation assumed serious proportions, with political prisoners inside the jail violating the jail regulations and undermining the authority of the jailor.[85]

The government thus was forced to declare the AICC Working Committee and other such bodies within the province as illegal. On 16 August 1942, at Bari, Mangala Devi made a gigantic effort to "free the Congress ashram which had been attacked and taken over by the police".[86] She was arrested along with other women workers when she was trying to burn the seized property and uniform

[82]O fellow travellers
We would have to cross over
The arduous expansive sea
And overcome the insurmountable
Heights of mountains
In the night's fathomless hour
Be aware.

[83]V. Rajendra Raju, op. cit.

[84]Home Pol., File No.3/31/42.

[85]V. Rajendra Raju, op. cit., p. 81.

[86]See *The Indian Historical Review*, Vol. XXI, op. cit., p. 90.

belonging to the police. Other women to have been arrested by the police were Rama Devi, Malati Choudhury, Priyambada Devi, Godavari Devi and some other Congress workers. Annapurna Moharana, along with a group of agitators, demanded their immediate release and broke the police cordon. In order to bring the situation under control, the police had to resort to firing.[87]

In places like Jagatsingpur, Tirtol and Balikuda, the situation was quite grave with people becoming violent and setting on fire some government institutions like post offices, police barracks, etc. In order to check this violence, the ADM and the Additional Superintendent of Police announced imposition of many fines on people. Annapurna Moharana once again made her presence felt by strongly protesting against the imposition of fines. She was again arrested by the police and was sent to Cuttack jail which, on that memorable occasion, was filled with women Satyagrahis.[88] People at Eram in the Balasore district prevented the government officials from carrying out their duties which was a provocation enough for the police to resort to firing.[89] In the melee which ensued, a number of women Satyagrahis were injured and one of them—Pari Bewa—died on the spot. One Jambuvati Devi of Sambalpur "crossed the Orissa border and led a procession starting from Ghoramora Training School to Tumuka in Bihar. She attacked the district court of Turika, was arrested by the police, suffered injuries in the process, and died in Bihar on 15 July 1943".[90]

Nandini Devi,[91] a student leader, took an active part in the movement in the Ravenshaw College. She was arrested by the police and, because of her active involvement in

[87]Ibid.

[88]Annapurna Moharana, "Bara Number Ward" (in Oriya) (Ward No.12), *Sucharita* (January 1985), p. 34. This article is based on Annapurna's own experience.

[89]*Orissa Review*, Vol. XLIV, No. 1, August 1987, p. 11.

[90]*Who's Who Freedom Workers*, Vol. III, p. 22.

[91]She later became the Chief Minister of Orissa.

political activities, was subsequently rusticated from the College.

During the Quit India movement, some Oriya women spread the patriotic spirit through literature. The most notable example in this respect is that of Sitadevi Khadanga, who wrote a number of books propagating the message of Gandhi. In her work *Posyaputra*, she made an earnest appeal to the masses to make all possible sacrifices for the sake of the country's liberation.[92]

The women who made remarkable contributions by way of making the Quit India movement popular in Orissa were: Malati Choudhury, Rama Devi, Sarala Devi, Annapurna Moharana, Mangala Devi, Suryamani Devi, Gunamanjari Devi, Champa Devi, Hemalata Devi, Suryamma, P. Taramma, A. Laxmibai, Parvati Devi, Jambovati Devi, Radhika Devi, Sitadevi Khadanga, and some others. The contributions made by them were all the more commendable, particularly considering that all the prominent male leaders at that time were behind the bars. Gandhi paid a compliment to them in the following words: "I have had the privilege of mixing with tens and thousands of India's women, I have seen them at work. But nowhere have I seen anything quite like what Ramadevi and her little band have been found to do, so gracefully and so naturally".[93]

Bihar

In Patna, the Mahila Charkha Samiti was actively associated with the Quit India movement. On 9 August 1942, members of this Samiti took out a big procession. After passing through the entire town, the procession finally stopped at Congress Maidan where a meeting was held in which Bhagwati Devi, Rampyari Devi and Sundari Devi made forceful speeches exhorting the government servants to

[92]Sitadevi Khadanga, *Sitadevi Granthalaya* (in Oriya) (Cuttack, 1978), Vol. I, p. 142.

[93]*Harijan*, 15 June 1934.

resign and the lawyers to leave their practice.[94] Among the many women who took part in the movement in Bihar, the names of Sarala Devi, Usha Rani Mukherji and Saroj Das of Palamau district stand out prominently.[95] Other women who were involved in the movement were Prabhawati, Priyamvada Nandkeoliyar, Krishna Devi, Girija Devi, Manorama Devi and Shakuntala Devi.[96]

In the Monghyr district also, women were actively associated with the movement. In Ruiyar village under Chautham police station, people became victims of police atrocities. On 2 September 1942, the police resorted to firing in which many women died along with their kids. "Mrs Hunkeri Telin died along with her three-year old daughter and seven-year old son. Surti Devi died with her three-year old child".[97] Mrs Hakni and Mrs Sampatia along with her daughter died in a police firing".[98]

In Palamau district, Kumari A.R. Das played an important role in making the August Revolution successful. In the Manbhum district of Purulia, a number of women were arrested. The police raided the Shilpa Ashram in Purulia and took into custody Lavanya Prabha Ghosh and her daughter Kamla Ghosh.[99]

In Hazaribagh district, Saraswati Devi made her presence felt when she took over the mantle of leadership consequent upon the arrest of prominent male leaders. She organized a big procession on 11.8.1942, but was arrested the same day. On 12 August, when she was being transported to Bhagalpur jail along with another woman prisoner, a group of students freed her from police custody in Nathnagar and she was brought in a procession to Bhagalpur.[100] At Bhagalpur, she addressed a

[94]K.K. Datta, *Freedom Movement in Bihar* (Govt. of Bihar, Patna, 1957), Vol. III, p. 32.

[95]Shiva Pujan Sahay, op. cit., p. 321.

[96]Ibid., p. 321.

[97]Niroj Sinha, op. cit., p. 171.

[98]Shiv Pujan Sahay, op. cit., p. 320.

[99]K.K. Datta, op. cit., p. 50.

[100]Niroj Sinha, op. cit., p. 171.

gathering of students in Lajpat Park. She was again arrested on 14 August while entering the office of SDO.[101]

In Santhal Parganas, Jamvati Devi and Prema Devi headed a big procession on 18 August 1942. Sharda Devi also organized huge processions in Rajmahal and Sahabganj. She was sentenced to an year's imprisonment.[102] Viraji Madhiain of Ghoramara village was killed by police bullets.[103]

Bengal

The people of Midnapore district had played an important role in the Quit India movement. Among the "national governments" which were formed in some areas was the Tamralipta Jatiya Sarkar formed at Tamluk in Bengal. It had its own army called Vidyut Vahini and a Sisters' Corps attached to it. This national government which functioned within the limits laid down by the Congress Committee kept on functioning till 8 August 1944. It was dissolved at the instance of Gandhi.[104]

The women of Tamluk organized a number of processions, and in one of these seven women were arrested and an imprisonment of two years was awarded to each.[105] Manangini Hazra, a woman of seventy-two, had led one such procession with the purpose of occupying the Thana. The police started inflicting blows on her hands, but she never loosened her grip and made sure that the flag which she was holding did not drop. At the Thana, she urged the officials to give up their jobs and join the national movement. Unfortunately, a bullet was fired at her which proved to be fatal.[106]

[101] K.K. Datta, op. cit., p. 50.

[102] Niroj Sinha, op. cit.

[103] Shiva Pujan Sahay, op. cit., p. 321.

[104] P. Chakraborty and Bejin Mitra, ed, *The Rebel India* (Calcutta, 1946), p. 22.

[105] Ibid., p. 25.

[106] Ibid.

On 9 January 1943, six hundred soldiers surrounded three villages of Masuria, Dalmasuria and Chandipur in Mohishadal Thana. Apart from plundering these villages, the soldiers resorted to indecent behaviour and criminally assaulted as many as forty-six women on a single day.[107] In order to protect their honour and self-respect, the women formed an organization called Bhagini Seva Sangh. Some of the women affiliated to this organization kept weapons with them so as to protect themselves from criminal assault. Two women were prosecuted under the Arms Act for drawing out daggers in self-defence.[108]

Apart from Orissa, Bihar and Bengal, women in other states also took part in the Quit India movement. In Assam, on 20 October 1942, Kanak Lata Barua, a teenaged girl, led a procession of five hundred people towards Gohapon Thana;[109] in Punjab, Rajkumari Amrit Kaur took an active part in the Quit India movement and led a number of processions from 9 August to 16 August 1942; in Dharwar (Karnataka), on 23 October 1942, two young women—Hemlata Shenolikar and Gulvadi—entered the District Courts and hoisted the tri-colour on the judge's seat.[110]

IV
The Indian National Army: Captain Lakshmi Swaminathan's Role

The role of women in the national movement did not remain confined to India. Outside India also they were actively associated with the national movement, the most notable example being their association with the Indian National Army of Subhas Chandra Bose.[111] Bose, whose

[107]Ibid., p. 28.
[108]"August Struggle Report", op. cit., p. 78.
[109]P. Chakraborty and Bejin Mitra, op. cit., p. 3.
[110]Manmohan Kaur, op. cit., p. 217.
[111]G. Forbes, op. cit., p. 212.

political ideology was much different from that of Congress, left Calcutta for Berlin in January 1941 to strike a deal with Hitler. An year and a half later he reached Tokyo by submarine where he took charge of Indian prisoners of war. These prisoners were taken to Singapore where an army of liberation was to be formed.[112]

The Indian Independence League was formed on 16 January 1942 at Kuala Lumpur. Subsequently, its branches were formed at Thailand and other places. At that time the number of Indian prisoners at Kuala Lumpur had swelled to five thousand. Captain Mohan Singh urged them to join the Indian National Army to fight the British in Malaya and at other places.[113]

In March 1943, women's section of the Indian Independence League came into being. On 9 July 1943, Subhas Bose was made the President of the League's branch at Singapore. In the course of the speech delivered by him, Bose emphasized the need to involve women in the national movement. He said that he wanted "a unit of brave Indian women"[114] to make his mission successful. In keeping with his immense faith in the woman power, he added a Department of Women's Affairs to the League and appointed Dr. Lakshmi Swaminathan as its head.[115]

Daughter of Barrister S. Swaminathan and Ammu Swaminathan—the first woman worker of Madras Congress—Lakshmi Swaminathan was a doctor by profession. She passed her M.B.B.S. in 1937. During the Second World War, she was in Singapore, where she had founded a hospital and served her countrymen. She offered her services at Netaji's call and took over as Commander of the Women's Rani Jhansi Regiment. She served as Minister of Social Welfare and Medicine in the Azad Hind Cabinet. As a result of the efforts made by her, the number of

[112]Ibid.

[113]K.S. Giani, *Indian Independence Movement in East Asia* (Lahore, 1947).

[114]G. Forbes, op. cit., p. 212.

[115]Ibid.

women fighters of the Rani Jhansi Regiment increased from 175 to 2000. Apart from general services this women force displayed great courage in the famous battle of 'Imphal' on the Indian border, and emerged victorious over the British.

> In 'Maulmen', during the defeat of the 'Azad Hind Force', Captain Lakshmi and her force persevered bravely till Netaji passed out safely, only after which she surrendered. She was captured and her Regiment was disbanded in 1945 and most of the girls were sent away to Singapore from Rangoon. Lakshmi was also sent to Rangoon jail. There was a great deal of agitation for her release and the government had to yield, and released her on the condition that she would not make any public speech. But she defied the order and spoke on the anniversary of the Azad Hind Force on 21 October 1945. She was again arrested and was flown to 'Meikilita' from where she was taken to 'Kalawa' in a military car. She was released after a year. She came to India and was married to Captain Sehgal of the Indian National Army.[116]

V

Women's Role in the Evacuation of Refugees

At the midnight hour of 14-15 August 1947, when the dawn of freedom was being celebrated in Delhi, Gandhi was in Calcutta where communal riots had taken an ugly turn. In order to restore communal harmony he went on a fast. It was only when on 4 September that all the communities gave him a written assurance, that he came to Delhi. In Delhi too be continued with his efforts for the restoration of

[116]Home Pol., File No.1/8/45. Also see *The Tribune*, 7 March 1946.

communal harmony right till his assassination on 30 January 1948.

After taking over as Prime Minister of India, Nehru too made all possible efforts, both at the administrative and personal levels, to bring about communal harmony. At the suggestion of Gandhi, Nehru's daughter Indira too took the plunge and played a remarkable role in restoring the spirit of camaraderie between the two communities. Indira Gandhi recalls:

> We used to go out at five in the morning and come back long after dark. We got the streets cleaned. We went to the Town Hall. The ration shops were there, but to get the rations, nobody would give us conveyance.... The sweepers were not prepared to go because they said they would be killed. We had to provide two young men for each sweeper as a guard....
>
> We went to the Hindu *mohallas* and said: 'Is there a Muslim in this particular neighbourhood who, you would say, had been quite secular and had done nothing against Hindus?' They would say: 'Oh! yes, there is so and so'. Then we went to the Muslims and asked: 'In all this rioting, is there a single Hindu who you can say has either positively helped you or at least not done anything wrong?' They said: 'Yes, there is so and so'. Then we said, 'Are you willing to meet them'? They would say: 'No, we simply can't meet'. We had to go backwards and forwards from place to place.... In between my father started getting rather threatening letters saying: 'Our daughters have been raped and killed and now she is working amongst the Muslims and we are going to do this to her'... but finally we did get a small group to sit in a place and talk and agree that this had to be ended.[117]

[117] *What I am* (Indira Gandhi Memorial Trust, New Delhi, 1986).

Another important woman from the Nehru family who was actively involved in ensuring the safe journey of refugees at the time of partition was Rameshwari Nehru, who was staying in Lahore with her husband Brijlal a few months preceding the partition. Just as Muslims in Delhi were in a state of terror and were being harassed, so were the Hindus in Lahore. Thousands of Hindu and Sikh families from Rawalpindi, Multan, Gujranwala and Peshawar had assembled at Lala Lajpat Rai Bhawan in Lahore from where they were to be evacuated to India. Rameshwari Nehru recalls:

> My husband and I ... went to Lala Lajpat Rai Bhawan every day to look after refugees and as far as possible arranged their safe journey to India in a reliable company. It appeared at that moment that it was impossible for any Hindu-Sikh family to stay on in Punjab with dignity. My husband wrote to Gandhiji then defending the people of Noakhali, as to 'what should we do?' Prompt came the reply, 'You should not leave Lahore. Even if you die, I shall not shed tears'.[118]

It was only when the last batch of refugees was evacuated from Lahore in October 1947 that Rameshwari Nehru and her husband Brijlal came to Delhi. Indeed, their effort was highly commendable, particularly considering that they did all this at the risk of their lives. In his biography, O.P. Paliwal paid rich compliments to Rameshwari in the following words: "Rameshwari was a source of comfort and solace to the minority community on this side—to the Muslims in India as much as she was attentive to the 'minority' on that side of the fence in Punjab".[119]

In her capacity as Hony Adviser to the Ministry of Rehabilitation in Delhi, Rameshwari Nehru did everything she could to restore the abducted persons to their families.

[118]Aruna Asaf Ali, op. cit., 1991, p. 149.
[119]Ibid.

Mridula Sarabhai too joined Rameshwari in this noble work with utmost enthusiasm and zeal.

Concluding Remarks

After the passing of the Quit India resolution in August 1942, a new generation of women—which was prepared to undertake dangerous and challenging tasks—began to emerge. This period saw the women play a much more aggressive role as compared to the 1930s. The August Revolution became so widespread that even people of rural areas and tribals started taking a keen interest in the movement and played a significant role in the last phase of the freedom struggle. It would be interesting to note that in the Koraput region of Orissa, even those tribal women who had no idea of politics had joined this movement, notable examples being Mrs Misti Kasturi, Subarna, Sutank, Aryati, Kumari Jhara, Mrs Jamuna, Mrs Jani, Kumari Tandra and Kumari Draupadi.[120] Thus, the traditional image of women as weak and helpless creatures underwent a radical transformation. Their levels of confidence increased manifold and they had a new role to play in the national mainstream.

[120] See *The Indian Historical Review*, Vol. XXI, op. cit., p. 91, fn. 111.

CHAPTER VI

THE ASSESSMENT

A Critical Analysis of Gandhi's Role

In the early years of the twentieth century, the number of women associated with political activities was marginal. Moreover, the participation of women was restricted only to those belonging to the elite classes whose presence was symbolic rather than active political participation. The partition of Bengal in 1905 and the entry of Annie Besant into politics in 1914 did infuse a new patriotic spirit among women, but still the participation of women in the national movement on a mass scale was lacking. This could partly be attributed to the social environment of those times which was too conservative to allow women to associate themselves with such activities.

But with the advent of Gandhi on the political scene of India, a radical transformation took place in the attitudes of women and they began to come forward in increasing numbers to contribute their humble mite to the cause of the country's emancipation. To start with, however, the participation of women in the Non-cooperation campaign (1920-22) was not on a big scale and was "mainly confined to those, whose husbands, fathers, brothers or sons had already joined the struggle and were in jail".[1] But by the

[1]Aparna Basu, "The Role of Women in the Indian Struggle for Freedom", in B.R. Nanda, ed, *Indian Women: From Purdah to Modernity* (Vikas, New Delhi, 1976), p. 22.

time the Civil Disobedience movement started in the early 1930s, women began to associate themselves with the national movement in increasing numbers in different parts of the country and started taking part in activities like picketing of shops selling foreign cloth and liquor, salt-making, public demonstrations, propagation of *charkha* and *khadi*, etc.

And with the passing of the Quit India resolution in August 1942, a new generation of women—which was prepared to undertake dangerous and challenging tasks—began to emerge. In contrast to the *desh sevikas* of the 1930s who were clad in orange and white sarees, the 1940s saw women play aggressive roles. A conspicuous feature of the 1940s was that women from both the middle and lower class families became victims of police brutalities. But this did not dampen their spirits, and they stuck to their task with utmost determination. In many provinces and districts women became 'dictators' to run the Congress movement. All this went a long way in transforming the self-perception of women and "gave them a new sense of power, a new self-view".[2] Indeed, full credit goes to Gandhi who succeeded in mobilizing women in large numbers and in motivating them to fight for the country's independence. However, the questions that arise are: what made it possible for women to take part in nationalist politics, when other forms of politicization, indeed other means of public activity, were strictly denied to them? How come that even after having played such an important role in the national movement, women reverted to their age-old traditional roles at home after the attainment of the country's independence?

Transformation of nationalism into religion was one of the important factors which facilitated women's participation in the movement. Freedom struggle was looked upon as *desh puja*. It was by virtue of Gandhi's image as a saint and the perception of the patriotic struggle as essentially a religious duty that the feminine role could be combined

[2]Rajan Mahan, *Women in Indian National Congress, 1921-1931* (Rawat Publications, Jaipur and New Delhi, 1999), p. 304.

with nationalist politics. This meant that despite their active involvement in the national movement, women could not become a part of the political process. To quote Tanika Sarkar: "The stress on the personal saintliness of Gandhi, a subtle symbiosis between the religious and the political in the nationalist message under his leadership, enabled nationalism to transcend the realm of politics and elevate itself to a religious domain.... Patriotism was subsumed within religion, the country became a vivid new deity added to the Hindu pantheon, and, by a sleigh of hand, became at once the highest deity from the moment of her deification: 'it is your image that we worship in the temples' ".[3] The motherland was identified with mother Goddess, and sacrifice of the highest order was required if the motherland was to be liberated. This was particularly relevant to women, who were supposed to be the manifestations of the Supreme Shakti herself. The nationalists capitalized on this and succeeded in mobilizing women by asserting that "unless the vital principle of Shakti imprisoned in women is released, the great act of sacrifice will not be complete".[4] Though the strong traditional moorings of the national movement did facilitate the participation of thousands of women in the national movement, yet at the same time the idea of any permanent reversal of the customary roles of women was never considered by Gandhi.

It may further be noted that Gandhi interpreted women's political participation as an extension of their traditional roles. He placed before women the example of the suffering Sita who was his ideal woman. Gandhi believed that women's involvement in the freedom struggle was necessary both for ideological and practical reasons. If women could be involved, the national movement could be

[3]Tanika Sarkar, "Politics and Women in Bengal—the Conditions and Meanings of Partition", in J. Krishnamurthy, ed, *Women in Colonial India: Survival, Work and the State* (OUP, New Delhi, 1989), p. 238.

[4]Ibid.

linked to every home in India.[5] Gandhi very ingeniously used the extended family concept as a powerful metaphorical construct for the extension of women's role outside their homes into the areas of public activity in the context of the national movement.

Another important programme through which Gandhi had ensured the participation of women in large numbers in the national movement was the *khadi* programme. This programme was particularly evolved for women. A large number of women was associated with this programme in its various dimensions. Many women took part in the picketing of shops selling foreign cloth, while others had cultivated the habit of spinning the *charkha*. Many widows also got engaged with spinning activity with the purpose of earning some money.[6] Mothers encouraged their sons to earn their livelihood through the manufacture and sale of *swadeshi* goods. Above all, at many places *mahila shilpamelas* were organized where handicrafts and *khadi* clothes were sold.[7] In many patriotic songs women were depicted as making an earnest request to their husbands to buy *charkhas* for them so that they could carry out their religious duties and also supplement their family income. The importance which women attached to *khadi* is depicted in the following patriotic song:

> I request you, O Lord, with folded hands and lying prostrate at your feet to bring for me a *swadeshi* sari. I will wear *chunari*. This is *singar* of *sohagin*, the *saput* of widows .... Fill with wealth and purify the body of mother.

[5]Gail Minault, "Introduction—The Extended Family as Metaphor and the Expansion of Women's Realm", in idem, ed, *The Extended Family: Women and Political Participation in India and Pakistan* (Chanakya Publications, New Delhi, 1989), p. 11.

[6]Geraldine Forbes, "The Politics of Respectability: Indian Women and the Indian National Congress", in D. A. Low, ed, *The Indian National Congress* (OUP, New Delhi, 1988).

[7]Radha Kumar, *The History of Doing* (Kali for Women, New Delhi, 1993), pp. 42, 57-58.

> I will spin yarn and weave cloth as sanctioned by *dharma*. The excess of scarcity is now really intolerable, O dear, raise my veil a little and teach some arts to me.
>
> Don't forget the old traditions. *Charkha* worship is written in *karma kand*.[8]

One important reason why the nationalists attached a special significance to *khadi* was that as a result of the import of a large amount of foreign made cloth by the British authorities, the indigenous weaving craft got a big setback. The Swadeshi movement thus aimed at reviving the local textile industry. In due course, handloom weaving became a powerful symbol of moral and spiritual regeneration in India. Spinning became a spiritual activity which could purge the spinner of all impurities. The wheel also assumed the status of being one of the members of the family. Gandhi repeatedly emphasized the spiritual aspect of spinning and said that through this activity a person could become a noble human being. The nationalists tried to infuse into the minds of people the idea that Indian men and women became poor and naked because of the consumption of foreign goods worth millions of rupees. Gandhi particularly emphasized the image of female nakedness and shame, as can be seen from the following statement:

> "The tyrants stripped off the clothes from the body of our sisters on road. We shall never put them on again.... It is our duty to use the spinning wheel and cut off the fetters of bondage

[8]Bihar Special Branch, Proscribed Leaflet, "Bhanda Phore", L III/21, "Charkha Vinode", 1631/1921. Cited in Lata Singh, "Gender, Nationalism and Khadi: Rendering Women as Domestic(ated) and not Political Subjects", in Aparna Basu and Anup Taneja, ed, *Breaking out of Invisibility: Women in Indian History* (ICHR Monograph Series 7, New Delhi, 2002), p. 153.

> and to save Mother India from the shame of being stripped naked like Draupadi.[9]

The nationalist leaders were thus able to associate women with the *khadi* programme through the constant use of themes like protection, female nakedness, shame, etc. *Khadi* became a religious symbol. And any programme which had religious overtones, greatly facilitated mobilization of women in large numbers. In the following statement, the religious aspect of spinning has been highlighted:

> The *sohagin* adjusted the *charkha*, fitted the handloom and took up the gin. When she sat on the stool and began to spin yarn, she woke up the yoginis. When she put on the newly-woven cloth and set out for the market even good women began to feel jealous of her.[10]

Spinning was particularly recommended for every woman who was inclined towards spirituality. Moreover, participation in this activity did not contradict the socially accepted roles of women within the home; on the contrary it strengthened that role.

However, it would be interesting to note that even though Gandhi urged women to take the *swadeshi* vow and to spend some time each day in spinning, yet he never had the notion of women's identity as wage-earners. In fact, Gandhi asserted that the spinning activity would reaffirm the ancient status of women.[11] The image of women as nurturers rather than wage-earners was predominant in the minds of the nationalists at the time when they were trying to involve more and more women in this activity. The role of spinning was merely confined to

[9]Bihar Special Branch, Proscribed Leaflet, "Bharat Mata Ka Sandesh" (CID), 1921. Cited in Lata Singh, op. cit., p. 153.

[10]Bihar Special Branch, Proscribed Song, "Charkha Vinode", L III/1922. Cited in Lata Singh, op. cit., p. 153.

[11]*Collected Works of Mahatma Gandhi*, Vol. XV, pp. 290-92, 322-26.

supplement the family income, as can be seen from the following statement of Gandhi:

> Every yard of *khaddar* purchased means a few coppers in the hands of women. It is for the women of India, a large number of whom do not get even an anna per day, that I am going about the country with my spinning wheel and my begging howl. The same money which you spend on foreign cloth may be very usefully employed in covering the naked bodies of a few of the poor sisters.[12]

Gandhi never favoured the idea of economic independence of women. He looked upon spinning and weaving as religious acts which were suited to the gentle nature of women. He regarded women as the embodiment of suffering and sacrifice; their entry into the political field would purge the system of all the corrupt practices. Thus, Gandhi's perception in regard to an equal status for women was limited to the religious sense of the term which was in conformity with patriarchal norms under which women's role was complementary to that of men.

To Gandhi, chastity of women was more important than her right as a worker. He strongly recommended the spinning of *charkha* to women because it gave them dignity and honour. To quote him:

> Millions of people are starving. They feel the pinch of hunger, but they cannot go to the costly works that the government has opened for them. The work there mostly consists of breaking stones for the roads or carrying metal. And what are the conditions under which this work has to be done. The majority of them are women and they have to work under the supervision of the overseers who have no character to lose or keep and

[12]K.K. Datta, *Writings and Speeches of Mahatma Gandhi relating to Bihar, 1917-47* (Government of Bihar, Patna, 1960), pp. 223-24.

> who are lustful. These women who ought to be as dear to you as your mothers or sisters, if you have any regard for them, have been weaned from this class of labour. This *charkha* gives them all that they need. It gives them dignity. An old lady of 60 years walks two miles to obtain silvers from my son and says 'tell your father he has given me something which is a blessing to me because it has given me a dignity which I did not have before'. Today there are millions of such men and women in Champaran to whom *charkha* would give independence. The wages of women there are anything between 5 and 6 pices per day, those of boys between 3 and 4 pices and those of men between 8 and 10 pices.... How are they earning this income? No insolent overseers who rob these sisters of their shame and take one rupee as their *dasturi* of the three rupees that they give to them, but by working under the observation of clean lads who will regard their honour as sacred as of their own sisters and give them money with a smile. It makes all the difference in the world whether you receive 8 or 10 annas from insolent hands or four pice from hands sanctified with work. This is the dignity of *charkha*.[13]

Thus, women's participation in the *khadi* programme was merely an extension of their domestic roles. On the basis of this, women could not claim an equal status with men in society. The nationalist ideology thus subjected women to a **new patriarchy**. The nationalists had little concern for the emancipation of women.

All this criticism, however, does not detract from the immense contributions made by Gandhi to the cause of Indian women's emancipation. "Like all solutions, Gandhi's

[13]K.K. Datta, *Gandhiji in Bihar* (Government of Bihar, Patna, 1969), pp.95-96. Also see Lata Singh, op. cit., pp. 158-59.

solution had its own strengths and weaknesses. Yet whatever be these strengths and weaknesses",[14] the fact cannot be denied that it was because of Gandhi's influence that a mass mobilization of women could take place in different parts of the country. His achievement becomes all the more significant when we consider that a large number of *purdah* bound women abandoned this unhealthy custom and started working alongside men for the cause of the country's freedom.[15]

Devaki Jain songs that for many women leaders in pre-independent India, Gandhi's call for Satyagraha opened the door for their own liberation from oppressive social customs. In the ashrams of Gandhi great importance was attached to reverence for women. The ashram life thus made it possible for a large number of women to come out of the narrow confines of their homes and to interact with a wider community. Thus in a way Gandhi met the Indian tradition half way. "He directed it away from its establishment structures and towards its changing dynamics".[16] Devaki Jain further argues that it was this capacity to meet the Indian tradition half way that enabled women to extricate themselves to a certain extent from the firm grip of the male-dominated patriarchal norms. Though Gandhi's approach was reformist and moderate in nature, he proved to be tactically effective as his approach provided vehicles and options for charge.

Also, it would not be proper to evaluate Gandhi's role on the basis of the Western feminist standards of the present-day times. In order to have a balanced perspective of the contribution made by Gandhi to the women's cause, it is

[14]Ravinder Kumar, "Nationalism and Social Change", Occasional Papers on History and Society, NMML, No. 3, 1983, p. 43.

[15]Uma Rao and Meera Devi, "Glimpses: U.P. Women's Response to Gandhi, 1921-30", paper presented at the Second National Conference on Women's Studies held at Trivandrum from 9-12 April 1984, mimeographed, p. 8.

[16]Devaki Jain, "Gandhian Contributions towards a Feminist Ethic", in *Speaking of Faith—Cross-Cultural Perspectives on Women, Religion and Social Change* (New Delhi, 1986), p. 265.

important to consider the social environment of the times —1920-1948—during which the various Gandhian movements, starting from the Non-cooperation movement of the early 1920s, took place. Also, one must not overlook the fact that for a long time India had remained a colony of Britain; the primary concern of the nationalists therefore was to secure the country's freedom. Moreover, patriarchy was so deep-rooted in the Indian psyche that it was difficult to eliminate it completely. Therefore, given the constraints of those times, women's participation in such large numbers in the national movement was in itself a big achievement. Indeed, Gandhi deserves the highest accolade for being able to mobilize women on such a mass scale and to motivate them for actively participating in the national movement.

It is also not true to say that all women became passive and reverted to the age-old structure once the country became independent. It is not denied that the majority of women completely dissociated themselves from political as well as social life after the country's independence, but at the same there was a considerable number of women leaders (who took an active part in the national movement) who continued to be actively associated with Indian political and social life, notable examples being Vijaylakshmi Pandit, Sucheta Kripalani, Sarojini Naidu, Subhadra Joshi, Aruna Asaf Ali, Rameshwari Nehru, Mridula Sarabhai, and so on. There were others who continued to work for the women's cause through organizations like the AIWC.

We may conclude the discussion by saying that the pride of having fought for the country's freedom, the experience of working outside the home, and the act of participating shoulder to shoulder with men and the memories of jail and *lathi* charge went a long way in infusing a spirit of self-confidence and self-respect among the women of India, and in elevating their position in society.

BIBLIOGRAPHY

PRIMARY SOURCES

Papers and Files

Nehru Memorial Museum and Library, New Delhi
Jawaharlal Nehru Papers
Rajkumari Amrit Kaur Papers
Vijaylakshmi Pandit Papers
Brij Kishan Chandiwala, Urdu Diary, Private Papers of B.K. Chandiwala, F. No. 9.
All India Congress Committee Papers
File No. G-151, 1930-31, Foreign Cloth Picketing
File No. G-48, 1927, Boycott of British Goods
File No. 16, 1930, Correspondence with Bombay Swadeshi Market
File No. G-71, 1937, Women's Suffrage
File No. G-49, 1936, Women Volunteering
Report of the 1930 Satyagraha from different provinces File No. G-18, 1930; G-146, 1930; G-145, 1930; G-86, 1930; G-84, 1930; G-94, 1930; G-80, 1930
Gandhi Memorial Museum, New Delhi
M.K. Gandhi Papers

Interviews with Women Leaders

Oral History Section, Nehru Memorial Museum and Library, New Delhi
Chattopadhyaya, Kamaladevi

Dasgupta, Kamala
Deshmukh, Durgabai
Ghose, Shanti
Kripalani, Sucheta
Mehta, Hansa
Mehta, Usha
Menon, Lakshmi
Nehru, Rameshwari
Pandit, Vijaylakshmi
Ray, Renuka
Sehgal, Manmohini
Sen, Ashalata
Zutshi, Lado Rani

Government Records, Official Publications and Reports

National Archives of India, New Delhi

Records of the Home Department of the Government of India, filed as Home Public and Home Political— Home Political Files are divided into A, B and Deposit categories.

Bamford, P.C., *History of the Non-Cooperation and Khilafat Movements*, Delhi, 1925.

Rushbrook Williams L.F., *India in 1919*, Calcutta, 1920.

Rushbrook Williams L.F., *India in 1922-23*, Calcutta, 1923.

Coatman, J.A., *India in 1929-30*, Calcutta, 1931.

Coatman, J.A., *India in 1930-31*, Calcutta, 1932.

Coatman, J.A., *India in 1932-33*, Delhi, 1934.

Coatman, J.A., *India in 1933-34*, Delhi, 1935.

The Civil Disobedience Movement 1930-34, Delhi, 1936.

Hale, H.W., *Political Trouble in India 1917-1937*, reprint Allahabad, 1974.

Reports

All India Women's Conference, Annual Reports

Indian Statutory Commission, The Summary Report, 1930

Indian National Congress, Proceedings and Reports of Annual Sessions (Consulted from Report of the Thirty-fourth Annual Session held at Amritsar in 1919 till Report of the Forty-Eighth Annual Session held at Bombay in 1934).

The Rashtriya Stree Sabha, Report of the Desh Sevika Sangha, 1930-31.

Towards Equality: Report of the Committee on the Status of Women in India, Delhi, 1974.

Women's Indian Association, Annual Reports

Delhi Satyagraha Report, 1930.

Collections of Documents, Letters and Other Source Material

Annie Besant: *Builder of New India*, (Adyar, 1942).

Bose, S.K., ed, *Subhas Chandra Bose: Correspondence 1924-32,* (Calcutta, 1967).

Datta, K.K., *Writings and Speeches of Mahatma Gandhi Relating to Bihar* (Govt. of Bihar, Patna, 1960).

Datta, K.K., *Gandhiji in Bihar* (Govt. of Bihar, Patna, 1969).

Desai, M., *Day with Gandhi: The Diary of Mahadev Desai,* Vol. I to VII, Varanasi, 1968 onwards.

Fragments from the Past: Selected Writings and Speeches of Aruna Asaf Ali, (New Delhi, 1989).

Gandhi, M.K., *The Collected Works of Mahatma Gandhi,* Publications Division, New Delhi.

H.N. Mitra and N.N. Mitra, ed, *Indian Annual Register, 1919-35,* Calcutta.

Jain, Pratibha, ed, *Reflections on Women: Selections from Nehru's Writings and Speeches,* (Jaipur, 1989).

Nehru, Jawaharlal, *Selected Works of Jawaharlal Nehru* (edited by S. Gopal), (Orient Longman, New Delhi).

Nehru, Jawaharlal, *A Bunch of Old Letters,* (Bombay, 1960).

Speeches and Writings of Sarojini Naidu, (Madras, 1925).

Old Journals, Newspapers and Periodicals

Amrita Bazar Patrika

Bambodhini Patrika

Bharati

The Bombay Chronicle

Chand

Dainik Asha

Dainik Chandrika

Harijan

The Hindu

The Hindustan Times

The Leader

Madhuri

Modern Review

Navjivan

Sandhya

Stree Darpan

Stri Dharma

The Tribune

Young India

SECONDARY SOURCES

Books, Monographs, Original Writings, Autobiographies, Biographies and Memoirs of Women Leaders

Abraham, Taista, ed, *Women and the Politics of Violence,* (Delhi: Har-Anand, 2003).

Agnew, Vijay , *Elite Women in Indian Politics,* (Delhi: Vikas, 1979).

Alexander, Horace, *Gandhi Through Western Eyes,* (Bombay: 1969).

Ali, Aruna Asaf, *Resurgence of Indian Women,* (Delhi: Nehru Memorial Museum and Library and Radiant Publishers, 1991).

Alteker, A.S., *The Position of Women in Hindu Civilisation: From Prehistoric Times to the Present,* (Delhi: Motilal Banarsidass, 1973, first published, 1938).

Athalye, D.V., *The Life of Mahatma Gandhi,* (Pune: Swadeshi Publishing Co., 1923).

Baig, Tara Ali, *India's Woman Power,* (Delhi: S. Chand, 1976).

Women of India, (Delhi: Publications Division, 1958).

Bakshi, S.R., *Documents of Home Rule Movement,* (Delhi: 1989)

Bala, Usha, *Indian Women Freedom Fighters* 1857-1947, (Delhi: Manohar, 1986).

Basu, Aparna, *Mridula Sarabhai: Rebel with a Cause,* (Delhi: Oxford University Press, 1996).

Basu, Aparna and Ray, Bharati, *Women's Struggle: A History of the All India Women's Conference* (1927-2002), (Delhi: Manohar, 2003).

Basu, Aparna and Taneja, Anup, ed, *Breaking out of Invisibility: Women in Indian History,* (Delhi: ICHR and NBC, 2002).

Besant, Annie, *How India Wrought for Freedom,* (Madras: 1915).

Bhandare, Murlidhar C., *The World of Gender Justice,* (Delhi: Har-Anand, 2002).

Borthwick, Meredith, *The Changing Role of Women in Bengal,* 1849–1905, (New Jersey: Princeton University Press, 1984).

Brown, Judith M., *M. Gandhi: The Prisoner of Hope,* (Delhi: OUP, 1990).

Butalia, Urvashi, *The Other Side of Silence: Voices from the Partition of India,* (Delhi: Viking, 1998).

Chaudhurani, Sarala Devi, *At the Point of Spindle,* (Madras: Ganesh and Co., 1922).

Chakravarti, Uma, *Rewriting History: The Life and Times of Pandita Ramabai,* (Delhi: Kali for Women,1998).

Chakravarti, Uma and Gill, Preeti, ed, *Shadow Lives: Writings on Widowhood,* (Delhi: Kali for Women, 2001).

Chanana, Karuna, *Socialization, Education, Women,* (Delhi: 1988).

Chandra, S., *Enslaved Daughters: Colonialism, Law and Women's Rights,* (Delhi : Oxford University Press, 1998).

Chaudhuri, Maitrayee, *Indian Women's Movement: Reform and Revival,* (Delhi: Radiant Publishers, 1993).

Chen, M.A., ed, *Widows in India: Social Neglect and Public Action,* (Delhi : Sage, 1998).

Cousins, M. E., *The Awakening of Asian Womanhood,* (Madras: Ganesh and Co., 1922).

Dastur, Aloo J. and Mehta, Usha H., *Gandhi's Contribution to the Emancipation of Women,* (Mumbai: Popular Prakashan, 1991).

Devi, N. Seeta, *Life History of Durgabai Deshmukh,* (Madras: 1977)

Dube, L. Leacock and Ardener, S., ed, *Visibility and Power: Essays on Women in Society and Development,* (Delhi: Oxford University Press, 1986).

Dutt, Guru Sadaya, *A Woman of India: Being the Life of Sarojini Nalini,* (London: Hogarth, 1929).

Embree, E.T., *Charles Grant and British Rule in India,* (London: 1962)

Engels, D., *Beyond Purdah, Women in Bengal,* 1890-1939 (Delhi: Oxford University Press, 1996).

Erikson, Erik, *Gandhi's Truth,* (New York: W. Norton and Co., 1969).

Everett, Jana, *Women and Social Change in India,* (Delhi: Heritage, 1979).

Forbes, Geraldine, *The New Cambridge History of India, IV. 2: Women in Modern India,* (Cambridge University Press, 1996).

Gandhi, Indira, *What I am,* (Delhi: Indira Gandhi Memorial Trust, 1986).

Gandhi, M.K., *The Story of My Experiments with Truth,* (Penguin, 1983).

Women and Social Justice, (Ahmedabad: Navjivan, 1942).

Letters to Rajkumari Amrit Kaur, (Ahmedabad: Navjivan, 1961).

Ganguli, B.N., *Gandhi's Social Philosophy,* (New York: John Wiley and Sons, 1973).

Gedge, E and Choksi, M., ed, *Women in Modern India,* (Bombay: 1929).

Ghadially, R., ed, *Women in Indian Society: A Reader,* (Delhi: Sage, 1988).

Ghose, I., ed, *Memsahibs Abroad: Writings by Women Travellers in 19th Century India,* (Delhi: Oxford University Press, 1998).

Ghosh, P.G., *Mahatma Gandhi As I Saw Him* (Delhi: S. Chand, 1968).

Grover, V. and Arora, Ranjana, *Great Women of India,* (Delhi: Deep and Deep, 1993)

Heimsath, Charles, *Indian Nationalism and Hindu Social Reform,* (New Jersey: Princeton University Press, 1964).

Jain, Devaki, ed, *Indian Women* (Delhi: Publications Division, Government of India, 1976).

Jassal, Smita Talwar, *Daughters of the Earth: Women and Law in Uttar Pradesh,* (Delhi: Manohar, 2001).

Jayawardena, Kumari, *The White Woman's Other Burden: Western Women and South Asia During British Colonial Rule,* (New York and London: Routledge, 1995).

Jeffrey, Patricia, *Frogs in a Well: Indian Women in Purdah,* (Delhi: Manohar, 2000).

Jethmalani, Rani, *Kali's Yug: Empowerment, Law and Dowry Deaths,* (Delhi: Har-Anand, 2003).

Kalarthi, M., *Ba and Bapu,* (Ahmedabad: Navjivan, 1962).

Karlekar, Malavika, *Voices from Within: Early Personal Narratives of Bengali Women,* (Delhi: Oxford University Press, 1991).

Kasturi, Leela and Mazumdar, Vina, ed, *Women and Indian Nationalism,* (Delhi: Vikas, 1994).

Kaur, Manmohan, *Women in India's Freedom Struggle,* (Delhi: Sterling, 1985).

Kaur, Rajkumari Amrit, *Incidents of Gandhi's Life,* (Bombay: 1949).

Challenge to Women, (Ahmedabad: Kitabistan, 1946).

Kishwar, Madhu, *Off the Beaten Track: Rethinking Gender Justice for Indian Women,* (Delhi: OUP).

Kishwar, Madhu and Vanita, Ruth, ed, *In Search of Answers: Indian Women's Voices from Manushi,* (London: Zed Books Limited, 1984).

Kosambi, Meera, *Pandita Ramabai Through Her Own Words: Selected Works,* (Delhi: OUP).

Kripalani, Krishna, *Gandhi: A Life,* (Delhi: NBT, 1968).

Kripalani, Sucheta, *An Unfinished Autobiography,* edited by K.N. Vaswani (Ahmedabad: Navjivan, 1978).

Krishna Raj, Maithreyi, *Women's Studies in India: Some Perspectives,* (Mumbai: Popular Prakashan, 1986).

Krishnamurthy, J., ed, *Women in Colonial India: Essays on Survival, Work and the State,* (Delhi: Oxford University Press, 1989).

Kumar, N., ed, *Women as Subjects: South Asian Histories,* (Delhi: Stree Publications, 1994).

Kumar, Radha, *Gender, Work and Power Relations: A Case Study of Haryana,* (Delhi: Har-Anand, 1998).

The History of Doing, (Delhi: Kali for Women, 1993).

Llewellyn, J.E., *The Legacy of Woman's Uplift in India: Contemporary Women Leaders in the Arya Samaj,* (Delhi: Sage, 1998).

Mahan, Rajan, *Women in Indian National Congress, 1921-1931,* (Jaipur and Delhi: Rawat Publications, 1999).

Mazumdar, Vina, ed, *Symbols of Power: Studies on the Political Status of Women in India,* (Mumbai: Allied, 1979).

Mayo, K., *Selections from Mother India,* (Delhi: Kali for Women, 1999).

Mehrotra, S.R., *Towards India's Freedom and Partition,* (Delhi: Vikas, 1979).

Mehta, Hansa, *Indian Women,* (Delhi: Butala & Co., 1981).

Menon, Ritu and Bhasin, Kamla, *Borders and Boundaries: Women in India's Partition,* (Delhi : Kali for Women, 1999).

Menon, Visalakshi, *Indian Women and Nationalism: The U.P. Story,* (Delhi: Har-Anand, 2003).

Metcalf, Barbara Daly, *Perfecting Women,* (Delhi: Oxford Univerity Press, 1992).

Minault, Gail, *The Extended Family: Women and Political Participation in India and Pakistan,* (Delhi: Chanakya Publications, 1981).

Secluded Scholars: Women's Education and Muslim Social Reform in Colonial India, (Delhi: OUP).

The Khilafat Movement: A Religious and Political Mobilization in India, (Delhi: OUP, 1982).

Minturn, I., *Sita's Daughters: Coming out of Purdah,* (New York: Oxford University Press, 1993).

Mody, Nawaz B., ed, *Women in India's Freedom Struggle,* (Mumbai: Allied, 2000).

Mukherjee, A., ed, *Women in Indian Life and Society,* (Calcutta: Punthi Pustak and Institute of Historical Studies, 1996).

Mukhopadhyay, Swapna, ed, *In the Name of Justice: Women and Law in Society,* (Delhi: Manohar, 1998).

Mukta, P., *Upholding the Common Life: The Community of Mirabai,* (Delhi: Oxford University Press, 1994).

Naidu, Sarojini, *My Experiences as a Legislator,* (Madras: Current Thought Press, 1930).

Nair, J., *Women and Law in Colonial India,* (Delhi: Kali for Women, 1999).

Nanda, B.R., *Mahatma Gandhi: A Biography,* (Delhi: OUP).
In Search of Gandhi, (Delhi: OUP, 2003).

Nanda, B.R., ed, *Indian Women: From Purdah to Modernity,* (Delhi: Vikas, 1976).

Nanda, Reena, *Kamaladevi Chattopadhyay: A Biography,* (Delhi: OUP)

Nehru, Rameshwari, *Gandhi is My Star,* (Patna: Pustakbhandar, 1950).

Oldenburg, Veena Talwar, *Dowry Murder: The Imperial Origins of a Cultural Crime,* (Delhi: OUP).

Pawar, K., ed, *Women in Indian History: Social, Economic, Political and Cultural Perspectives,* (Delhi: Vision and Venture, 1996).

Rai, Ganpat, *Gandhi and Kasturba: The Story of Their Life,* (Lahore: Kasturba Memorial Publications, n.d.).

Ramaswamy, V., *Walking Naked: Woman, Society, Spirituality in South India,* (Simla: Indian Institute of Advanced Study, 1997).
Divinity and Deviance: Women in Virasaivism, (Delhi: Oxford University Press, 1996).

Ramaswamy, V., ed, *Researching Indian Women,* (Delhi: Manohar, 2003).

Raju, V. Rajendra, *Role of Women in India's Freedom Struggle,* (Delhi: 1994)

Ray, B., ed, *From the Seams of History: Essays on Indian Women,* (Delhi: Oxford University Press, 1995).

Ray, B., *Early Feminists of Colonial India: Sarala Devi Chaudhurani and Rokeya Sakhawat Hossain,* (Delhi: OUP).

Ray, B. and Basu, A., ed, *From Independence Towards Freedom: Indian Women Since 1947,* (Delhi: Oxford University Press, 1999).

Ray, Rajat Kanta, *Exploring Emotional History: Gender, Mentality and Literature in the Indian Awakening,* (Delhi: OUP, 2002).

Ray, Renuka, *My Reminiscences: Social Development During Gandhian Era and After,* (Delhi: Allied, 1982).

Rayaprol, A., *Negotiating Identities: Women in the Indian Diaspora,* (Delhi: Oxford University Press, 1997).

Reddy, Muthulakshmi, S. *Autobiography,* (Madras: 1964).

Roy, Kumkum, ed, *Women in Early Indian Societies,* (Delhi: Manohar, 1999).

Sahgal, I., *A Revolutionary Life: Memoirs of a Political Activist,* (Delhi: Kali for Women, 1999).

Sangari, Kumkum and Vaid, Sudesh, ed, *Recasting Women: Essays in Colonial History,* (Delhi : Kali for Women, 1989).

Women and Culture, (Mumbai: 1985).

Saradamani, K., *Matriliny Transformed: Family, Law and Ideology in Twentieth Century Travancore,* (Delhi: Sage, 1999).

Sarkar, Sumit, *Modern India, 1885-1947,* (Delhi: Macmillan India, 1983).

Sarkar, Tanika, *Words to Win: The Making of Amar Jiban: A Modern Autobiography,* (Delhi: Kali for Women, 1999).

Sarkar, Tanika and Butalia, Urvashi, ed, *Women and the Hindu Right: A Collection of Essays,* (Delhi: Kali for Women, reprint, 1996).

Sengupta, Padmini, *Sarojini Naidu: A Biography,* (Mumbai: Asia Publishing House, 1966).

Sen, S., *Women and Labour in Late Colonial India: The Bengal Jute Industry,* (Cambridge University Press, 1999).

Shah, Shalini, *The Making of Womanhood: Gender Relations in the Mahabharata,* (Delhi: Manohar, 1995).

Sinha, Mrinalini, *Colonial Masculinity: The "Manly Englishman" and the "Effeminate Bengali" in the Late Nineteenth Century,* (Delhi: Kali for Women, 1997).

Slade, Madeline, *The Spirit's Pigrimage,* (New York: Longman's, 1960).

Sogani, Rajul , *The Hindu Widow in Indian Literature,* (Delhi: OUP, 2002).

Southard, Barbara, *The Women's Movement and Colonial Politics in Bengal: The Quest for Political Rights, Education and Social Reform Legislation (1921-36*), (Delhi: Manohar, 1995).

Srilata, K., ed., *The Other Half of the Coconut: Women Writing Self-respect History,* (Delhi: Kali for Women, 2002)

Sunder Rajan, R., *Real and Imagined Women: Gender, Culture and Post-Colonialism,* (London: Routledge, 1993).

Sutherland, S.J., ed, *Bridging Worlds: Studies on Women in South Asia,* (Delhi: Oxford University Press, 1992).

Tendulkar, D.G., *Life of Mahatma Gandhi,* (Bombay: K. Jhavery and D.G. Tendulkar, 1940).

Thapan, M., ed, *Embodiment: Essays on Gender and Identity,* (Delhi : Oxford University Press, 1997).

Thapar, Romila, *Shakuntala: Texts, Readings, Histories,* (Delhi: Kali for Women, 2000).

Venkatarangaiya, M., *The Freedom Struggle in Andhra Pradesh*, 1921-31, (Hyderabad: 1965).

INDEX